The King and the Catholics

Antonia Fraser is the author of many widely acclaimed historical works which have been international bestsellers. The prizes she has won include the Wolfson Award for History and the Norton Medlicott Medal of the Historical Association. She has been President of English PEN, chairman of the Society of Authors, and chairman of the Crime Writers' Association.

Antonia Fraser was made a DBE in 2011 and a CH in 2018 for services to Literature. She was married to Harold Pinter who died in 2008. Her previous books include *Mary Queen of Scots*, *Cromwell, Our Chief of Men*, *King Charles II*, *Marie Antoinette*, *The Gunpowder Plot: Terror and Faith in 1605*, *The Six Wives of Henry VIII*, *The Weaker Vessel*, *Warrior Queens*, *Love and Louis XIV* and *Perilous Question: The Drama of the Great Reform Bill 1832*. She has also written two memoirs, *Must You Go? My Life with Harold Pinter* and *My History: A Memoir of Growing Up*.

Also by Antonia Fraser

THE KING AND THE CATHOLICS

The Fight for Rights 1829

ANTONIA FRASER

WEIDENFELD & NICOLSON

First published in Great Britain in 2018

This paperback edition first published in 2019
by Weidenfeld & Nicolson
an imprint of The Orion Publishing Group Ltd
Carmelite House
50 Victoria Embankment
London, EC4Y 0DZ

An Hachette Company UK

1 3 5 7 9 10 8 6 4 2

A CIP catalogue record for this book
is available from the British Library.

ISBN: 978 1 4746 0194 8

Typeset at The Spartan Press Ltd,
Lymington, Hants

Printed and bound by CPI Group (UK) Ltd,
Croydon, CR0 4YY

www.weidenfeldandnicolson.co.uk

CONTENTS

ILLUSTRATIONS

AUTHOR'S NOTE

The subject of this book is timeless: the rights of people to practise their own religion. There is a side issue concerning the possible duties to the State which exist alongside those rights. It is, however, limited to one particular time in British history: thus the narrative begins with the Gordon Riots against Catholic Relief in 1780 and ends roughly fifty years later with the parliamentary Act for Catholic Emancipation.

During that period the phrase 'the Catholic Question' – used by people of very different views on the subject – came to dominate British and Irish politics. At one point an exasperated Anglican clergyman even referred to it as 'the Abominable Cath. Quest. which made it impossible to eat or drink or see or think'. There are obvious parallels with other periods of religious dispute and ferment, including the present day, which readers will draw for themselves. During this time the conscience of the reigning monarch played an important part, hence the symbolic use of the word 'King' in the title of this book, although there were two Kings on the throne during this period.

On a personal note, I should say that I am not a 'Cradle Catholic', as those born into the Catholic Faith are sometimes known; my parents' families were Church of England (or Ireland) and Unitarian respectively. Following their conversions to Catholicism, some years apart, I was allowed to make my own choice to convert at the age of fourteen, just when history was beginning to obsess me. The result was a lifelong fascination with Catholic history which found expression in a study of the events leading up to the Gunpowder Plot of 1605, published in

1996. *The King and the Catholics* is, in one sense, the sequel to that book.

I should add that my direct descent, on my father's side, from the Irish Protestant Ascendancy, including such characters as Brunswick Tom, 2nd Earl of Longford, gave an added piquancy to my researches.

Antonia Fraser
Feast of All Saints, 2017

NOTE ON MONEY

I have from time to time given rough estimates of the value of particular sums of money in our own day, using round figures for convenience. In this way, £100 in 1800 is taken to be worth approximately £7,500 in 2018. The website of the Bank of England provides a proper detailed guide.

ACKNOWLEDGEMENTS

I wish to thank Her Majesty Queen Elizabeth II for permission to quote from the Royal Archives, and Miss Allison Derrett, Archivist (Volunteers Manager), for her assistance. I am grateful for being able to work at the Jesuit Archives, Farm Street, and to Rebecca Somerset, Province Archivist.

I wish to thank the staff of the following: the Bodleian Library, Oxford; the British Library including Jamie Andrews and Jonathan Pledge; the Museum of London; the Public Record Office, Kew; and the Public Record Office, Northern Ireland; Thomas and Valerie Pakenham guided me in the Pakenham Archives, Tullynally Castle. The late Cardinal Cormac Murphy-O'Connor gave advice and encouragement.

The following people were helpful in many different ways, including suggestions about reading, answering queries or providing information. I thank Jonathan Aitken; Kenneth Baker; the late Sir Christopher Bland; Mark Bostridge; Fr. Michael Campbell-Johnston SJ; Judith Curthoys, Archivist of Christ Church, Oxford; Richard Davenport-Hines; Eugene Downes; Professor Roy Foster for encouragement at a critical moment; Sally Gardner; Professor Patrick Geoghegan; Geordie Greig; Lady Celestria Hales; the Very Rev. Dr John Hall, Dean of Westminster; the late Lord Hutchinson of Lullington for his enthusiastic response to the title; Dr Serenhedd James; the late Lucy Jebb and Louis Jebb for the engraving of the Gordon Riots; Linda Kelly; Dominic Lawson; Allan Mallinson; Dr Leslie Mitchell; Charles Moore; Fr. Stephan Morgan and Mrs Cathy Pickles, Church of Our Lady of Mercy and St Joseph, Lymington; Nigel Morris, Chairman,

The Peel Society; Sir Tom Oakshott, Professor David Parrott; Professor Munro Price; David Raymont, Librarian, The Actuarial Profession; John Martin Robinson; John Ronayne; Dr Ruth Scurr; Fr. Nicholas Schofield; Fr. Michael Seed; Anne Southworth; James Stourton; Sir Roy Strong; Canon Tony Trowles; Hugo Vickers; Katie Waldegrave; Robert Wright for research on European religious discrimination; Adam Zamoyski.

My agent, Jonathan Lloyd, was as helpful as ever; so was my publisher and friend Alan Samson, together with Lucinda McNeile, Linden Lawson and Christopher Phipps; Linda Peskin at home provided invaluable assistance. My family were as usual extremely supportive.

Lastly, Professor Boyd Hilton, Sir Anthony Kenny and Michael Walsh kindly read the manuscript at my request and provided valuable corrections; the interpretations – and any remaining errors – are my own responsibility. The book is dedicated jointly to an historian and a publisher: Hugh Thomas and George Weidenfeld, with each of whom I enjoyed a friendship lasting over sixty years.

PROLOGUE

Sky like Blood

*'Such a scene my eyes never beheld, and I pray God
I may never again... The sky was like blood with
the reflection of the fires'*

Lady Anne Erskine, Clerkenwell, 1780

THE STORY BEGINS with violence: in the summer of 1780
London was the scene of the worst riots the city had ever experienced, and which were to prove the 'largest, deadliest and
most protracted urban riots in British history'. The death toll
was probably about 1,000 people altogether (in proportion to the
population of the capital, this remains the highest percentage of
deaths in a riot yet known). The physical damage to the structure
of the city would not be surpassed until the Blitz in the Second
World War. Known to history as the Gordon Riots – famously
commemorated by Dickens in *Barnaby Rudge,* when he wrote of
'a moral plague' running through the city – they were deliberately
initiated by the militantly Anti-Catholic son of a Scottish duke,
who was a Member of the British Parliament.[1]

Riots were certainly not unknown in eighteenth-century
London: there had been the so-called Wilkes Riots in the 1760s
and the Keppel Riots after that; but in degree of violence, the

Gordon Riots excelled them. Symbols of the State were attacked. Ten Downing Street, already the official residence of the Prime Minister, Lord North, was assaulted at two o'clock in the morning by protesters bearing lighted flambeaux and faggots: they had to be driven off by twenty dragoons on horseback. Meanwhile the Prime Minister's dinner guests climbed onto the roof in order to see the fires burning as far as the horizon.

If prime ministers were obvious targets for attack, private individuals were not safe either. Lady Anne Erskine was a Scottish lady living quietly in a house attached to Spa Fields Chapel in Clerkenwell. She wrote: 'Such a scene my eyes never beheld, and I pray God I never may again. The situation of the place which is high and very open gave us an awful prospect of it. We were surrounded by flames. Six different fires – with that of Newgate towering to the clouds... with every hour we were in expectation of this house and chapel making the seventh. The sky was like blood with the reflection of the fires.' Ten years later, the literary Ladies of Llangollen, gazing at a fierce crimson sunset, were still irresistibly reminded of the Gordon Riots.[2]

Susanna, sister of another literary lady, Fanny Burney, was living just off Leicester Fields (the modern Leicester Square); the house had formerly belonged to Sir Isaac Newton and still had his old observatory attached. From here the twenty-five-year-old Susanna heard the violent shouts and huzzas as all the furniture of their neighbour was piled up in the square, and his servant forced to bring a candle to light the bonfire: 'my knees went knicky knocky,' she confessed. The next night was worse. She watched another house in her own street totally emptied and set alight. The rioters, covered in smoke and dust, looked like 'so many Infernals' in the firelight.[3]

Suddenly the little group in the window, consisting of Susanna, her sister Esther and brother-in-law, caught the attention of the crowd below: 'They are all three Papists!' was the cry. It was a dangerous acclamation. 'Call out *No Popery* or anything,' said Esther urgently to her husband. (They were not in fact Catholics.) In a similar fashion, the Jews in Houndsditch would inscribe 'This house is a true Protestant' on their dwellings to preserve themselves. One foreigner simply wrote 'No Religion' outside his own house, although he also more explicitly draped himself in the blue ribbons of the rioters in the cause of self-preservation.

The mere word 'Popery' was in fact inflammatory in its own style. Many of the ignorant crowd, when not seriously bent on plunder as such crowds tend to be, were aware of 'Popery' as an evil which needed to be restrained (with 'Papists' being those who practised it) without seeking any further information. There were 10,000 stout fellows, as Daniel Defoe had written earlier in the century in *The Behaviour of Servants,* who would spend their last drop of blood against Popery but 'do not know whether it be a man or a horse'.[4]

An illustration of this was the bewilderment of a certain group at the time of the actual Riots when called to attack a house 'as there were *Catholics* there'. They replied: 'What are Catholics to us? We are against *Popery*.' Maria Edgeworth, in her novel featuring these events, *Harrington,* picked on another area of ignorance. A certain woman observer was amazed at the assault on a particular carriage, and the breaking of the windows of a house; for surely these were not 'Romans'. When assured they were: 'How is that, when they're not Irish? For I'll swear to they're not being Irish...' This particular mob responded with lethal simplicity: 'We require the Papists to be given up for your lives,' and then added for good measure: 'No Jews! No wooden shoes!' This was the kind of mindless cruelty which was responsible for the deliberate incineration of the canaries belonging to a rich silk merchant named Malo, on the grounds that they were 'Popish birds'.[5]

From her observation post, Susanna's heart ached for her Catholic friends, mainly Italians (she was having a delicate romance with an Italian singer at the time). They could not even venture to complain about the destruction of their houses and property because their religion made them so vulnerable. Instead, they mainly took their suspicious foreign names off the door, and one even put his own *No Popery* notice on it. The summit of the crowd's wilful, even absurd destruction occurred when a house was attacked – just because the notices outside were in French.

These ferocious riots were in fact a protest against the Catholic Relief Act which had received the Royal Assent of George III in June 1778. It might legitimately be supposed that this Relief Act had enacted widespread, even revolutionary, relaxation of the Penal Laws against Roman Catholics, to provoke such a scabrous assault. In fact the Relief was relatively mild. It was the reaction which was extreme.

To sum up the actual state of the law in England and Scotland before June 1778:* first of all, no Catholic could receive political office, neither in the House of Lords nor the House of Commons, or engage in anything else of an official nature. No Catholic in England and Scotland was allowed to buy or inherit land. Exercising the function of a Catholic priest or running a Catholic school were both activities punishable by life imprisonment. Catholics could not receive commissions in the army or navy, or officially be soldiers or sailors. In the same way, Catholics who declared themselves as such could not attend universities, let alone take degrees.

There was one prohibition in particular with enormous potential social consequences. Even if both bride and groom were Catholics, they could not get married legally by a Catholic priest in a Catholic church: such a ceremony would have no status under the law, with all the consequent penalties. The Marriage Act of 1753, which had relaxed the rules for other dissenting religions, left out the Catholics. For Catholics, in order to avoid complications to do with inheritance and other matters, there had to be an alternative (Protestant) ceremony, even if the participants by definition regarded these vows as empty.

Inheritance was, in fact, another awkward question. There were penal tax laws. Catholics could not in theory inherit property – giving rise to the unpleasant possibility of one member of the family declaring adherence to the official Protestant religion of the State, and demanding to inherit property otherwise destined for a Catholic heir. Six years before the passage of the Act for Relief, the case of the Widow Fenwick became notorious. The

---

* The laws in Ireland were a separate matter at this point.

Catholic heiress Anne Benson had married the Protestant John Fenwick. When Fenwick died, his Protestant brother claimed his sister-in-law's property with no other justification than her proscribed religion. Mrs Fenwick was fortunate: she attracted the attention of the benevolent Lord Camden, and finally she secured a settlement by a private Act of Parliament.[6] But the threat remained, and it was a genuine threat under the law.

There were minor issues: religious dress – that of nuns, monks and priests – could not lawfully be worn in the streets. Ostentatious signs of the Catholic religion, such as the sound of bells being tolled at Catholic chapels, were specifically forbidden. Furthermore, there is an important clue to the world which lay beyond the arid sentences of the law: anyone who chose to provide information leading to the conviction of a Catholic priest could expect a payment of £100 (about £7,500 today). Nor had this law been a dead letter in recent years: in 1767 the Informers Act was used to secure the successful prosecution of a priest. The informer was one William Payne, who made a living out of such dubious activities. As a result of this denunciation a certain Father Maloney was sentenced to life imprisonment, although subsequently released after four years with a Royal Pardon on condition he left the country to become 'an exile for Christ', in the words of a Catholic bishop.[7]

What then did this Act for Relief, so savagely resented, provide for? First and perhaps most importantly, the laws concerning the arrest and prosecution of Catholic priests were repealed, and the keeping of a Catholic school was no longer punishable by life imprisonment. Catholics could buy land and inherit it just like anyone else, according to the laws of the country, without the potential menace of a Protestant heir, however remote, intervening. All of this affected the lives of ordinary people, or at any rate those prominent enough in society to attract the attention of the land law.

The existence, however, of that notorious controlling authority, the foreign Pope, was not ignored. Catholics were now explicitly commanded in a new Oath of Allegiance to deny that the Pope had any 'temporal' (worldly) jurisdiction as opposed to spiritual authority; which meant that the Pope could not any more declare Catholics able to murder their 'heretic' Protestant princes (or princesses) without sin. The Pope was also no longer allowed to absolve Catholics from keeping faith with heretics – in so far as he ever had. On the positive side, there were to be prayers for the King in the Catholic churches and chapels newly freed from their illegal status.

The leader – the initiator – of the ferocious protests against this mild relaxation of the Anti-Catholic laws was a curious individual even to his contemporaries. Lord George Gordon's unusual appearance – long red hair to his shoulders, and slightly protuberant blue eyes – added to the startling impression which he left upon observers, and inspired Horace Walpole to call him 'the lunatic apostle'. Whether it detracted from the effect he had, or secretly added to it, Gordon had the reputation of a libertine in his private life. It was significant that when he denounced the Protestant Archbishop of Canterbury as 'the Whore of Babylon' for his Catholic sympathies, a wit commented that this particular whore was the only whore that Gordon disliked. [8]

Lord George was the sixth child of the Duke of Gordon. His education at Eton College was conventional, a note of eccentricity in his family circle being struck by his mother, the Duchess: on being widowed, she chose to marry a young American soldier. It was the Duchess who decided on her son's early career in the navy. Lord George was twenty-nine at the time of the Gordon Riots, and had been a Member of Parliament for Ludgershall in Wiltshire since the age of twenty-two: it was a seat, in the un-reformed House of Commons, which had been bought for him by General Simon Fraser, the Member of Parliament for Inverness.

Gordon was a complicated character. His fierce hostility to the idea of Catholic Relief should be contrasted with other views which would be considered positively liberal in the modern sense of the word.* Undoubtedly possessing great personal charm, he was kind and tender to his social inferiors. Mistreatment of the sailors during

---

* Liberal as an adjective, meaning generous and tolerant, would come to be used in a critical political sense: but there was no Liberal Party as yet in Britain.

his naval career appalled him and he said so: he was 'the sailor's friend', in the words of a biography written shortly after his death. Visiting Jamaica, he studied the conditions in which the inhabitants lived and was indignant at what he called 'the bloody treatment of the negroes'. In America, by way of contrast, he admired the free-and-easy way of life and independent spirit which he found in the people. Later, as an MP, influenced by Burke, he was marked by his violent opposition to the 'mad, cruel and accursed American war' against the would-be independent colonies.[9]

This was also a man who, as the son of a duke, felt entitled to call on King George III, and exercised his birthright twice. In the second of the two interviews, he chose to indulge himself in a rant about the historic banishment of the House of Stuart for its encouragement of Popery and arbitrary power, with the obvious implication for the future of the King himself, given the Relief Act he had sanctioned. Unsurprisingly, Gordon was denied access to the royal presence a third time.

As all this demonstrates, as well as the charm and the compassion, there was something deeply erratic in Gordon's nature. On the one hand, it enabled him to exercise a hypnotic influence over large numbers of people. On the other hand, it could take an extremely aggressive form which brought its own consequences. Horace Walpole's lunatic apostle was on another occasion described by him as Lord George Macbeth.* There was a saying that there were three parties in Parliament, the ministry, the Opposition and Lord George Gordon – to which the man himself characteristically responded that he belonged to a fourth party, the party of the people. Another reference was made to the 'whirligig' nature of his political speeches, which contrasted with the 'elegant young gentleman of engaging manners' who went out in Society.

When the Catholic Relief Bill was originally introduced into the House of Commons on 15 May 1778, not many Members were present and interest in it was lacklustre. It was not long,

---

* It is possible that Gordon would be diagnosed as bipolar in the twenty-first century.

however, before stories began to spread and play upon the sus-
ceptibilities of what seemed like a self-perpetuating Anti-Catholic
mob. In Scotland a separate bill was proposed in 1779, but met
with organized hostility in which Gordon took a keen personal
interest. As a result, he was elected leader of the Scottish Protestant Association.

One anecdote seems to sum up that mixture of good manners and ardent Anti-Popery which characterized Edinburgh. As
the good Catholic Bishop Hay was returning home, a woman
explained to him with great courtesy why the way was blocked:
'Oh, Sir, we are just burning the Popish chapel and we only
wish we had the Bishop to throw in the fire.'[10] She evidently
believed her behaviour to be perfectly normal, or at any rate to
need no further justification. There were torchlight processions in
Glasgow and other demonstrations; Gordon was able to report
to the House of Commons that many of the Scots were quite
sure that King George III was actually a 'Papist'. The Bill was
abandoned in February 1779.

All of this was highly encouraging to the English Anti-Papist
zealots: in the autumn of 1779 an English Protestant Association was formed with the declared aim of getting the Relief
Act repealed. The title page of the *Appeal from the Protestant
Association* by Bishop Sherlock did not mince words: 'To design
the Advancement of POPERY is to design the Ruin of the State,
and the Destruction of the Church, it is to sacrifice the Nation
to a double Slavery, to prepare chains for their Bodies and their
Minds.' This theme was continued in the text. Popery had long
been 'chained' in Britain and the consequences of unchaining it
would be dreadful to posterity: 'to tolerate Popery is to encour-
age what by Toleration itself we mean to destroy, a spirit of
persecution of the most notorious kind'.[11] In parallel, Gordon's
speeches in the House of Commons, never calm, became notably
wilder as the months passed.

Meanwhile signatures were gathered for Petitions to Parliament, the lawful contemporary method of protest. In London
over 40,000 people put their names to one Petition, leading to
strange incidents such as the distinguished Catholic Lord Petre

calling upon Gordon in Welbeck Street, and having to push through a crowd of people waiting to sign a Petition against all his co-religionists. London Petitioners included a handful of women. Susanna Burney believed in fact that the women were more active than the men, but another commentator cynically blamed the odd female intervention on drink – 'shocking intemperance' – rather than political commitment. Personal testimonies were added to signatures: 'John Castle protests against the Doctrine of Popery'; 'Joseph Sloane, Cooper and Freeman of London and Popery I do deny.'[12]

Rumour, Shakespeare's Rumour 'painted full of tongues', was ever present. Benedictine monks in Southwark were said to have poisoned all the flour. Even more frighteningly, there were tales of 20,000 Jesuit priests lurking in tunnels beneath the Thames, only waiting for orders from Rome to blow up the banks and bed of the river in order to flood the whole of London.[13] This was a bizarre echo of the details of the Gunpowder Plot 175 years earlier, when Guy Fawkes had reached Parliament via the river, and probably owed something to folk memory of it.

It was the presentation of the London Petition to Parliament on 2 June 1780 which led to the escalation of protest to the next, very different stage. The weather matched the mood of the crowd: it was intensely hot, with occasional flashes of lightning. At least 60,000 people gathered in St George's Fields in Southwark (now the site of Waterloo Station, then an area notorious for beggars on the one hand and illicit love encounters on the other).

Upon which, 'King Mob' took things to another stage and began a massive march on Parliament. There were Scots there too, led by a Highlander in a kilt with a drawn sword, and cockades for sale with 'No Popery' on them. At least one fifteen-year-old boy from nearby Westminster School joined in. Naturally, not every member of this growing army was animated by idealism; drink began to play an inevitable part, the drunken merging happily with the zealots.

Finally, the whole vast throng surged into Palace Yard and began hooting at the MPs and peers as they arrived. It was not long before hostile words gave way to deeds: the mob moved to pelting mud, and was soon jostling and even assaulting the law-makers of the country. Lord Bathurst was first insulted as 'the Pope and a silly old woman' – surely contradictory – and then hit in the face. The Duke of Northumberland had a bad time when he was mistaken for a Jesuit priest. The Protestant Archbishop of York was manhandled, while the Prime Minister, Lord North, had his hat snatched off his head, with pieces sold off as souvenirs for a shilling each.

Soldiers eventually dispersed the rioters from Parliament itself but the mob simply moved on to what it did best: crude but effective attacks on targets chosen according to their own equally crude prejudices. In this way the chapels of the 'Catholic' Embassies were sacked. Most visible was that of Sardinia in Duke Street, Mayfair, 'the Cathedral of London Catholicism'; then there was the Warwick Street church originating from the Portuguese, then the Bavarian Embassy chapel in Golden Square.*[14] The Venetian, the Spanish and the French chapels all suffered devastation.

If chapels were wrecked, so, at the other end of society, were prisons. Newgate was set on fire, which would result in a dramatic scene as described by Dickens, with Barnaby Rudge himself being held in the prison at the time. Other prisons were attacked, including the Fleet prison and the new prison at Southwark. Houses of prominent Catholics – or supposed Catholic sympathizers like the Lord Chief Justice, Lord Mansfield – were destroyed. Sir George Savile, as the initiator of the Bill, had his house completely destroyed even though he was a Protestant. The Catholic Bishop Challoner, the Vicar-Apostolic, who was in his late eighties and had dedicated his life to religion, had to be hustled away from his house in Queen Square to a place of safety in Finchley at the home of a Catholic merchant; he had a stroke as a result and died the next year.[15]

There were exceptions. A building at Hammersmith which was well known in the neighbourhood to be a Catholic convent

* Rebuilt, designed by Joseph Bonomi, in 1790, as Our Lady of the Assumption and St Gregory; today it is the only surviving eighteenth-century Catholic chapel in London.

was saved by the historical myth that Queen Elizabeth I as a girl had been educated there. Lord Petre was fortunate in that his house at the upper end of Park Street was protected by the encampment of soldiers in Hyde Park just opposite.[16] But a certain Catholic gentleman, Thomas Fitzherbert of Swynnerton, physically collapsed after his fearful exertions in fortifying his London house, and died the next year at the age of thirty-seven – with the unintended consequences, for royal history, of leaving his much younger wife Maria Fitzherbert a widow.

Along with these indignities and worse there were instances of admirable behaviour, headed by King George III. 'My attachment is to the laws and security of my country', along with 'the protection of the lives and properties of all my subjects', was the line he took.[17]

It may well be questioned why the soldiers took so long to demolish the resistance of people who were certainly not so efficiently armed, if properly armed at all. Officially the soldiery had to wait for the Riot Act to be read by a local authority, according to the rules of the time. But it has to be remembered that the enemies of England against whom wars had been fought sporadically throughout the century were actually Catholics. There were nasty stories that the troops had been bribed with money and, even more importantly, alcohol.[18] Lord Stormont, for example, pointed out that since the army's oath included support for the Protestant Succession, aiding Catholics might actually be illegal.

This is not to suggest that all non-Catholic contemporaries were similarly and lethally bigoted. John Newton was an evangelical Anglican clergyman who had begun life as the captain of slave ships before his conversion and subsequently wrote the hymn 'Amazing Grace'; he founded the so-called Clapham Sect. Now in his fifties, and the recently appointed vicar of St Mary Woolnoth, Lombard Street, he was horrified by these events and declared himself firmly against the 'mistaken zeal' of the Protestant Association. 'Surely the Son of Man came not to destroy men's lives but to save them,' he observed pointedly. Asked to condemn the Papacy by some of its members, he had an acerbic answer: 'I have read of many Popes but the worst Pope I ever encountered was Pope Self.' Newton was also dismayed that this should be happening at a time when Protestants were gaining more liberties in Papist countries.[19]

On the other hand, John Wesley, for the Methodists, as early as January 1780 had deplored the increase in Catholicism in the population in a way that was hardly conducive to peace. In the case of the riots, it was not until 5 June that the Protestant Association came to its senses and proclaimed that all true Protestants be requested to show their attachment to their best interest by 'a legal and peaceable deportment'. Anything else would only distract the MPs from paying proper attention to the united prayers of the Protestant Petition. It was Lord George Gordon who signed the proclamation. But still the riots raged on.

Gradually peace returned and the fires died down. The wretched Catholics who had been told to lie low and attract as little notice as possible began to creep back into the streets again. In the aftermath, there was general agreement by observers on the strange tranquillized state of the city, although there were soldiers instead of merchants on the Royal Exchange, and red coats instead of black infesting St Paul's Cathedral. The authorities remained profoundly nervous about possible future explosions. Thus the thirteenth-century church of St Christopher-le-Stocks, with its tower, in Threadneedle Street was deemed to be a potential 'vantage point' from which to storm the Bank of England. It was purchased and knocked down (to be replaced by the Bank's own buildings). It became known that other areas had been subject to similar Anti-Popish violence, notably Bath in the west. Other churches and chapels had been destroyed, such as St Charles Borromeo in Hull.[20]

As a signification that order was being restored, Lord George Gordon himself was arrested in his Welbeck Street house and taken to the Tower of London. He was indicted for High Treason but subsequently acquitted, thanks to a determined defence who pointed out successfully that Lord George and the mob were two quite different things. And one of his legal defenders was not above invoking the Protestant past in a highly emotional manner: 'I will not call up from the graves of martyrs all the precious blood that has been spilt in this land to save its established government and its reformed religion from the secret villainy and the open force of Papists.'[21]

Lord George Gordon's own *Narrative* of these tumultuous events is not marked by any regrets: this, despite the colossal destruction and loss of life which had followed the presentation of the Petition which he had masterminded.[22] In the face of examination, according to Lord Jersey, he had kept 'a tolerable good countenance' and answered all the questions with great cunning; but shrank when his crime was explained to him. In his own account, he describes vividly his fears that *he* would be attacked by Papists, and his need for guards. He denied strongly having any connection to the rioters: 'he thanked God his conscience was perfectly easy and at rest'. Had he used the word 'Persevere', urging on the people in the lobby of the House of Commons? Lord George admitted that it was possible, but always in the sense of persevering 'in constitutional measures'. He had certainly continued to supply them with bulletins throughout the proceedings.

Such a conflicted individual, at once liberally far-sighted and morally blind, was not destined for an easy life, despite this particular acquittal. Further troubles led to further imprisonments, and Lord George Gordon finally died of fever at the age of forty-two in Newgate, that prison once set on fire by the crowd he had inspired. For some time before his death, his interest had moved from Protestantism to Judaism. Five years after the Gordon Riots, he wrote from prison to the Austrian Emperor Joseph II about his policy towards the Jews. He was converted in 1787, growing a beard and taking the additional name Abraham.

The story of Catholic Emancipation, then, began with violence, the sky like blood. Lord George Gordon, by his strange life story, symbolized in an extreme form the enormous obstacles which lay in its path, the embedded Anti-Catholicism in England and Scotland. This was the emotion which would animate a preacher at the conclusion of the Riots, who referred to England as 'the Capital of the Protestant world'. Here was a man who was able to envisage the sufferings of negroes, independent-minded American colonists and Jews, but, far from being able to encompass the need for so-called Catholic Emancipation, felt it his duty to raise the country against it.*

The question was whether the story would also end in violence. As the historian Gibbon, who lived through the period, wrote: 'the month of June 1780 will ever be marked by a dark and diabolical fanaticism which I had supposed to be extinct'.[23] There was another question about the fight for Catholic Emancipation: when would it end, if it ever did? One way or another 'the Catholic Question' would loom over the next fifty years of British history.

---

* The word 'Emancipation' means freeing from legal, social or political disabilities, hence its application to women and slaves as well as the professed adherents of a particular religion.

PART ONE

THE DANGEROUS MIXTURE

'Time will explain this mass of falsehood and intrigue – but when religion is mixed with politics, only misfortune can be expected.'

Hyacinthe Roland (Marchioness Wellesley),
on Catholic Emancipation, 1801

CHAPTER ONE

That Fallen Worship

'She was a Catholic...
And deemed that fallen worship far more dear
Perhaps because 'twas fallen...'

Lord Byron, *Don Juan*

IT IS TIME TO CONSIDER the Catholic world which the savagery of the Gordon Riots of June 1780 was intended to destroy. A year and a half earlier, shortly after the passing of the Catholic Relief Act, the whole household of Lord Petre at Thorndon Hall in Essex was in a state of joyous preparation. This was because King George III and his wife Queen Charlotte, together with their travelling royal panoply, had proposed themselves for a visit timed to coincide with the inspection of some troops in Essex. In English Society, distinguished birth evidently trumped the theoretical disability of a proscribed religion.

In the present instance, Lord Petre was in every way a suitable courtier and host – with the exception of his Catholicism. Cardinal Newman would later describe the English Catholics as having spent decades 'in the shadows', and then added: 'more accurately the shadows of obscure country houses'. This was certainly not true of all the ancient surviving Catholic families:

some of the houses were very large and grand and, in Newman's sense, diffused a good deal of sunlight. Had not Lord Petre's father been given a licence by the Archbishop of Canterbury to marry his mother in 1732 – although both were well known to be Catholics?[1]

Lord Petre was confident of his position in the world, which he regarded with a certain hauteur. This was a man who, with a lofty sense of priorities, paid his Jesuit household chaplain £20 a year but his cook £40. (A generation later Sir William Jerningham paid *his* chaplain a princely £300; as he happily remarked when the man died, now he could give the salary as pin money to his wife.) At the same time Lord Petre was markedly charitable to the less fortunate, and in fact expended 'his time, his mind and his fortune' helping them, in the words of Charles Butler in his *Historical Memoirs respecting the English, Irish and Scottish Catholics,* published in 1819.[2]

A particular indication of his esteemed personal status is given by the fact that he was actually nominated Grand Master of the Masonic Order in 1772, this being before the Papal condemnation of the Freemasons. The new Meeting Hall in Great Queen Street, London, was dedicated to him, in recognition of his sterling work in raising money for it. His portrait* shows a fine, upstanding man of great dignity, whom the Freemasons would later salute: 'In an age of religious bigotry he rose superior to the partisanship of all faiths and creeds... A true and liberal Christian.' Another nineteenth-century ecclesiastic, Cardinal Manning, said that he knew the Church was built on the foundations of St Peter, but he had discovered it was also built on those of Lord Petre.[3] It seemed appropriate to his rank to entertain his Protestant sovereign, although he would be devastated when his daughter married a Protestant (subject).

The largest landowner in Essex, with financial resources backed up by owning a great deal of timber, Robert Edward, 9th Baron Petre came of an ancient family which had managed to hold on to their wealth despite potential penalties. Sir William

---

* Which still hangs there.

Petre had been Secretary of State to Henry VIII, Edward VI and Mary Tudor in succession; the first Lord Petre was created in 1603. Unfortunately, there was a reverse towards the end of the seventeenth century, when the Lord Petre of the time was imprisoned in the Tower of London as a result of the false denunciations of Titus Oates in the so-called Popish Plot.

This malevolent fantasy of 1678, a hundred years before the Catholic Relief Bill, resulted in the execution of various innocent Catholics, including priests. Four priests died in prison, one at the age of eighty-four, probably as a result of being thrown down three flights of stairs.[4] Lord Stafford endured a lifetime's imprisonment and died in the Tower. It remained a vivid if vicious part of the Anti-Catholic propaganda which reached its culmination in the Gordon Riots. In that capacity it could be linked to other legendary episodes of horror in which innocent Protestants were persecuted by villainous Catholics. The fact was that these episodes were horrendous either way: whether true – as some were – or fabricated – as many others were.

One of these was the (genuine) Massacre of St Bartholomew's Day of 1572 in which 3,000 French Huguenots died in Paris and as many as 70,000 in the rest of France. It was notable that a pamphlet was issued in 1678, the time of the Popish Plot, entitled *A Relation of the Barbarous and Bloody Massacre of about an hundred thousand Protestants, begun at Paris, and carried on all over France by the Papists, in the Year 1572*. Lest anyone forget, it ended with a specific denunciation of the Pope: 'Nor did the Pope think there was yet Blood enough shed, but that which all the World condemned as excessive Cruelty, he apprehended was too gentle.' In short, in the words of a recent historian, since the sixteenth-century Reformation, Catholicism had been regarded 'as a form of national treachery'.[5]

In 1666 it had been an automatic reflex to link the tragic accidental Great Fire of London which ignited in Pudding Lane to 'the Papists'. On the first day, there was a rumour that 5,000 French (Catholic) troops had landed in the south of England.[6] Given the primordial desire for some kind of visible target as spurious comfort in a time of disaster, who better than the

Papists? The Jesuits were as always convenient targets: Titus
Oates, recalling that the Jesuits had been implicated in the Gunpowder Plot, accused them of having another go in 1666.* At
the time an hysterical false confession, probably under torture,
by a deranged Catholic watchmaker called Robert Hubert had
conveniently implicated the French and given the slender proof
that was needed. (He was hanged for it despite the doubts of the
judges concerned.)

In 1681, a plaque clearly blaming the Catholics was put up
commemorating the Great Fire on the house where it had started
in 1666: 'Here by ye permission of heaven, hell broke loose
upon this protestant city from the malicious hearts of barbarous
papists, by the hand of their agent Hubert, who confessed, and on
ye ruines of this place declared the fact for which he was hanged
that here began that dredfull fire.'† Similarly, a monument erected
to the Fire by Christopher Wren had an Anti-Catholic message
carved on its east side in 1681, which caused Alexander Pope,
himself a Catholic, to deplore its message in the next century:

> London's column, pointing at the skies,
> Like a tall bully, lifts the head, and lies.[7]

If one delved further back into the unconscious of the sixteenth-
century mob, not to say the Protestant memory, one might find the
deaths of Protestant martyrs decreed by the last English monarch
who was openly Catholic throughout her life. Queen Mary Tudor,
known as 'Bloody Mary', was estimated to have killed 300 people
for the sake of religion (the executions carried out in the subsequent reign of her half-sister Elizabeth – 123 priests and more
than sixty laymen, including women – were of course part of the
Catholic memory, not the Protestant one, and in any case took

---

* The Society of Jesus would actually be suppressed by the Franciscan Pope
Clement XIV in 1773, a fact which did not trouble the mob.

† This plaque, taken down on the accession of James II, then reinstated,
disappeared at one point; it was rediscovered and is now in the Museum
of London.

place over a far longer period of time).[8] Foxe's *Book of Martyrs,* first published in 1563 at the beginning of the reign of Elizabeth, went through several new editions, including cheap instalments, in the eighteenth century. Here brutal religious persecution was linked with Catholicism and foreign intervention, whereas the Protestant martyrs represented 'everyman', including women and babies.

Where individuals were concerned, it was the Pope who was so often the problem. When the Jesuit Father Edmund Campion was sentenced to death, he declared with the eloquence of the future martyr: 'In condemning us [the Catholics] you condemn all your ancestors, all the ancient priests, bishops and kings, and all that was once the glory of England, the island of saints, and *the most devoted child of the See of St Peter*.'[9] It was the last phrase which was lethal.

And yet in the Protestant memory there was that notorious Bull *Regnans in Excelsis* of Pope Pius V of 1570, following the accession of Elizabeth in 1558, excommunicating her. Far from helping the fortunes of so-called 'recusants' or Catholics, it had a devastating effect. By formally releasing Elizabeth's subjects from their loyalty to a heretical sovereign, it enabled them all to be treated as potential traitors in the eyes of the government. The Catholic Cardinal William Allen, for example, did not pretend to believe that Catholics and Protestants could live together, and aimed, on the contrary (if unsuccessfully), at the reconversion of England by a form of conquest.[10] He assisted in the planning of the invasion of the Spanish Armada of 1588.

Most potent of all, perhaps, because it had become an annual ritual of cheerful Anti-Popery, was the image of the bonfires set alight throughout the country on 5 November, in memory of the so-called Gunpowder Plot of 1605. This was another genuine plot, even if the details were not as straightforward as the government of the day pretended. Ever since, an effigy representing the most memorable conspirator, Guy Fawkes, in his trademark black slouch hat, might be burnt on a village green or similar public space to universal glee; alternatively, some image of the Devil or the Pope (in so far as there was perceived to be a difference) provided good sport.

The vilification of the Pope, the cardinals who surrounded him, and all the other trappings of the Roman Catholic Church was amply demonstrated in the scandalous satires of the eighteenth century. The ostensible celibacy of both men and women in religious orders was mocked, as in a couplet of 1733: 'Their Church consists of vicious *Popes*, the rest Are whoring *Nuns* and bawdy *bugg'ring Priests*.'

By way of illustration here were cardinals, identifiable by their hats and robes, lewdly kissing; their love objects were not necessarily female, although when women were involved the dress, if any, was scanty, the flesh by way of contrast lavish, and the sex often visibly unnatural. As the blasphemous text beneath one such picture, *Le Magnificat de Priappe*, had it: here was the physical demonstration of the famous words, 'My soul doth magnify the Lord'.[11]

Enormous British interest, with numerous newspaper articles and best-selling translations of the legal briefs, was taken in salacious reports of a case for abuse brought in 1730 by a twenty-year-old French woman in Toulon against a Jesuit priest described in a popular jingle as:

> That compound of a goatish Lecher
> And a most edifying preacher.

There were numerous newspaper articles and best-selling translations of the legal briefs. One letter to a newspaper hoped that 'every British subject and true Protestant' would now understand 'by what villainous and diabolical Arts' Catholic priests maintained 'absolute Dominion' over the consciences as well as 'the Persons' of their devotees.[12]

All this was the work of passion – and the work of prejudice. But there was a whole other aspect to Anti-Catholicism which might be termed 'politics and foreign policy'. The Stuart threat to the Hanoverian dynasty on the throne had once been a real one, with two armed invasions, coupled with rebellions, in 1715 and 1745.

Furthermore, they had been backed by Catholic powers.

Earlier it was the French in the form of Louis XIV who had supported the Catholic James II to fight the new Protestant King of England, William III, in Ireland. James fled to France after his deposition and, following his defeat at the Battle of the Boyne, Louis XIV gave him refuge for the rest of his life. In short, throughout the eighteenth century the English were regularly involved in wars with Catholic France and Catholic Spain. There might be said to be a hereditary enmity of which their different official religions were symbolic, even if there were many other causes as well.

In 1778 reality was different. The past could not be altogether obliterated: the mother of Lord Petre, for example, host at Thorndon Hall, was the daughter of the Earl of Derwentwater, who had been executed for his part in the rebellion of 1715. But the Stuarts were represented in 1778 by Charles Edward, King Charles III in loyal Stuart parlance. This man, grandson of the king deposed by William III in 1688, had once been known as the Young Pretender, and even as Bonnie Prince Charlie. By this time he no longer represented youth and adventure, but had 'a melancholy, mortified appearance', in the words of a contemporary.[13] He was now approaching sixty, with his 'countenance heavy and sleepy', a bloated red face due to excessive drinking, a lugubrious gaze, his big frame bowed down – in other words, no hero figure to anyone.

Charles Edward had no legitimate heir, and on his death the Stuart claim, if pursued, would thus pass to his only brother Henry. This was the man now designated as Cardinal Henry of York, who had been ordained as a priest and was long resident in Rome. It was true that both men had spoken English since childhood – Henry was described in later years as speaking English 'pretty well for a foreigner' – but his cardinalate was obviously held against him in a Protestant country, even if Charles Edward had had a secret 'conversion' to Protestantism in 1750 on a clandestine visit to London. When it came to the two royal houses, Stuart and Hanover, it could not be questioned that the Hanoverians were by now thoroughly Anglicized by residence for over sixty years since 1715, whereas the Stuarts, in contrast, were aliens. (In his eighty-two years, Cardinal Henry, the Stuart heir, spent twenty months outside Italy, but none of them in England.)[14]

Pointing again in the direction of tolerance was the Quebec Act of 1774. Following the treaty which ended the Anglo-French wars in North America, Canada passed to the British. Yet the largest part of the population was Catholic. Later on, George III personally expressed understanding, and referred to 'the old inhabitants whose rights and usages ought by no means to be disturbed'.[15] Certainly, he acquired at this point about 70,000 new 'Popish' subjects. And there was the practical matter of security. Anti-Catholic penalties had not developed here, animated by passion and prejudice: where politics and foreign policy were concerned, it would be dangerous to impose them. So the Quebec Act was passed, guaranteeing free practice of the Catholic Faith, and, in a significant foretaste of what was to be so controversial in Britain twenty-five years later, removed a reference to the Protestant Faith from the Oath of Allegiance.

The English Catholic world in the eighteenth century, in contrast to such stirring events, presented outwardly a curiously untroubled appearance, given the technical illegality of so many of its practices. Estimates of the actual numbers of Catholics vary, as any estimate of a body practising a religion forbidden by the law of the country must inevitably do. There were probably about 70,000 or 80,000 British Catholics in the 1770s, out of a population of seven million, with estimates of the specific Scottish Catholic population varying between 12,000 and 19,000.

In the future, the rise of the middle classes in the burgeoning industrial cities would be a significant factor. For the time being the continuing influx of Irish workers, who were all Catholic, was an unsettling element, as everything about Ireland at that time was unsettling to the class known as the Protestant Ascendancy which ruled it. In the meantime, the county families who pursued the way of life of their ancestors could do so largely without interference except in times of national danger, as it was perceived by the authorities.

It hardly needs saying that county families who expressed

their restless worldly ambitions, if any, by a keen competitive interest in racing (like the Petres) were very much part of English life. Then there was cricket. John Nyren, the great early chronicler of the game in *The Young Cricketer's Tutor*, was born at Hambledon in Hampshire in 1764 into a Scottish Catholic family which had been implicated in the earlier Jacobite risings and fled to England. Nyren was educated by a Jesuit. His father, Richard Nyren, was founder and member of the famous Hambledon Club which gave laws to English cricket, and his daughter Mary went on to be Abbess of the English convent at Bruges – a conventional path for a girl of her religion at that time. The original list of members of what was then known as the Mary-le-Bone Cricket Club included wealthy Catholics such as a Stonor and Thomas Lord himself, a Catholic by birth, whose name is still commemorated by the ground.[16]

The harsh laws and the live-and-let-live reality were two very different things. This world was divided into the upper classes, the aristocracy and the gentry, and what were literally the working classes. Undoubtedly, the survival of Catholicism in the past was due largely to the dogged, but hopefully inconspicuous, protection provided by the former to the latter. Country neighbours, Anglicans and Catholics, lived amicably together in keeping with this *laissez-faire* reality.

If we take the Welds, an ancient Catholic recusant family established in Dorset, it was significant that at the time of the Forty-Five Rebellion, when all Catholics were supposed to be suspect – not unreasonably – there was trouble for them at Poole Harbour. Rumours were abroad of a plot to release Catholic prisoners held at Plymouth, along the coast. Nevertheless, the local magnate, the Lord Lieutenant, found these charges 'malicious and improbable'. Edward Weld was equally accommodating in turn, and sent his coach horses to a neighbour's stables 'that I may not be in any way obnoxious to the government'. There was general agreement in the neighbourhood that the Welds would give no trouble, and Lord Shaftesbury went further: 'you might have your horses whenever you pleased'.[17]

Meanwhile the lower classes, such as servants of various

degrees and farm workers, miners, mill workers and trades-
men, responded with loyalty, hard work and gratitude for the
opportunity to practise the faith of their fathers (and even more
importantly, in many cases, their mothers). Their contribution
should certainly not be ignored, even if it is for obvious reasons
more difficult to uncover than that of their theoretical superiors.
The unspoken survival of the Catholic community in England,
despite the Penal Laws, depended also on these local families
unknown to history whose existence is recorded as Catholics in
Anglican parish registers. That of Walton-le-Dale parish church,
near Preston in Lancashire in 1781, for example, records 178
families, with 875 individuals as 'Papists'. Where baptisms are
concerned, parental occupations are stated as weaver, husband-
man and labourer, with names such as Turner, Wilcock, Baldwin
and Charnley.*[18]

Records of graveyards bear witness to the kind of benevolent
indulgence by which local people seen as harmless have always
managed to get by. Thomas Errington, a noted London silver-
smith, father of a future archbishop, bought a large estate in
1800 at Clints in Swaledale in Yorkshire. On 8 October 1779
Anne Preston, the cook at Clints, died: 'She was a Papist *but*
[underlined three times] had the Burial Service read as usual.' On
the other hand, 'Bryan son to Miles Stapleton Esq. of Clints and
Lady Mary his wife born *not baptized by me* as the family are
papists.'[19] Evidently neither of these events caused any disruption
as, according to the law, they might have done.

The great houses had their chapels, which might perhaps for
the sake of form be described as libraries, just as chapels had
been secret upper rooms in the dangerous times of the sixteenth
century. Priests, on the other hand, were openly acknowledged
as such, where once they had been described as tutors. (In the
1590s the Jesuit Father John Gerard had the great advantage
of gentlemanly birth and manners: his skill on the hunting field,
especially falconry, made him a plausible family tutor.) Yet

---

* In the 1950s these were still the surnames of schoolchildren in a Black-
burn school.

technically they were illegal: as we have seen, it was still possible to impose a sentence of life imprisonment upon a Catholic priest. In a survival from the bad old days (from the Catholic point of view), the Mass was carefully described in public as 'Prayers'.

Lord Byron, in *Don Juan*, unfinished in 1824 when he died, created a romantic character in Aurora Raby, a sixteen-year-old girl famous for her purity who attracted the passing fancy of the Don. She was an adherent of 'that fallen worship', Catholicism, and 'deemed that fallen worship far more dear / Perhaps because 'twas fallen'. This loyalty, this solidarity, was another residue of the bygone age of danger and execution, equivalent to the folk memories of the Popish Plot. For obvious reasons the Catholic aristocracy was heavily intermarried. Petres, Dormers, Fitzherberts, Stonors, Gages, Welds, Stourtons, Throckmortons, Howards – the leading family of the Dukes of Norfolk – all found partners among themselves with relentless regularity; with, it has to be admitted, occasional slippings-away of great families, when the lure of more obvious worldly advancement was felt to be too great. But, more conventionally, in two generations the Petres made three prestigious interconnected Norfolk marriages. The 9th Lord married, first, Anne Howard, the niece of one duke, and, the year after her death, Juliana Howard, sister of another. His son married Mary Bridget Howard, the sister of Juliana, his own stepmother.

Preparations for the royal visit to Thorndon Hall began ten days before the projected arrival of the royal party on 2 October.[20] They were certainly on a royal scale, just as the house itself, a huge, newly built Palladian mansion with a Corinthian portico, was fit to be a palace. Damask for furnishings was sent from London, with the proviso (which has a curiously modern ring) that it should be *English* damask. In the end Indian damask was also needed, of 'a very beautiful green', for the Drawing Room and the King's Dressing Room, while the Queen's Bedchamber had a more restful 'low-coloured Damask'. A few days later two whole coaches of female upholsterers, gilders, japanners, cabinet-makers and painters arrived, which with the addition of men and women hired locally came to about a hundred people toiling away. A procession of French cooks began, accompanied by their professional moulds, and special confectioners. Another coach full of cooks arrived on the eve of the visit. Except that, as it turned out, it wasn't.

On Friday, 2 October, when all was prepared, an express message came from Lord Amherst. The King had decided to postpone the visit by nearly three weeks to 19 October. The cooks stopped cooking. Everything that was edible had to be eaten up, with special local dinner parties arranged for 'those dishes that would not keep, very good things,' wrote Lord Petre afterwards. (Given his benevolent attitude to the local poor, one assumes that they also benefited.) So the cooks departed.

On 14 October back came the cooks, and the preparing started all over again. Grandees such as Lord Waldegrave, Lady Mildmay and the Duke of Norfolk himself had lent gold plate. The whole scene glittered when, at ten minutes past three, in the words of Lord Petre's journal: 'behold in the Avenue the finest sight of the kind I ever saw'.[21] The sun was bright and shone on the soldiers drawn up on each side as the King and Queen appeared. The massive artillery was engaged in a perpetual noisy salutation, which echoed back from the woods and joined the enthusiastic shouts of the people. The whole county, some on horse, some on foot, were assembled.

The man who now stepped into view was aged forty and had occupied the throne he inherited from his grandfather George II for the last eighteen years; well built but not overweight, with the florid looks which would become associated with his family. John Adams, as America's first Minister to the Court of St James, would deliver the following verdict on him a few years later: King George III had all the 'affability' of Charles II and all the 'domestic virtues and regularity of Charles I'[22] (a reversal of these judgements would certainly make for a much less suitable occupant of the throne).

There was no public hint at this point of the mental – or was it physical? – instability which would haunt the later years of his reign. In fact, his principled firmness at the time of the Gordon Riots was the subject of comment: 'Never had any people a greater obligation to the judicious Intrepidity of their Sovereign', in the words of Sir Nathaniel Wraxall. It was symbolic of his equability – at this date – that he had actually been born in Norfolk House, belonging to the leading Catholic peer, the 9th Duke of Norfolk, with the strong-minded Mary Blount, who was said to be able to 'act the man' when necessary, as his Duchess.[23] And this Duke of Norfolk was the uncle of Lady Petre, his hostess. In both cases, the values of the aristocracy trumped those of the illegal religion.

Queen Charlotte, the German princess the King had married sight unseen soon after his accession, was neither 'tall nor a beauty' but very pale and thin, according to Horace Walpole, describing her at the Coronation which followed shortly after the marriage. On the other hand, she seemed 'very sensible, genteel and remarkably cheerful'.[24] Now in her mid-thirties, Queen Charlotte had proved herself right royally (in the way many queens did not) as a deliverer of princely progeny. She was already mother of twelve out of the fifteen children she would bear altogether; the eldest, George Prince of Wales, was sixteen at this time.

The visit itself was on the same magnificent scale as the arrival, including the fact that the King and Queen were grand enough to need separate dining arrangements. Having escorted them to bed at one, the hosts then enjoyed their own supper at three o'clock in the morning. The royal couple arose for a special breakfast *à deux* in the noble Presence Chamber: 'all sorts of cakes were served up'. The military review which provided the focus for the visit took place in the morning, a special stand having been built so that the Queen could watch. The next day the royal couple departed for the house of Lord Waldegrave, leaving behind a gracious present of 100 guineas for the servants.

The cost to Lord Petre was estimated at over £1,000 (about £75,000 today). Judging from his response to the King, it was all more than worth it. And yet the message was not without its political significance: 'I shall always feel it as the most flattering circumstance of my Life,' wrote Lord Petre, 'that your Majesty gave me an opportunity of shewing him in the ordinary course of life that respect, Loyalty and affection which the laws of my country prevent me from doing on more important occurrences.' He meant his inability as a Catholic peer to sit in the House of Lords.[25] It was an attitude eloquently displayed by his fellow Catholic Lord Arundell of Wardour, who was painted by Reynolds in his official peer's robes – despite the fact that he was barred from taking his seat.

On the one hand the Catholic Relief Act of 1778 aroused further political hopes, as delicately hinted by Lord Petre; on the other hand the violent reaction which followed it in June 1780 confirmed the difficulties which lay ahead before Emancipation and freedom from legal restraints could be achieved. The setting-up of the so-called Catholic Committee brought into prominence a third and potentially lethal feature of the debate: a split between the well-born Catholic laity, the natural governing class had it not been for their religion, and the Church itself. In short, the laity was seen, not without some justification, as trying to free itself from ecclesiastical control in the interests of worldly advancement. 'That system of lay interference' was the angry description of Bishop John Milner later – a key figure in all this, but not on the side of the aristocracy.

The original Catholic Committee consisted of a group of lawyers called together by Lord Petre, to discuss how to bring Relief Acts before Parliament. They had gathered before the 1778 Act in the Thatched House Tavern in Essex Street, taverns being the traditional place for such meetings. At this point the ancient Bishop Challoner, he who would die shortly after the Gordon Riots, gave cautious approval. Challoner, however, born in the previous century, represented the more passive English Catholic Church of yesteryear. Four Apostolic Vicars presided over various geographical areas, with priests beneath them – none of them of course with any legal status, rather the reverse, in the United Kingdom.

The Catholic Committee was reconvened in 1782, and refounded in 1787 with Lords Petre, Stourton and Clifford among the peers, Sir John Throckmorton and Sir William Jerningham – all distinguished Catholic names – among the others. The decision it now took to present a Petition was a fateful one for the English Catholic community because of its nature. The Petition suggested that Catholics should take a new oath of loyalty to the King explicitly denouncing the Stuart claims to the throne. So far, so good, or rather so placatory. But the oath was also to contain another clause even more important for the future: Papal jurisdiction in England was also to be explicitly denied. William Sheldon, the first Secretary of the Catholic Committee, rejected any idea that the Catholic clergy in England should be consulted over temporal, that is, political matters. Their authority – like the Pope's – was to be spiritual only.

The thirty-year-old Sir John Throckmorton wrote pamphlets on the subject which he distributed free of charge. They proposed the election of bishops by the laity according to ancient tradition, and in general advocated less Papal interference. 'I have no other object in this Address to you,' wrote Sir John, 'than the desire of seeing our religion practiced in its primitive purity.' Less engaging was his bald announcement in April 1785 to the Catholic Committee: 'We don't want Bishops [at the meeting].'[26]

This attitude among the prominent English laymen came to be known as 'Cisalpine': that is to say, 'on this side of the Alps', as opposed to the rest of Italy, where lay the magnetic force called Rome. It was a state of mind which made it easy to understand why the heir to the throne, George Prince of Wales, might describe the Catholic religion as 'the religion for a gentleman'. The easy contacts with Catholics made by young aristocrats during their Grand Tours of Europe (the equivalent of the modern gap year) were not likely to turn their minds towards personal bigotry on return. In the same way, Charles James Fox enjoyed 'Popish libraries' abroad, and Whigs whose lack of doctrinaire beliefs made them tolerant would not distinguish between Catholic friends and others while laughing at the ridiculous nature of Popish beliefs.

There was, however, a problem with the Cisalpine philosophy. It might or might or not appeal to the King of the country of which they were proud to be nationals, but it was not calculated to appeal to their own Catholic clergy getting their authority from Rome. In the years to come the English Catholic clergy, above all the abrasive Bishop John Milner, saw this for what it was: a radically different approach to Emancipation from the mere request for Relief. If the Catholic Church was not to be directed by the Vicar of Christ, currently resident in Rome, then by whom? The distinction drawn by the Petition between *spiritual* direction and *temporal* orders relating to national affairs was one which might satisfy the Catholic gentry, longing to be full members of the society to which their families had belonged since ancient times. But, as the clergy perceived, it could be highly dangerous from the point of view of their own status.

Who, for example, should appoint bishops? If the clear answer was the English Catholic Church to which they belonged, then did not the monarch have any say in the appointments – on grounds of security, in view of the Catholic past of rebellion and disaffection? There were many possibilities which might satisfy the need for a formally good relationship between the King and the Catholics. Perhaps the King could be presented with a short list and choose one from among the names on it. Perhaps the King could have a 'Veto' on the Catholics' own choice – the word Veto was to become extraordinarily contentious in the future, not so much between the King and the Catholics, but among the Catholics themselves, including the Catholic Church in Ireland.

The contribution of the working class has been mentioned. There was one particular way in which the sons of labourers and farmers, mine workers and others of hereditary physical stamina exercised a strong, unintended influence on the progress of Emancipation. This was by serving in the army.[27] Theoretically the army could not include Catholics, owing to the need for an Oath of Allegiance which precluded such, and theoretically all the men – who enlisted as 'Protestants' – had to attend Anglican services. In practice, with Scottish Highlanders and with Irish fighters, no such distinction was exercised. Where Ireland was concerned, in 1774 the Irish Parliament passed an Act to allow subjects 'of any persuasion' to swear allegiance. In 1777 it was considered safe to use Scottish Highlanders.

When it was a question of Canada, the Catholicism of the

native inhabitants was treated by the army with respect from the first, for good pragmatic reasons. There were standing orders to the British garrison of Quebec in 1759 that officers were to pay 'the compliment of the hat' to any Catholic processions made in the public streets: it was a civility due to 'the people who have chosen to live under the protection of our laws'. After the capture of Montreal, it was noted with alarm by one Anglican clergyman that the soldiers of the garrison frequently married French women and then had 'Romish Priests' to baptize their children. But since there were few Protestant clergy around (and presumably few Protestant women), it was all part of an inevitable process of practical assimilation by the army.

The generals, not the most obvious class of politically tolerant men at first sight, were in practice extremely realistic, as they needed to be. They saw more clearly than prejudiced dignitaries at home the absolute absurdity of denying their men their Mass, and indeed compelling them by law to attend Anglican services, when it was physical strength and devotion to the military struggle which was demanded of them, not spiritual allegiance. And there was another kind of social absurdity, by the standards of the time, when Lord Petre raised 250 men in 1796 for the French wars, expecting that his son should command them: Mr Petre, however, was sternly told to serve in the ranks, to the 'sensible mortification' of the noble Lord. (It was also arguably illogical, since if his Catholicism did not preclude service in the ranks, why should it bar him from command?)

The British Army in India included many Catholic soldiers who naturally wanted their own priests to tend to them, whatever the law. At Dinapore in 1808 the Anglican Company Chaplain described the visit of 'an Italian padre'; when he came into the barracks 'the Catholics crowded about him by hundreds' and pointed in triumph to his decorous dress (he was actually a Franciscan friar), contrasting it with that of a clergyman of the Church of England, 'booted and spurred and ready for a hunt'.[28]

The need for recruitment, especially in the Scottish Highlands, became acute at the time of the revolt of the American colonies against British monarchical rule. And there was another huge shadow, in this case across the European, not the American, map: this was the threat of revolution in the country just across the Channel. The storming of the Bastille by a revolutionary mob on 14 July 1789 was the first unmistakable public manifestation of what would be known with hindsight as the French Revolution.

CHAPTER TWO

Nothing to Fear
in England

*'We will make every effort to procure you that happiness
and peace which you could no longer enjoy in France;
take courage, therefore, you have nothing more to fear.'*

Greeting to refugee nuns arriving on
Shoreham Beach, 1792

As THE ENGLISH CATHOLIC LORDS petitioned and quarrelled with their own priests, the public attitude to the Catholics in England underwent a transformation based on two very different things: patriotism and compassion.

It was not the campaign of the would-be governing class for Catholic Relief which was responsible, although this continued. It has to be said that even among the great Catholic lords there were different approaches towards participation in the ruling life of the country. Conspicuous for his apparent apostasy was the Premier Peer and Earl Marshal, Charles 11th Duke of Norfolk, who succeeded his father in 1786.[1] In general, such conformity for the sake of integration into the national life had always been known among the Catholic aristocracy and gentry – even if not in quite such a flamboyant form. The Duke, for example, declared that if he was going to hell, he would rather go to hell from the House of Lords than anywhere else. Others of his class and kin preferred a more subtle approach to conformity, with an alleviation of the controversial Oath of Allegiance which Catholics had previously found it impossible to take.

A Relief Bill was prepared by Charles Butler, who would be the first Catholic barrister and was a man undaunted by controversy. A memorial was presented to the Prime Minister, William Pitt, in May 1789. A proposed new oath, formed by the Catholic Committee, was published in June 1789 – and condemned by the four Catholic Vicars Apostolic for the various districts of the country, who disapproved of its language regarding the Papacy. The wrangling continued. Other bishops condemned the oath in January 1791.

Then the priest John Milner attacked the Catholic Committee in February. The peculiar character of Milner was to play a marked part in the history of Catholic Emancipation, not always to its advantage. Here was no gracious descendant of noble but suffering Catholics down the years: Milner, born in 1752, was the son of a tailor in Lancashire and his appearance throughout his life was held to mark his origins – an unwieldy figure and thick, strong neck, florid face marked by heavy, dark, bushy eyebrows. He dressed by preference 'like a farmer' in a greatcoat and beaver hat, 'driving his gig at a spanking pace'.[2]

'Asperity' was the quality his kinder critics gave Milner and he certainly had a weakness for angry rhetorical outbursts. He was also an unqualified opponent of aristocratic dominance over the Church – which implied of course the exact opposite, the dominance of the Church over the aristocracy. There were inevitable comparisons to Thomas à Becket in this respect. A mid-nineteenth-century biography, on the other hand, referred to Milner as the man who had been the Catholics' Moses in their days of bondage, leading them out of the wilderness: in other words, one of the giants of the Faith. There were many tributes also to his tender pastoral care of lesser people, inspired by the principles of the New Testament. It is possible to see that these two pictures, if slanted in different directions, were not incompatible, especially if other discreet comments are borne in mind: Milner, it was said, undervalued 'the little etiquettes of society', and 'the strength of his language gave a handle to his enemies'.[3]

Milner the tailor's son was educated at the English College at Douai in France from the age of sixteen, on the recommendation of Bishop Challoner, and ordained priest in 1777. Returning to England, he ended up in Winchester, a place where Catholic worship of a sort had been openly tolerated since the end of the seventeenth century. But it was Milner who oversaw the building of a Catholic chapel in the Gothic style to replace the inconvenient garden shed and priest's house where it had previously taken place.

The new Bill was eventually passed by Parliament in June 1791. The Relief begun officially in 1778 was continued: the Penal Laws were at last abolished and celebration of the Mass legalized. Milner was now nearly forty, and in the future would become Vicar Apostolic with the rank of bishop for the Midland District.* His strong dislike of the political influence of the aristocracy, however, combined with his equally strong propensity for aggressive argument, remained. The demands of the Catholic Committee to be consulted on ecclesiastical management were not forgotten.

One satire on these demands of laymen to have some say in the appointment of their religious ministers probably dates from late in 1791 or early 1792. It took the form of a spoof Petition entitled The Rights of Women – an amusingly ludicrous concept at the time, when the feminist Mary Wollstonecraft was described by Horace Walpole as a 'hyena in petticoats'. Found in the Weld Archives, it was supposed to be addressed to the Catholic Committee from 'Ladies, Widows, Wives and Spinsters, Housekeepers, Cooks, Housemaids and other female persons professing the Roman Catholic Religion, conceiving themselves to be sorely aggrieved by the subtraction of their inalienable rights'.[4]

Hitherto, although born in a free country, they had only been

* There were no legal bishops at this period with United Kingdom dioceses.

able to exercise their authority 'in the paltry concerns of domestic management' to which their husbands and masters had abandoned them. But 'it would be an evident injustice to exclude one half of the flock, from a right which is now demonstrated to belong to the whole' – that is, the nomination of their spiritual directors. There was a further admonition: remember the 'distinguished' part women have played in the French Revolution. This was more heavy sarcasm, given the contemporary attitude of horror towards the vociferous and uncontrolled women in the French mob.

As for choosing bishops, women could elect deaconesses from among themselves, deaconesses being the glory of the ancient Church and the extinction of that order 'a grievous hardship of the sex' and 'a most lamentable abuse of ecclesiastical discipline'. Now, these imaginary Petitioners hoped, an 'indolent acquiescence in established abuses' would come to an end, and the rights of one half of the Catholic body, i.e. the female half, henceforth be free and untainted.

None of this internecine combat affected the future of Catholicism quite so much as the dramatic, often horrifying events in France. In August 1792 a decree by the new French Legislative Assembly ordered all priests who refused the revolutionary oath to be expelled from the country. The King, Louis XVI, was put to death in January 1793 and in February France declared war on England.

England now became like a Paradise for those who fled from France and the Low Countries. One letter from a certain John Pugh received by a Catholic priest explained the generosity of the welcome:[5] 'I am a Protestant and love the cause of real liberty; but these unhappy men are strangers, thrown by unavoidable accident, not crime, on our shore, and in my humble opinion have the claim which distress not tainted by crime always should have.' These were words which might stand for the compassion due to refugees down the ages.

It was Sir Samuel Romilly who commented in 1792 on a new 'phenomenon': you couldn't walk 100 yards in any London street without meeting two or three French priests, and this was only twelve years after the Gordon Riots. The Abbé Barruel put it lyrically: 'the soul seemed to awaken from a terrifying dream of fiends and monsters, into a scene of perfect ease and liberty'. Some French Catholics who were welcomed by the English Protestant aristocrats Lord and Lady George Cavendish were more crudely explicit: 'Here we are not stunned with the ferocious sound of *Ça Ira*, nor the brutal *carmagnole*, rows of strewed bayonets, uplifted.' In short, France was once more the enemy, as she had been eight times during the past century – but a very different enemy.

Hitherto Britons had had a mental picture of the French as, in the words of Linda Colley, 'superstitious, militarist, decadent and unfree'.[6] It was the unhappy (Protestant) Huguenots, notably after the Massacre of St Bartholomew, who had sought to escape France and settle in England. Now the picture had changed. France was no longer a Catholic enemy, but an enemy representing Unbelief who was thus an enemy of Catholicism. It was a country in which nuns and priests were likely to be murdered, or imprisoned and executed during the Terror of 1792. Nor were the horrors short-lived: a terse entry in the diary of a middle-class Frenchman for the summer of 1794 reads: 'Today, 40 individuals had their heads cut off, including 16 Carmelite nuns.'*

Horror stories spread to England and lost nothing in the telling, particularly as there were escapes by members of prominent families such as Stonor, Plowden and Dormer. One party of priests with a host of English boys in their care made a daring crossing to Hull in Yorkshire, and so traversed the north of England to hospitable Lancashire. Naturally the French priests who arrived in England responded with ardent prayers for the King and the Royal Family at Mass.

Benedictine nuns at Cambrai were imprisoned at Compiègne, and since they had no money to subsidize their prison keep – having made lifetime vows of poverty – were limited to a grudging diet of bread and water by their jailers. Mary, daughter of Charles Stonor, born in 1768, had become a nun while still at her convent school in Paris; there she remained, using the term

---

* The plot of Poulenc's opera *Dialogues des Carmélites*.

Citoyen when writing to her brother Thomas and prudently designating herself *Citoyenne* (although she offered a Mass for Louis XVI after his execution). The convent was made into a women's prison, and only the death of Robespierre saved Mary from the guillotine: she was now Prioress, a tall and severe figure who would impose the religious rules of abstinence even on sick children – but she had survived.[7]

The refugees fell into two main categories. There were actual Catholic priests: it has been reckoned that French émigrés may have constituted as much as ten per cent of the Catholic clergy in England at one point.[8] Then there were the English Catholics, some quite young, who were being educated out of their own country, the only opportunity acceptable to them, Catholic education being forbidden at home. This discreet slipping off abroad was one way of keeping a low profile. Places like Douai and St Omer in France flourished. Naturally some of these same children, upon reaching adulthood, decided to enter the religious life themselves. Sons remained to train as priests, or take their vows as monks; daughters who felt a vocation to the religious life (instead of marrying one of their cousins in England – the obvious alternative at the time) settled into a kind of world which was familiar since childhood, despite being far from home. It was after all a process which had been going on since the Reformation.

Charlotte Jerningham, for example, daughter of the lively observer Frances Lady Jerningham and the solid Norfolk squire Sir William, was deposited by her parents in the Ursuline Convent of the Blue Nuns in Paris in 1784. It was a conventional move for a girl of her class. But it was the same need that had driven English Catholic women during far more frightening times in the seventeenth century. Mary Ward was part of the vast, active Catholic cousinage which had produced several Gunpowder Plot conspirators, but herself was inspired by the more laudable aim of promoting girls' education. She founded the Institute of the Blessed Virgin Mary abroad, an order of nuns, for that purpose.* The Reformation, which had necessitated the flight of the

* The I.B.V.M. is still in existence.

convents and their treasured nun–teachers from England, was a positive disadvantage to the cause of girls' education – unless the girls could go abroad.

Back in England, nuns were therefore another phenomenon, in Romilly's phrase, not seen for 250 years. Thomas Weld of Dorset, whose daughters had been educated abroad and become nuns, called them 'terrestrial angels', on the grounds of their music, now heard once more. (Other nuns, however, felt awkward in their unaccustomed everyday dress – 'a strange appearance in those unused to it' – especially as they were forbidden to carry their familiar breviaries, the prayers books which encased their rituals, in public.) One of Weld's daughters, who made her vows as a nun in 1795 at Winchester, was probably the first to do so since the Reformation.[9]

John Milner established Benedictine nuns who had fled from Brussels, and Franciscans from Bruges. Lady Stourton hosted some canonesses from Liège at Holme Hall in Yorkshire. In the words of the Prioress, the Stourtons 'expressed the greatest satisfaction to have it in their power to afford us an asylum in our present distress', even if the villagers were said to be greatly alarmed to see so many people dressed 'in a peculiar manner', just as others gawped at 'Frenchmen dressed in women's clothes' – who were of course actually priests with their long skirts.[10] The Benedictine schools for boys at Douai and Dieulouard in Lorraine were given refuge by Sir Edward Smythe at Acton Burnell Hall in Shropshire. The chaplain of Lady Anne Fairfax at Gilling Castle in Yorkshire was Dom John Anselm Bolton, who had held his position for thirty years. Now he arranged for Ampleforth Lodge to be given to his community of St Lawrence, made homeless by the Revolution.*

Where money was concerned, appeals were singularly successful, and nearly £34,000 was raised in a few weeks (roughly £2.5 million in today's money) from the University of Oxford, and cities such as Bristol, Portsmouth and Winchester. The language

---

* His name is still commemorated today at Ampleforth School in the steep hill known as Bolton Bank.

of the appeals was highly emotive, with its references to the assaults committed against the wretched Catholics caught up in the Revolution: 'several women... dedicated to religion, in the peculiar exercise of a sublime charity attending sick in hospitals, stripped naked and barbarously scourged in public, women driven out, many old'. There was a significant reminder of the history they all shared: 'It is hoped that a difference in religious persuasion [Catholic as opposed to Protestant] will not shut the hearts of the English Public against their suffering brethren, the Christians of France.'[11]

One moving episode at Shoreham Beach in Sussex seemed to sum up the strange contradictions in the English Catholic world. In 1792 French nuns who for years had been established at Montargis in the Loire Valley, having been rudely expelled, expected to go to Catholic Belgium via England. When they arrived at Shoreham, however, where the captain of the ship had warned the inhabitants, the beach was crowded with a large number of carriages and a mass of people.[12] The nuns cannot have failed to have felt apprehension, to put it at its mildest, given that they were disembarking on an island where for over two hundred years their religion had been proscribed.

But the women scarcely had time to scramble out of their tiny boats before there was wild cheering. 'Come, come and forget amongst us all that those villains have made you suffer.' They were then taken to a neighbouring house for an enthusiastic welcome: 'We will take away the least trace of your misfortunes.' The salutations continued: 'You will find here none but feeling and compassionate hearts, who will esteem themselves happy in repairing the injustice and cruelty of your fellow countrymen.' Others still said: 'We will make every effort to procure you that happiness and peace which you could no longer enjoy in France; take courage, therefore, you have nothing more to fear.'

It was at nearby Brighton that the nuns learned of a remarkable piece of intervention on their behalf. It was the heir to the throne, George Prince of Wales, now aged thirty, who had offered to defray expenses in the town where he himself had begun to build a regal so-called pavilion in 1784. He also sent his own physician to see them the morning after their arrival to enquire after their welfare; in a subsequent visit the physician persuaded the Reverend Mother not to journey on as had been intended but rest in England. Later George met the community and, with what was the true politeness of princes, left before too long. That is to say, when it became obvious that the lack of chairs meant the exhausted nuns had to stand so long as he remained, he turned to his companion and suggested tactfully that they left. Who was this companion who had been part of the welcoming party at Shoreham and had undoubtedly alerted the Prince? She was a certain widow, Mrs Maria Fitzherbert, and it was widely believed that she was the Prince's (Catholic) wife.

Born as Mary Anne Smythe, granddaughter of a baronet, Maria Fitzherbert, as she was now known, was in her thirties, six years older than the Prince. Maria had in fact been twice widowed, in both cases without children. Her previous husbands were also from the higher echelons of the Catholic gentry: Edward Weld, who died after falling from a horse, and Thomas Fitzherbert of Swynnerton, who had died following the Gordon Riots; the latter left her wealthy.

During the 1780s the Prince of Wales's love for this famously sympathetic woman – 'sweet by nature' – had become the stuff of gossip. Her fellow Catholic (or 'Cat' as she put it), Frances Lady Jerningham, wrote in 1786: 'Mrs Fitzherbert has I believe been married to the Prince. But it is a very hazardous undertaking... God knows how it will turn out – It may be to the Glory of our Belief, or it may be to the great Dismay and destruction of it.' The details of her lifestyle impressed Society: 'She has taken a Box to herself at the Opera, a thing which no Lady but the Duchess of Cumberland ever did – 100 guineas a year. The Prince is very assiduous in attending her in all public places.'[13]

The Prince was, in fact, said to have first glimpsed Maria at the opera, probably in the box of her friends Lady Anne and Lady Margaret Lindsay in 1784, and become smitten. Yet her physical appearance was evidently not the whole key to Maria Fitzherbert's engaging personality. Her hair was luxuriant, it was true, and she had soft hazel eyes; but her figure was lavish, or as Lady Jerningham put it to one who was evidently not an admirer: 'Do you remember seeing her when she was the Widow Weld? You found her *far too fat*.'[14] One suspects that the answer lay in a mixture of the ardent, the maternal (always an element in the Prince's later love affairs) and sheer niceness.

Maria Fitzherbert was not only a good Catholic, but she was a good, kind, charitable person: the two virtues, after all, as with any religion however venerable, were not necessarily to be equated. One of the proofs of this virtue was the very fact that their publicly close relationship definitely indicated to the outside world that in some way Maria believed herself married to the Prince. There is evidence of a wedding on 15 December 1785, performed in a private house by a clergyman of the Church of England, after the Prince caused a report of his despair and shortly ensuing death to be carried to her.[15] The wedding, valid in the eyes of the Catholic Church, was enough to satisfy Maria's conscience. (There was no requirement at this date to get married in front of a Catholic priest in England, where the decrees of the Council of Trent had not been promulgated.) Henceforth the couple acted unashamedly as husband and wife.

But this validity in the eyes of the Catholic Church was where the complications of the situation became evident. Except for its dramatic royal connotations, the whole episode was no different from the many anomalies and irksome restrictions faced by Catholics in eighteenth-century England. Here was the heir to the British throne. If the Royal Marriages Act of 1772 applied to anyone, it applied to him. Yet this Act demanded the assent of the sovereign to the marriage of George III's descendants, without which it had no official status. Any children born to such a union, for example, would be illegitimate. For the future it was significant that the Prince of Wales was still theoretically free to wed (and beget heirs). In the meantime, nice Mrs Fitzherbert graciously lorded it in London – and in Brighton. The destitute nuns of Shoreham Beach were the beneficiaries.

Thomas Weld of Lulworth Castle was the younger brother of Maria's husband Edward, from whom he inherited in 1775. Weld was another Catholic oligarch, to use a modern phrase, who combined landed power, philanthropy for his co-religionists, and a real friendship with King George III. His nature was not that of a political activist and he had in fact refused to join the Catholic Committee in 1782. Weld was certainly known for his individuality within the confines of his class. His co-religionist Robert Clifford criticized him at one point for some property deal which Clifford felt belied Weld's great reputation for piety. How much better to save a noble family in distress – the religion of hundreds depended on it – than say the breviary at four o'clock in the morning! He added sardonically that everybody had their own method of seeing things, 'as the Welshman said when he kissed the cow'.[16]

Weld the determined individual was said to be 'the handsomest small man in England'. If a small man, he certainly owned a lot of large properties, and was rumoured to be the second-largest landowner in England:[17] there were Chideock and Pylewell Park in the south-west, as well as Lulworth, whose proximity to Bath at the time of the Gordon Riots, together with his own prominence, had caused Weld to worry about security. Then there were Leagram and Stonyhurst in Lancashire and Britwell in Oxfordshire.

The Welds had a huge family born between 1773 and 1789. There was a priest, besides the eldest son, also Thomas, who first married and had children, then became a cardinal, giving up his properties. There were intermarriages, naturally enough, with families such as the Stourtons. It was Charlotte Stourton, married to Joseph Weld, who was installed at delightful Pylewell Park, near Lymington, while Catherine Weld, 'the Dorset Rosebud', married the future Lord Stourton.

There were also three daughters who had become nuns abroad as Sisters of the Third Order of St Francis at Bruges and had to be rescued. Weld's agent sent a coded message conveying the success of his mission: he was despatching 'three black mares'. Weld's request was that they should wear bonnets and black veils, not those giveaway nuns' hoods. Nuns must not dress 'to frighten the crows'. The King nodded benevolently in the direction of the holy paraphernalia they needed to bring with them, technically forbidden: 'Tell them to bring their Church vestments, breviaries and such like. I will give orders that they shall pass the Custom House.' The propinquity of the King's favoured seaside resort, Weymouth, to Lulworth Castle obviously played a part in this friendship between monarch and Catholic gentleman. Who would not want to ride across the sands to nearby Lulworth Cove, over which loomed a romantic Elizabethan castle? It was a castle, incidentally, which had been acquired by the Welds in the middle of the last century and much renovated since.

In August 1789 a more formal visit took place, for which Thomas Weld had his own private agenda. Just as the wretched French royal family, ejected by the mob from Versailles, were trying to settle into the Tuileries in Paris, the King and Queen of England arrived by frigate at Lulworth Cove, where they found carriages waiting to convey them to the castle. At Lulworth itself, the steps were covered with 'carpetry'. There was a medallion of the King over the door flanked on either side by two great statues festooned with a broad label of Garter Blue silk inscribed with the words: 'Long Live the King'. Colours were also flown from the top of the castle. Eight of the Weld children lined the steps, singing 'God Save the Great George', and the Queen was later greeted by the whole lot drawn up in order of age in the Hall.[18]

The only awkward moment was when Thomas Weld's sister was spotted going barefoot and bare-legged, giving food to the poor. George III made his lack of approval for such informality clear: 'God might be served as well with shoes and stockings on as without them,' was his acid comment.

The crucial part of the visit – at any rate from the point of view of the host – was the reaction of the King to the Great Chapel, which Weld had started building in the grounds in 1786 (and would in fact be consecrated by three bishops late in 1790). Previous chapels had been attached discreetly to country houses, doubled as upper rooms or in some other way built so that their true purpose was capable of polite dissimulation. At Lulworth there had obviously always been some room for prayer or a hidden chapel, traditionally below the floor of the North East

Tower, and later in the muniments room, but this was a radical step forward. There was a story that King George had, with a wink, proposed that his friend was actually building a free-standing family mausoleum (a perfectly legal endeavour, unlike the chapel). At any rate one may imagine the collective sigh of Weld family relief when the royal inspection passed without incident except for the most gracious observations.

Now Thomas Weld was able to write to his co-religionist and neighbour Lord Arundell, whose chapel at Wardour Castle was a few years earlier, but more or less discreetly still constituted part of the house: 'I am very glad this business is over. I hope it will answer the purpose I have solely in view. I think the King's seeing the Chapel in that public manner must be a kind of sanction to it.'[19]

While the Catholics in England benefited from the effects of the French Revolution, which developed into outright war between England and France, the effects in Ireland were very different. Here was a largely Catholic country, riddled with patriotism of a very different sort, if equally sincere. Long ago the future Jesuit martyr Edmund Campion, who knew Ireland in the middle of the sixteenth century, described it as being like an egg, lying aloof in the West Ocean. This aloofness could no longer be counted upon. The position of Ireland, so near to England in terms of geography, so distant in terms of religion, made it a perpetual security threat in times of war from the perspective of the British government and the so-called Protestant Ascendancy who ruled it. The perspective of the Irish, who wished for independence from what they considered to be English rule, was naturally very different. War, especially with France, was their opportunity. The example not only of the French Revolution, but the successful bid for independence by the former colonists in America, inspired rebellion.

'The 1798' – the Irish revolt of the United Irishmen against English domination, potentially backed by French forces – was led by the Protestant Wolfe Tone. In a powerful pamphlet, *An Argument on Behalf of the Catholics of Ireland,* issued seven years earlier, Wolfe Tone had evoked the outcry of Shylock against persecution of the Jews: 'Shall they not say to us "Are we not men as ye are... Hath not a Catholic eyes, dimensions, organs, passions? Fed with the same food, hurt by the same weapons, healed by the same means, warmed and cooled by the same summer and winter, as a Protestant is?"'* Wolfe Tone proposed that Anti-Catholicism belonged to 'the dark ages of superstition', not 'the days of illumination, at the close of the eighteenth century'.[20]

Wolfe Tone and others were arrested and found guilty, although Wolfe Tone cheated the hangman and died by his own hand. Lord Edward Fitzgerald, a rebel from the ducal family of Leinster, died in prison. But the whole troubling episode convinced the English government under William Pitt that a proper joining-up of the governments with only one Parliament, and that in London, was the essential method to preserve general British security. It was for this reason that the Act of Union of 1801 was promulgated.

Was there perhaps an opportunity here for those (not all Catholics) who believed that Catholic Emancipation was also in the best interests of the country? Catholic Emancipation, like any other Bill put before Parliament, did of course need the Royal Assent; that is to say, the agreement of King George III, good friend of Thomas Weld, benevolent patron of the escaping Weld nuns.

---

* Shakespeare's original lines from *The Merchant of Venice*, Act 3 scene i began: 'Hath not a Jew eyes?... warmed and cool'd by the same winter and summer as a Christian is?'

CHAPTER THREE

The Royal Conscience

*'The agitation of it had been the cause
of a most serious and alarming illness to
an illustrious personage'*

The Duke of York on George III
and Catholic Emancipation

IRELAND NOW HAD its Parliament formally swallowed up in
that of the United Kingdom by an Act which came into force
on 1 January 1801. This was a country with a huge Catholic
population. It has been variously estimated as three-quarters or
even five-sixths of the total, with the remainder divided between
the Established (Protestant) Church and Dissenters.[1] But Catholicism, although without question the dominant religion, was not
spread evenly across the various classes. On the contrary, the
ruling classes, as the phrase Protestant Ascendancy indicates,
tended one way, while their social inferiors, whether servants,
farmers or soldiers, were almost universally Catholic.

These peasants, as they were seen from across the English
Channel, were routinely derided with the word 'barbarous', or
barbarian, deriving from the Latin *barbarus* for stranger. However, they were of course the natives of the island, and it was the

Protestant Ascendancy whose history stretched back to invasion, notoriously that of Cromwell in 1649, and subsequent settlement in the great estates of the land. Nevertheless there was an endemic attitude of scorn – often affectionate scorn – towards the Catholic peasantry on the part of those who were their social superiors.

Not only were these peasants but they were lawless peasants, as Robert Peel pointed out early in his political career, when he was sent to Ireland as Chief Secretary in 1812: 'You can have no idea of the moral depravation of the lower orders in that country.' This was accompanied by a 'fidelity towards each other' which was 'unexampled, as they are in their sanguinary [blood-thirsty] disposition and fearlessness of the consequences'. Only the occasional compassionate voice would be raised, as when Maria Edgeworth, a Protestant, exclaimed to her sister about a noble chimney sweeper's boy spending hours climbing: 'I only wish the Anti-Catholics could have seen how poor Catholics were labouring here ... They are a most generous people ... wretched boys in rags refused shillings from me,' reminding her she had paid before although she would otherwise have blithely done so twice.[2]

Like all forms of racial or religious prejudice, this attitude could produce ludicrous incidents or amusing comments which provided at the same time a guide to contemporary values. Edward Bulwer entertained the Irish hero Daniel O'Connell in his London house at the height of the latter's early triumph. The story was that Mrs Bulwer directed the cleaning arrangements in the dining room the next day: she explained that she was 'fumigating in order to get rid of the brogue'.[3] Most of the Catholic peasantry would never see the inside of a gracious London household, but the treatment they received from birth, which was linked demographically to their religion, was inspired by the same fundamental contempt for 'the brogue' and what it stood for.

When Alexis de Tocqueville cast his cool eye on Irish society, he described the typical Protestant lord: 'His dogs are large and fat and fellow beings are dying at his door. Not only does he never help the poor in their need, he profits by their necessities to extract enormous rents and goes to France and Italy to spend the money he has gained.' In the meantime it was the poorest who had the most children, out of despair. It was small wonder that the Irish people believed firmly in another world, wrote de Tocqueville, 'because they are unhappy in this one'.[4] In its own way, this was a similarly prejudiced view, ignoring the numerous benevolent landlords, but it did express the vast difference in the two ways of life, so clearly visible to an outsider.

There could be a variety of attitudes within this contempt. The historian David Hume, pronouncing in 1767 that the Irish, 'from the beginning of time, had been buried in the most profound barbarism and ignorance', put it down to the fact that they had never been conquered by the Romans. Later the poet Robert Southey, inveterately hostile to the idea of Catholic Emancipation, asked himself the same question: why were the Irish people so barbarous? He blamed the Catholic aristocracy, their surviving landowners and their priests: it was their own leadership which deserved to be reproached. For all that, he was convinced that letting Catholics near political power would be 'the most perilous experiment that could by possibility be tried in a Protestant country'.[5]

There were those, the decent Protestant people of good intentions, who took comfort in the fact that the Catholics were actually the intolerant ones. This was an attitude summed up later by the nineteenth-century historian J. A. Froude: Ireland's 'Romanism' in the eighteenth century had aimed at domination, whereas the English attitude, infinitely less repressive, was one of *laissez-faire*. In short, the Catholics had no right to complain: 'They who had never professed toleration, had no right to demand it.'[6]

Another foreigner, the infinitely grand Prince Pückler-Muskau, took a more romantic view (despite being announced as Prince Pickling Mustard by the footman of the Irish novelist Lady Morgan): 'For all their crudity, these people combine probity with the poetic homeliness of the German, the quickness of the French and powers to best all the naturalness and submissiveness of the Italians.' He was therefore able to reflect with genuine pleasure, unconscious of complacency: 'I know no country in which I would rather be a great landowner.'[7]

It is true that changes were on the way. Towards the end of the eighteenth century, the Catholic middle class was beginning to germinate and grow as the career of Daniel O'Connell himself would demonstrate. But of course the middle class felt particularly hard done by according to the exclusive religious laws: as Sydney Smith wrote, there was not a parent who didn't feel 'his own dear preeminent Paddy would otherwise rise to the highest honour of state'.[8] It was to the advantage therefore of this class that in 1793 there was a Catholic Relief Act for Ireland. The prohibition against Catholics voting there was relaxed and the so-called Forty-shilling Freeholders – named after the value and status of their property – were emancipated (but they still could not stand for state office, of course). The Irish Catholics could also now inherit by the same rules as Protestants, and take 999-year leases, another overdue amelioration of their condition.

There was a rise in Catholic church-building after this date, including cathedrals in Waterford and Cork before the end of the century, and Dublin fifteen years later. The Royal College of St Patrick at Maynooth in Co. Kildare, 'for the better education of persons professing the popish or Roman church', to train priests, was voted public money by the Irish Parliament in June 1795 and after the Union its annual grants were fixed at nearly £10,000 a year (roughly £750,000 today).[9] The circumstances created by the French Revolution were once again part of the equation. The origin of the grant was a wish to prevent seminarists from crossing over to wartime France, whence they might return full of inappropriate revolutionary sentiments; but the effect was to bring Catholics generally closer into the Establishment.

At quite a different level, there was an increase in Catholic pilgrimages to places of ancient devotion at various points in the island. Croagh Patrick, nicknamed the Reek, in County Mayo near Westport, was one example, with its tradition of being climbed by pilgrims on Reek Sunday, the last Sunday in July, in honour of St Patrick's fast there. The name of the national saint was attached also to St Patrick's Purgatory, another ancient pilgrimage site on an island in Lough Derg, in Co. Donegal, mentioned in documents as early as the twelfth century.*

When the Act of Union came to be considered in detail, it made perfect sense for the subject of general Catholic Emancipation to be discreetly raised. Such a possibility – more than that, such a prospect – was delicately held out to the Catholic peers, and the liberal Protestants who advocated it for the sake of Ireland's future. Naturally the assent of the sovereign had to be secured, as with any proposed Act of Parliament: that was part of the British constitution.

The unexpectedly tumultuous episode which followed was centred on this Royal Assent. A shrewd comment about it was made in a letter soon afterwards: 'Time will explain this mass of falsehood and intrigue – but when religion is mixed with politics, only misfortune can be expected.'[10] The writer was Hyacinthe Roland, or Wellesley, as she would become: the French Catholic mistress and future first wife of Wellington's elder brother Richard, Marquess Wellesley. Certainly from the point of view of the 'Catholic Question', as the cause of Emancipation was generally known, 1801 represented an enormous setback which differed from that earlier setback the Gordon Riots in one major respect – the King was on the other side.

At some point the conscience of King George III, a decent, amiable, certainly not intolerant man, with good Catholic friends and compassionate towards unfortunate Catholic refugees, found itself stirred into a frenzy by the prospect of allowing these same Catholic friends and their children to participate in any way in the government of the country. There had been warnings over the years.[11] In 1795 he had declared that the subject was 'beyond the decision of any Cabinet of Ministers' and over the next years he issued further warnings such as this: 'I should become an enemy to it' – the Union – 'if I thought a change of situation of the Roman Catholics would attend the matter.'

It was a question of the oath which as sovereign he had

---

* Five thousand pilgrims were recorded even in the dark days of 1700, rising to 15,000 by 1826. It remains a place of pilgrimage today.

sworn at his Coronation forty years earlier on 22 September 1761. This was originally devised in 1689 after the Protestant couple William and Mary had replaced the Catholic James II. It naturally owed much to the seemingly perilous situation of the new English regime, threatened not so much by the exiled James as by his powerful backer Louis XIV.

In 1761 the key question was put to the young George III in Westminster Abbey by the Archbishop of Canterbury. It began as follows: 'Will you to the utmost of your power maintain the laws of God, the true profession of the Gospel, and the Protestant reformed religion established by law?' The Archbishop elaborated: 'And will you maintain and preserve inviolably the settlement of the united Church of England and Ireland, and the doctrine, worship, discipline and government thereof, as by law established, within England and Ireland, and the countries thereunto belonging?' He further named the rights and privileges of the bishops and clergy.

At the end King George rose up out of his chair in Westminster Abbey, and was assisted by the Lord Great Chamberlain, with the Sword of State carried before them, to the altar. Here he laid his right hand on the Holy Gospel contained in a great Bible. It had previously been carried in the procession and was now offered to him by the Archbishop kneeling before him. He made a solemn declaration.[12]

'The things which I have here before promised, I will perform and keep. So help me God.' After that the King kissed the Book. And then he was anointed. It was by the special request of the King that the anthem which followed was Handel's *Zadok the Priest*. It had been composed for the previous Coronation of his grandfather in 1727 with its awesome invocation: 'May the King live for ever. Amen, Allelujah.'

The King had made a clear public promise in 1761 – one whose meaning became clearer to him as time went on, with a little help from interested parties. On the other hand, it can never be known exactly what private promises were made in Dublin concerning future Catholic Emancipation in the run-up to the Act of Union. But promises there were.

One politician of rising importance was Viscount Castlereagh, heir to the Marquess of Londonderry but not yet a peer in his own right and thus able to sit in the House of Commons. Castlereagh was thirty-two in 1801. He had first taken office in 1797 and as Chief Secretary at the time of the Rebellion of 1798 had incurred some odium with the Irish. Yet he had his own clear philosophy regarding the two countries: in his role of Chief Secretary for Ireland beneath the Viceroy, 'I trust I shall never be an Irishman in contradiction to the Justice due to Britain, nor an Englishman opposing and betraying the interests of this country [Ireland].'[13] It was a noble sentiment, if more difficult to put into practice than to enunciate, given the sharp observation of Hyacinthe Wellesley on the subject of religion and politics.

Part of Castlereagh's personality was his undeniable charm. In the words of one interested observer of the political scene, Mrs Harriet Arbuthnot, confidante of the Duke of Wellington, he would come to present a fine commanding figure, with compelling dark deep-set eyes, rather a high nose and 'a mouth whose smile was sweeter than it is possible to describe'; he also had the perfect gallant manners of the aristocrat. A comparison was made to the young Augustus; alternatively Castlereagh had 'all the grace of the French and the manliness of the English and Irish...'.[14]

Time would show that one gift, that of oratory, had been denied this ladies' delight; but then the House of Commons was not the salon of Mrs Arbuthnot. He was a soporific orator, literally so: his compatriot Thomas Moore merrily versified on the subject twenty years later:

> Last night I tossed and turned in bed
> But could not sleep – at length I said
> 'I'll think of Viscount Castlereagh
> And of his speeches – that's the way.'[15]

In the late 1790s oratory was less important than the machinations which led to the successful presentation of the Act of Union. Castlereagh's Irish connection – like that of the Wellesley brothers – implied knowledge, but not necessarily sympathy for independence. For example, Castlereagh had come to believe strongly in the Union as a method of keeping the native Irish down; at the same time he had the patrician attitude of approval for the Irish in the army. 'Linked with England,' wrote Castlereagh, 'the Protestant Irish would feel less exposed, and become more confident and liberal, and the Catholics would have less inducement to look beyond that indulgence which is consistent with the security of our establishment.'

Emancipation, on the other hand, was a subject where his Irish connection acted the other way: it was possible for him to see how it might lead to a peaceful settlement of the country without incurring any proportionate danger. Castlereagh was therefore in a position to hold out hopes to the Catholic clergy and the Catholic members of the Irish establishment that Emancipation might follow Union.

In London, the chain of events was distressingly clear, at least on the surface. On 25 January 1801 a Cabinet meeting was held at 10 Downing Street, residence of the Tory Prime Minister, William Pitt the Younger, who had succeeded to office eighteen years earlier when he was only twenty-four.* As a result, the principle of Catholic Emancipation was approved. During the next two days the King was informed of what had happened. The results were disastrous.

The crucial event was the Royal *levée* of 28 January at St James's Palace, where official royal events took place, although Buckingham House at the head of the Mall had become the residence of the Royal Family in 1761. At this familiar event, imported originally by Charles II from France, it was the custom for politicians, soldiers and diplomats to be presented to the sovereign. It thus provided an opportunity for personal conversations at the monarch's choosing. Where George III was concerned, some of these could be uncomfortably frank. There

---

* The word Tory is used throughout this book for simplicity's sake in order not to distract from its theme, not according to contemporary practice.

was a further opportunity for impromptu declarations, of which the government would have no warning.

The royal *levée* of 28 January proved a catastrophe from the point of view of the government – and a nasty surprise to many of those present. George III publicly declared in a loud, 'agitated' voice that anyone who even proposed Catholic Emancipation forfeited his friendship. The terms in which he spoke were unequivocal. He used the term 'personal enemy'. When Henry Dundas, a minister and currently MP for Edinburgh, proposed a distinction between the King in private as an individual, and in his constitutional capacity, George III replied sharply: 'None of your Scotch metaphysics!' The King continued melodramatically: he would rather beg his bread 'from door to door through Europe' than consent to any measure that would betray his Coronation Oath.[16]

A meeting of the Cabinet was hastily called. Pitt remained in favour of Emancipation. Loughborough, Westmorland and Liverpool were against. On 1 February 1801 Pitt wrote to the King in the most reasonable terms he could design, pointing out that Catholic Emancipation would not harm the interests of the Established Church or Protestant interest in England or Ireland. The dangers from the Catholic people were gradually declining, and among the higher orders especially 'have ceased to exist'. The special new oath, for those taking office within the State, would take care of the situation, with its disclaimer of 'politically obnoxious' tenets and explicit refusal to be overridden by a priest's absolution. But, said Pitt, if the King disagrees, as he believes he does, Pitt will only remain in office long enough for him to find a successor.[17]

The King's response was unequivocal: any proposition which tended to destroy the maxim that employees of the State must be members of the Established Church could not be discussed. Anything else would result in 'the complete overthrow of the whole fabric'. On 2 February George III duly read his speech to the House of Lords at the Opening of Parliament with only one reference to the Union – not the one which so many of the leading Catholics and Pro-Catholics in Ireland were expecting.

Pitt resigned on 3 February as he had offered to do, and Henry Addington became Prime Minister in his place. It has been suggested that Pitt's own physical state was shaken by these events, leaving him as agitated as the King at the end of an audience.[18] Gout was an increasing problem. There were thus two healths involved, that of the King and that of the Prime Minister, not one. But from the point of view of Catholic Emancipation, it was Pitt's resignation which was the important, inexorable fact.

This was the monarch who had agreed to the rights of the French Canadians to their own religion, and was the genuine personal friend of Lord Petre and Thomas Weld. What had happened? The answer was in two parts. Partly he had been preyed on for political reasons by members of his court opposed to Pitt. One demonic force – from the Catholic point of view – was John FitzGibbon, created Earl of Clare in 1795 in the Irish peerage and later a Baron in the United Kingdom, enabling him to sit in the House of Lords. The former John FitzGibbon was now about fifty. The son of a successful lawyer, he was a man who had grown rich through the law in his own right, with an income estimated at nearly £7,000 in 1782. His sister had married into the prominent Beresford family, headed by the Marquess of Tyrone, which brought him noble connections added to those he himself had acquired.

Clare was a handsome, powerfully built man, and powerful in personality to match. He was also a heavy drinker: he would die, probably of cirrhosis, the year after the Act of Union and it was said that such was his unpopularity with the ordinary (Catholic) people that dead cats were thrown at his Dublin funeral. Certainly Clare was always profoundly Anti-Catholic, despite or perhaps because of his Catholic ancestors; these had been doctors and extremely minor gentry (although his enemies scoffed inaccurately at his peasant descent). As FitzGibbon he had for example savagely opposed the Catholic Relief Bill of 1778, a few months after his election to the Irish Parliament as Member for Trinity College, Dublin. He rose to become Attorney-General of Ireland in 1783 and Lord Chancellor in 1789.

This was a type very different from the Irish aristocrats of the Protestant Ascendancy to which he never quite belonged. A crucial speech stressed the active tyranny of Catholicism: if the new Bill was passed, the result would be the creation of a Catholic state in Ireland hostile to Protestantism. This speech was regularly reprinted as a body blow to the hopes of Catholic Emancipation. He was certainly a hardliner over the rebellion of 1798, and actually suggested that Wolfe Tone should not have been granted a trial, but hanged the moment he arrived in Ireland.

It was an obvious progression, as well as a cunning move, for the newly ennobled (FitzGibbon) Clare to stir up George III into believing that Catholic Emancipation would betray his Coronation Oath. He was naturally a strong proponent of the Union by which the Protestants would set about 'taming and civilizing' the barbarous Catholics, as was their duty. It seems very likely that he was the first to make the lethal suggestion of 'personal betrayal' to George III.

All the time, concealed in an apparently minor dispute on a matter of religious tolerance, was a constitutional point of enormous significance now and for the future.[19] The Revolutionary Settlement of 1689 had expressly excluded absolute monarchy: the King (or Queen) could not rule without Parliament. Finance and the army depended on laws passed annually. If that was what he could not do, what he could do was altogether more murky. The general feeling was that the sovereign had the right to try to find other ministers, if he disagreed with those to whom he had entrusted power.

In all this, of course, human nature played its part. George III was over sixty at the time of this crisis, his health, whether mental or physical, was demonstrably not good; the average male life expectancy in 1800 was about forty. (In fact the father of George III died at forty-four, even if his grandfather George II, who outlived his son, made seventy-six.) Surely the supposedly Pro-Emancipation views of his heir were an encouraging omen for a future without George III.

The unexpected factor was this: the granting of Catholic

Emancipation in the United Kingdom touched on a vein of developing paranoia in the King's nature. He had come to believe, as he told Pitt, that this was a decision beyond the sphere of any Cabinet minister.[20] It was this tragic paranoid condition which would rapidly turn to apparent madness, and bring about a seemingly permanent Regency for his son George Prince of Wales.

There had already been a bout of this madness in 1788 and 1789, with the younger George as temporary Regent.* Whatever the actual illness from which he periodically suffered, it included among the symptoms an obsessional quality which certain topics unquestionably aroused. Catholic Emancipation, that appalling prospect which would cause him to be damned for breaking his sacred vow, was prominent among them. This malevolent obsession itself was at the time more relevant to the Catholic Question than what the nature of the King's madness actually was.

The first witness to the connection was the King himself. On 21 February 1801 George III professed himself as feeling very ill. He was convinced that this nervous collapse was to do with the Catholic Question. By the night of 22 February he was delirious, and only recovered after a crisis on 2 March. When he learned that the Prime Minister had called, the King sent Pitt a message which was scarcely reassuring. 'Tell him that I am quite well – quite recovered from illness; but what has he not to answer for, who is the cause of my being ill at all?'[21]

The King instructed Addington to tell Pitt of the great danger of ever speaking to him on a subject 'on which I can scarcely keep my temper'. When conveyed this message, Pitt 'hastily' replied to the effect that he would not 'bring forward the Catholic Question' in future, whether in or out of office, and that he would try to defer it, should it be 'agitated'. A message came back from the King on 6 March: 'Now will my mind be at ease.'

---

* The causes of the 'madness' of King George III have been variously ascribed to inherited porphyria and, more recently, a bipolar condition; the existence of this condition of apparent 'madness', however, is not questioned.

The connection was now firmly made between the royal mental state – already the subject of anxious discussion following the previous collapses – and agitation over the Catholic Question. Twenty-four years later, the King's second son, the Duke of York, recalling the horror of that time from the point of view of the Royal Family, employed the same word when he pronounced in the House of Lords that 'the agitation of it had been the cause of a most serious and alarming illness to an illustrious personage'.[22]

In the same year as the Union, 1801, another event took place which would inevitably affect the issue of Catholic Emancipation, although it happened far from the shores of Britain. On 15 July a Concordat was signed between Napoleon and Pope Pius VII which reconciled the Revolutionaries and the Catholic Church in France. As part of this process of reconciliation, Napoleon was to select the bishops. This offered an even stronger possibility of interference than the more limited power of the so-called Veto, by which the King would merely have the right to block bishops from among those whose names were submitted to him.

As England and France veered for a short while uncertainly between peace and war with the temporary Peace of Amiens in 1802, the issue of Catholic Emancipation, forbidden in the Cabinet because of the explicit desire of the King, sank from notice in England. The Catholic aristocracy continued to bicker with the clergy over the issue of pragmatism. Was a royal Veto on Catholic clerical appointments to be allowed in return for toleration towards the religion generally? In fact, throughout Catholic Europe local princes were accustomed to having a say in episcopal appointments; England's status since the Reformation as a mission territory had meant that the bishops had enjoyed a particular independence. Or was there now to be a rigorous adherence to full Papal authority? This was a fundamental issue which needed to be settled. In the meantime, the question could not even be discussed in the Cabinet, by agreement of the Prime Minister with the King.

Under the circumstances, the point of view of Richard Wellesley is understandable: 'The obstacle of the coronation oath may be *respectable* but it is a gross error.'[23] It was however an error in which King George III remained resolutely, even stubbornly, uncorrected, describing anyone who gainsaid him as a personal enemy.

CHAPTER FOUR

Green Shores of Liberty

*'...thou art the isle on whose green shores I have desired
to see the standard of liberty erected, a flag of fire, a beacon
at which the world shall light the torch of Freedom!'*

Shelley, *An Address to the Irish People*, 1812

IN FEBRUARY 1812 Percy Bysshe Shelley, aged nineteen and
recently expelled from Oxford University, travelled to Ireland.
He brought with him his wife Harriet, with whom he had eloped
the previous year when she was sixteen. Shelley had the avowed
intention of supporting the Irish people: he wanted to draw
attention to their sufferings at the hands of a tyrannical England.[1]

In particular he advocated two reforms: Catholic Emancipation and the repeal of the Act of Union. All this was seen in terms
of liberty. Harriet Shelley fully shared his feelings: 'Good God
were I an Irishman or woman, how I would hate the English!'

Shelley had already written a poem to the Irish in 1809 which
included an allusion to 'the yelling ghosts' riding by on the blast,
incessantly crying, 'my countrymen! vengeance'. Now he published a pamphlet, *An Address to the Irish People*, of which 1,500
copies were printed, at the modest price of fivepence in order to
make it widely available. As the preliminary advertisement stated:

'The lowest possible price is set on this publication, because it is the intention of the Author to awaken in the minds of the Irish poor a knowledge of their real state, and suggesting rational means of remedy.'

The language was ardent: 'Oh! Ireland, thou emerald of the ocean... thou art the isle on whose green shores I have desired to see the standard of liberty erected, a flag of fire, a beacon at which the world shall light the torch of Freedom!' He also wrote a poem in tribute to Robert Emmet, executed in 1803 for his rebellion, and visited Emmet's grave. The Shelleys returned to Ireland the next year although to Killarney, not Dublin. Later the poet described this time as the most 'intensive period of practical political education that he had experienced in his life'.

This romantic view of a suffering Ireland needing 'a flag of fire' was in contrast to the practical steps towards Emancipation which continued to be taken in the newly united Parliament in London. As the Napoleonic Wars enveloped Europe and beyond, it was by no means clear which if either of the solutions – crudely summarized as Irish uprising or English political manoeuvring – would be successful. There was of course a third way: Irish political manoeuvring.

Shelley himself did not advocate violence: 'firmly, yet quietly resist. When one cheek is struck, turn the other to the insulting coward.' This was his recommendation in *An Address to the Irish People*. 'Disclaim all manner of alliance with violence,' he wrote, 'meet together if ye will, but do not meet in a mob.' In fact Shelley denounced at length the way the poor were put into uniform to kill each other: 'the folly of killing and fighting each other in uniform for nothing at all. It is horrible that the lower classes must waste their lives and liberty to furnish means for their oppressors to oppress them yet more terribly'. But in realistic terms, it was difficult to see how a people, not only without a Parliament of their own but the majority of whom had no representation in the Parliament designated for them in a far-off city overseas, were to achieve anything by turning the other cheek.

The enforced captivity of the Pope at the hands of Napoleon for six years, only ending in May 1814, was an additional complication. Following the Concordat of 1801, Pope Pius VII had travelled to France for the Coronation of Napoleon as Emperor in 1804 – although, significantly, it was Napoleon who placed the crown on his own head. After that there was a sharp deterioration in relations: the Pope in confinement was moved throughout the territories controlled by the Emperor. Inevitably his enforced absence would affect the response of the Catholic officials left behind in Rome to questions concerning the Papal authority. The proposed Veto (by a Protestant King) over the appointment of bishops was one such question, which grew in urgency with the Pope himself in confinement. It was certainly a vital one for the advocates of Emancipation in England and Ireland – but one on which there was no helpful uniformity of view, rather the reverse.

The death of William Pitt in 1806, restored to office but faithful to his promise not to raise the question of Emancipation, was followed by the so-called Ministry of All the Talents, under the prime ministership of Lord Grenville. The name indicated its avowed aim of political unity in the interests of securing peace with France. Unfortunately, not only was peace not secured, but the coalition government lasted little more than a year. It broke up in March 1807 over the issue of disabilities, the second government to do so since the beginning of the century. In this case the issue was the (official) admission of Catholics to the army, including 'foreign Papists', and the Oath of Allegiance. Once again the King refused at the fence; once again the incoming Tory Prime Minister, the aged Duke of Portland, promised his sovereign a government in which the subject of disabilities would not be raised.

Furthermore, the heir to the throne, the Prince of Wales, withdrew his own previous public support for Emancipation, so popular among his Whig friends, as being inappropriate in the circumstances. He feared that such open support would bring back the insanity of his father – and that he would be blamed.[2] The days of the unofficial (that is, invalid by the law of the country) marriage to the Catholic Maria Fitzherbert were over. George had married his Protestant first cousin, Caroline of Brunswick, in

1795; their child, Princess Charlotte, was born the next year. The Prince had in mind the prospect of a new Regency, as the King wheeled back into madness following the death of a daughter. The Prince of Wales officially became Regent in February 1811 for the foreseeable future of the old King's life. The ominous words of Hyacinthe Wellesley concerning the fatal mixture of religion and politics were once again proved true.

The principal advocate of Catholic Emancipation in the House of Commons during these years was Henry Grattan, an Irish Protestant MP. Grattan came from an established Anglo-Irish background, his father having also been an MP, and his grandfather Lord Chief Justice of Ireland. Originally elected for the Irish Parliament in 1775 at the age of twenty-nine, he now represented Dublin City in the British House of Commons. Grattan, unlike Castlereagh, was a distinguished speaker, one who had studied the fabled orators of the past such as Bolingbroke and Junius. With his narrow face, long, thin, aquiline nose drooping over his upper lip and determined set mouth, huge burning eyes and wild windswept white hair, he also presented an impressive physical sight.

The Whig cleric Sydney Smith paid him a moving tribute: 'The world could not bribe him,' he wrote. 'He thought only of Ireland; lived for no other object; dedicated to her his beautiful fancy, his elegant wit, his manly courage, and all the splendour of his astonishing eloquence.'[3] As a moralist Grattan strongly disapproved of the Irish penal code, which deprived three-quarters of the population of its civil rights: he was an explicit advocate of Emancipation, as positive as FitzGibbon-Clare was negative. But Grattan saw no objection to the Veto.

The formation of the Catholic Board in 1808, along the same lines as the Cisalpine Club but larger and more influential, appeared to mark a step forward along these pragmatic lines. The Secretary was Edward Jerningham, closely related to most of the members. Here were nearly thirty Catholic peers. Naturally Stourtons, Cliffords and Lord Petre featured in the list; there were also sons of peers and twenty-one baronets. A new pamphlet by Sir John Throckmorton concerning a Petition of Irish Catholics to Parliament put the Catholic Board's point of view very well.[4] He reiterated what the Catholics had already proclaimed 'a thousand times' but, as it seemed, without effect: they admitted to the Pope 'a power merely *spiritual*'. Throckmorton incidentally allowed himself a preliminary swipe at Henry VIII, aware of the festering matter of the Coronation Oath. It was Henry VIII who had begun by violating his own Coronation Oath 'and on that basis was laid the first stone of the Reformation fabric'.

With the Catholic Board prepared to be accommodating on the subject of the Veto, and Grattan himself agreeing to it, there was a moment, surely, of promise for the future. On 25 May 1808 Grattan and George Ponsonby MP, an Anglo-Irish barrister and now a British MP, Lord Chancellor of Ireland under the Ministry of All the Talents, referred in a House of Commons debate to the fact that the Veto had been agreed with the Catholics.

Unfortunately the idea of the Veto was officially rejected by the Irish bishops a few months later. Bishop John Milner, appointed their agent in England, reversed his previous attitude a year later, and with all the sarcasm and power of his language condemned it too. Henceforward Catholic Emancipation would be faced with two barriers of a very different nature: one was the declared refusal of the sovereign even to consider it; the other was a major dispute of policy between the powerful Church in Ireland and the equally powerful aristocracy in England on the subject of the Veto – which, ironically enough, had itself been advanced as a pragmatic compromise intended to make things easier rather than more difficult. Then there was of course the deep-rooted Anti-Catholicism in the soil of the English nature: this found happy accord with the theoretical stance of the King, and expression in the views of many Tory MPs.

Debates on the issue, which were defeated in both Houses of Parliament in 1810, culminated in a resolution proposed by George Canning. This was carried in the Commons by a majority of 129 in June 1812. Like so many of the politicians involved in the fight for or against Emancipation, including the Wellesley brothers and Castlereagh, Canning, now aged forty-two, had an Irish Protestant background: both his parents were Irish, his paternal grandfather coming from Londonderry, although he himself was born in London. One consequence of this background was that Canning maintained a keen practical interest in the subject of Catholic Emancipation.

Canning's father's died when he was a baby. His mother, Mary Ann Costello, then supported them both by working as an actress, originally under David Garrick and then in provincial theatres.[5] From this seemingly 'scandalous' world, a wealthy merchant-banker uncle rescued him and sent him to Eton and Christ Church, Oxford. Here he belonged to an elite debating society with 'D. C. P. & F.' on their cufflinks: for Demosthenes, Cicero, Pitt and of course Fox. The result of this education was a man famously brilliant in many different ways, an orator but also a wit capable of writing parodies which everyone scurried to read.

Canning first entered the House of Commons as MP for Newtown on the Isle of Wight in 1793 during the regime of Pitt, and himself described his reverence for Pitt as filial, something explained perhaps by his lack of a real father.[6] When Pitt resigned in 1801 over the King's refusal to consider Emancipation, Canning went too, despite his junior status. He was briefly Foreign Secretary in 1807 with the Duke of Portland as Prime Minister, and then out of office for several years.

What was constant in his life, apart from his admiration for Pitt, was his belief in the need for Catholic Emancipation to solve the security problem of Ireland, as opposed to religious toleration for its own sake. He did not, as it were, fraternize with Catholic priests and laymen, acquiring information indirectly or from the Catholic press. This aspect of 'the Catholic Question' was of course something others with an Irish background, such as the Wellesley brothers and Castlereagh, were also in a position to understand if they wished to do so. Such constancy was not, however, likely to recommend him to King George III; and there was an additional factor in the shape of his private life which was not likely to endear him to the Prince Regent. While Canning's relationship with Caroline Princess of Wales may have been ultimately innocent – for better or for worse, she acted as

godmother to Canning's first child after his marriage to an heiress
– it certainly did not prejudice the Regent in his favour.

Shelley's visit to Ireland symbolized how to many in Europe
(and the New World) the sufferings of Ireland had come to
epitomize the fight for liberty. Thus Catholic Emancipation was
no longer an equable wish by aristocrats to participate in the
government of the country, but something more radical and
potentially more dangerous. It was not quite clear in 1812 how
radical the lawyer Daniel O'Connell actually was. He was now
aged thirty-seven, having been born in the tiny village of Carhan,
Co. Kerry. It was the benevolence of a rich bachelor uncle, known
as 'Hunting Cap' O'Connell, which enabled him to be educated
abroad at Douai, with the further encouraging prospect of being
his uncle's heir. O'Connell then progressed to Lincoln's Inn in
London where he became a barrister, and so to the Dublin Bar
in 1796.[7]

This was the man who would one day be known as 'King
Dan' or alternatively 'the Liberator'. What is clear is that from
early on, O'Connell displayed that extraordinary charisma
which is the mark of exceptional people born in otherwise
unexceptional circumstances. He proved to be an orator of
unmatchable fervour: it was significant that while in London he
declared his admiration for the performance of the great actress
Sarah Siddons. O'Connell's modest estimation of his own talent
at about this time was as follows: 'While I apply myself to the
English language, I endeavour to unite purity of diction to the
harmony and arrangement of phraseology.'[8] His listeners put
it differently. Thomas Wyse, who knew him well, in a book of
reminiscences published in 1829 paid this tribute to his oratorical
style, which perhaps explains the charisma: 'He lends an eloquent
voice to the sentiments, the passions, and even to the prejudices,
of six million of men.' In short: 'He is a glass in which Ireland
may see herself completely reflected.'[9]

O'Connell's appearance, rather like that of his near-
contemporary the Duke of Wellington, became with time in-
extricable from the legend. Both men were born in Ireland
within six years of each other, the one in an elegant house in

Dublin, the other in a remote dwelling in the west of Ireland. In both cases, caricaturists were soon to rejoice in such a rich opportunity for satire, and in so doing helped the cause of the person: instant recognizability has, after all, never been a weakness in a leader. In the case of O'Connell, his big, burly figure seemed to indicate of its very nature health and strength; his handsome face with its bright blue eyes was rubicund, whether with good cheer or indignant passion; and as to the nature of that passion, according to Wyse there could be twenty different passions in two minutes.[10]

The diarist Creevey would call his style 'far too dramatic for my taste' while admitting that since the whole Irish nation was dramatic, they positively liked it.[11] O'Connell was certainly a showman. More than one commentator over the years referred to him strolling through Dublin with his umbrella shouldered as if it were a pike. Describing him a few years later to Lady Morgan, William Curran wrote that O'Connell was progressing 'in the full dress of a verdant liberator – green in all that may or may not be expressed, even to a green cravat, green watch-ribbon, and a slashing shining green hat-band', and, added Curran, 'he has a confident hope that "the tears of Ireland will prevent the colours from ever fading"'.[12]

O'Connell from the start was steadfast in his opposition to physical violence (as distinct from violence of eloquence) as a method of opposition, a principle he maintained and which was to prove of great significance in the years to come. This obviously divided him from the United Irishmen of the 1798 rebellion, when he would have been twenty-three, and Robert Emmet a few years younger. But his strongest desire was for the repeal of the Union, to which he was a dedicated adversary.

This meant that the Irish Catholic Committee, created in 1809 along the lines of the English Committee, in order to petition Parliament on the subject of Emancipation, was primarily seen by him as a political instrument rather than a religious one. This led inevitably to tensions within the Committee itself. There was a series of run-ins with the government on the subject of this Committee: on the grounds that it was contravening the law established in 1793 against petitioning for alterations in matters of Church and State, the so-called Convention Act.

It was this Catholic Committee to which the young Shelley, in the light of his *Address to the Irish People*, was invited in February 1812. In the course of his speech he referred to the decommissioned Irish Parliament building on College Green, sold to a bank after the Act of Union, as 'that edifice which ought to have been the fane [shrine] of their liberties converted to a temple of Mammon'. He also emphasized 'the necessity of Catholic Emancipation' as well as 'the baneful effects' of the Union. In a report to the English government, an informer who was present – actually a chief constable – referred to a certain Mr Shelley speaking 'who stated himself to be a native of England'. It was in fact the young poet's first political speech. Another pamphlet, *Proposals for an Association etc.*, followed.[13]

With time, Shelley moved towards the view that repeal of the Union would benefit the masses, whereas Catholic Emancipation, however desirable, was to the benefit of the great landlords, most likely the Catholic aristocracy: 'I do not like Lord Fingall or any of the Catholic aristocracy,' he wrote. 'Their intolerance can be equalled by nothing but the hardy wickedness and intolerance of the Prince [Regent].' His next visit to Ireland was a great deal less politically involved. Nevertheless his original intervention combined a denunciation of intolerance as literally unChristian, with a reference to the newly established United States: 'The original founder of our religion taught no such doctrine [penalizing people for religious belief]. Equality in this respect was general in the American States, and why not here?' This was one continuing aspect of the struggle for Emancipation: its symbolic value as representing the oppression of people. In the meantime, the practical political fight in Dublin continued, and Daniel O'Connell was an increasingly dominant figure.

In 1813 he acted as defence lawyer in the sensational trial of John Magee; this not only increased O'Connell's popular fame but it also focused the fierce light of official obloquy upon him. Magee was the editor of the heavily Pro-Catholic *Dublin Evening Post*, who had already been found guilty of libel against the Dublin police the previous year. At this point he was accused as editor and proprietor of a libellous article he had printed concerning the Duke of Richmond, Lord Lieutenant (or Viceroy) of Ireland. This was a resolution passed by a Catholic meeting in Kilkenny condemning the previous trial, which denounced both the government and the administration of Irish justice generally.

Now in his fifties, Richmond had been appointed Lord Lieutenant in 1807 and maintained a lavish state at the Viceroy's residences, Dublin Castle and his Lodge in Phoenix Park. Although social life in Dublin had distinctly diminished since the departure of Parliament, the Duke (and Duchess) maintained the old style, with the vast majority of guests coming from the Protestant Ascendancy. The Duke certainly had a magnificent concept of his duty as Duke and Viceroy; as for his wife, in Brussels later it would be the Duchess who was responsible for the famous ball on the eve of Waterloo.

Richmond was also a man noted for his charm and bonhomie, as well as being an ardent cricketer, qualities which it is to be hoped always coexist; he was a founder member of the Mary-le-Bone Cricket Club (MCC). The Duke also had time for drinking and skilful boxing, none of which reduced his bonhomie. He was obviously a member of the Church of England, but also a 'Protestant' in the way people were beginning to be defined, meaning that he did not support Catholic Emancipation. In keeping with his political convictions, Richmond had written in advance about his new Chief Secretary: 'Pray don't let them send me a Catholic [i.e. sympathizer] or a timid man.'[14]

The alleged libel on the Duke and his administration was certainly scabrous stuff. 'He [the Duke] came over ignorant – he soon became prejudiced, and then he became intemperate. He takes from the People their money, he eats of their bread and drinks of their wine, in return he gives them a bad government... His Grace commenced his reign by flattery, he continued it in folly, he accompanied it with violence, and he will conclude it with falsehood etc. etc.'

In a version of the trial, published the same year under

Magee's imprint, the introduction declared that 'the pen of Tacitus, good at Human Monsters, would fail before the Law-givers of Ireland', before referring to the 'unsparing scimitar' of Cromwell, and the Glorious Revolution of 1688 which cursed Ireland with 'a Slavery worse than African'.[15] One feature of the trial – as with all other trials – was of course the fact that the jury consisted entirely of Protestants, Catholics being debarred from jury service.

O'Connell's speech in defence was like a long blast on a trumpet, occasionally interrupted by William Saurin, the Attorney-General, with the angry toot of a rival instrument.[16] Saurin, the son of a northern Irish Presbyterian clergyman, now in his sixties, was an able lawyer; he was also virulently Anti-Catholic: one who believed unapologetically that the Catholic Church was the main cause of Ireland's problems and unlike, for example, Henry Grattan did not accept a compromise solution whereby the Irish state encompassed both religions.

Saurin objected to O'Connell denouncing Richmond's predecessors as Viceroy in such terms as these: 'They insulted – they oppressed – they murdered, and they deceived.' How could a man be included in the crimes of his predecessors? O'Connell was up to the challenge, emotionally if not in terms of the law. What Saurin said was true enough. 'But it is History; Gentlemen; are you prepared to silence the voice of History?' cried O'Connell. He then read out the allegedly libellous description of Richmond at length, before turning to the details of Richmond interfering in the late elections. Lastly O'Connell asked the court to imagine a dramatic reversal of circumstances in which 'The Protestant widow shall have her harmless Child murdered in the noonday.' All the while it was noticeable that Saurin was alternately 'green and livid' and flushed, with quivering cheeks and lips as white as ashes.

O'Connell continued the theme of role reversal by lashing out at the treatment of *Protestants* in *Catholic* Spain and Portugal: 'Do you enter into the feelings of Protestants thus insulted, thus oppressed, thus persecuted – their enemies and traducers promoted, and encouraged and richly rewarded... the emblems of Discord, the war-cry of Disunion, sanctioned by the highest authority, and Justice herself converted from an impartial arbitrator into a frightful partisan? Yes, Gentlemen, place yourselves as Protestants under such a persecution.'

At one point O'Connell turned, with a kind of prescience, to the newly appointed Chief Secretary. Richmond had certainly got what he asked for. This was no Catholic sympathizer. He was a certain Robert Peel, a brilliant, hard-working young man of twenty-five, the son of a rich industrialist whose middle-class birth, despite his own great talents, made him a target of snobbery. For one thing he retained the slight Staffordshire accent of his youth, which led one observer to say disdainfully that Peel could always be sure of an H when it came at the beginning of a word, 'but he is by no means sure when it comes in the middle'. O'Connell, nephew of 'Hunting Cap', was not immune from this snobbery, describing Peel on arrival as 'a raw youth, squeezed out of the workings of I know not what factory in England!'.[17]

It was perfectly true that the Irish establishment as a whole saw in Peel all that they resented and disliked about their Protestant rulers. This feeling matched Peel's own innate contempt for the Catholic aristocrats. In February 1812 he had spoken out against any concession to Catholic claims, and his first speech in office consisted of a strong defence of the Protestant Ascendancy: as a result he was nicknamed, predictably, Orange Peel. He was frank about it: 'Papal superstition' was the cause of one half of the evils of Ireland, the country he had been despatched to administer. The prevailing religion in Ireland, that is Catholicism, operated as an impediment rather than an aid to 'Civil Government'. Peel also opposed Catholic Emancipation in principle as the first dangerous step towards the repeal of the Union: any influential institution like a Church should be under the control of the State. 'A foreign earthly potentate' – that is, the Pope – had no place here.[18] The issue was one of security against attacks from outside, but it was also one of natural order, of which a State Church was a necessary part.

Peel's own religion was described later by his younger brother

Sir Laurence Peel in a memoir as 'of a home growth'. In their father's mind, and in their father's house, Anti-Catholicism was almost a religious faith.[19] It might be said of Robert Peel that he was born Anti-Catholic in the sense that the historian Guizot described him as being born a Tory. Good-looking in a healthy, florid way, with red hair and a fresh complexion, no one ever said of Peel that he was a brilliant orator; he was however an excellent debater. On the other hand he was an honest man, with natural integrity. Yet he did not conceal his innate opposition to any concessions to 'a set of human beings very little advanced from barbarism', as he would describe the Irish in 1816, after some violent incidents had taken place. It was a view shared by a large proportion of his fellow Englishmen; but in a politician of Peel's brilliance, it was a potential tragedy for the cause of Emancipation.

O'Connell, in turning to Peel, was appealing to the court on the subject of the Anti-Catholic *Hibernian Journal*, a newspaper which received public money. He also mentioned its limited circulation: how fortunate, given that it was 'a Paper of the very lowest and most paltry scale of talent'! And yet it was receiving thousands of pounds from the very men it 'foully and falsely' calumniated. 'Here Mr O'Connell turned round to where Mr Peel sat,' stated the report of the trial published by John Magee afterwards.[20] 'Would I could see the man...,' declaimed O'Connell, looking at him, that 'salaried and rewarded the Calumniator' responsible for prosecuting Magee 'merely because he has not praised public men, and has discussed public affairs in the spirit of Freedom and the Constitution'. He directly contrasted Magee's fate with that of the Proprietor of the *Hibernian Journal*, the one dragged to the Bar for a 'sober discussion of political topics, the other hired to disseminate the most horrible calumnies'.

The unprecedented violence of O'Connell's language – 'I hurl *defiance* at the Attorney-General' – ranged far beyond the actual case he was defending: at one point he actually threatened to 'chastise' Saurin, the Attorney-General. It became a question of whether O'Connell was not himself guilty of a more serious crime than the one he was defending. It explains why Magee now, in a remarkable development, disassociated himself from his counsel. It did not save him.

There was nothing even O'Connell could do to sway that jury in that court, something made quite clear by the concluding speech of Charles Kendal Bushe, the Solicitor-General: 'I look upon Ireland as identified with England,' he declared. 'I hold the impossibility of a separate existence. I consider Ireland identified with England, not only by law, but by language – by interests, by blood and affection.' Here Arthur Wellesley, currently Marquess of Wellington (advanced to Duke the next year), was introduced by virtue of his Irish descent: 'I see Ireland repaying England for the triumphs of Nelson, with the victories of Wellington.' The Solicitor-General, not for nothing known as 'silver-tongued Bushe', even dragged in Madame Roland, famously guillotined in 1793, and her immortal last words: 'Oh! Liberty, what crimes are committed in thy name!' He adapted them to his own satisfaction to the present case, where an innocent and distinguished man, the Duke of Richmond, was traduced: 'Oh! Toleration, what Intolerance is not practised in thy name!'[21]

The court report was terse. The jury retired and, 'after a short consultation', brought in a verdict of – Guilty. Magee was sentenced to prison for two years and six months, in separate terms, and fined as well. He was then immediately committed to Newgate Prison in Dublin, despite O'Connell's pleas. He asked first for Magee to remain at liberty with securities till the next term, for the proper judgment of the court. That was rejected. O'Connell then asked for the less rigorous Kilmainham Gaol; the Attorney-General said he would consider it and in the meantime Magee was taken to Newgate.

Peel and O'Connell were now ranged against each other in Dublin, the one in a position of official power, the other a rising barrister whose power depended on his own genius. It was a game which began originally within the green shores of Ireland, in Shelley's incantatory phrase. There would be a question of an actual physical duel between the two men in the future. In Europe, however, the long Napoleonic Wars were moving to some kind of ending, with consequences which directly affected Catholic Emancipation in its very heart. It was a question of that contentious issue: the Papacy.

CHAPTER FIVE

Cardinal Tempter

'In our familiar intercourse, the Prince Regent would
call out… "Hush, hush, Cardinal Tempter: when listening
to you I seem to see Henry VIII and his daughter
Elizabeth following me as avenging spirits."'

Mémoires du Cardinal Consalvi

THE TREATY OF FONTAINEBLEAU in April 1814 marked the final defeat – as it seemed at the time – of the Emperor Napoleon by the Allies. The Emperor abdicated and was exiled to the island of Elba, off the coast of Italy; Louis XVIII, younger brother of the guillotined King, resumed the Bourbon throne of his ancestors. A minor congress was planned in London in June to celebrate the peace, before the great Congress of Vienna later in the year, when the actual details of this peace would be worked out.

In that same month of April, when the map of Europe was still to be rearranged by the victorious powers, a highly concessionary document arrived from Rome in the shape of a letter called the 'Rescript'. The crucial phrase ran as follows: if the English legislators only wished to forbid ministers of the Catholic Church from 'disturbing' the Protestant Church or government by violence or arms, or 'evil artifices of whatever kind', then the

Papacy had no objection. That is to say, the Pope would accept Catholic Emancipation in Britain on these terms. Civil disturbance and other evil artifices were after all a matter of national security, not a spiritual concern.

The 'Rescript' was sent by Monsignore Quarantotti, Secretary to the office known as the Propaganda Fide (Sacred Congregation for the Propagation of the Faith); Quarantotti was in charge of affairs at Rome during the enforced absence of the Pope himself.[1] (The captivity of Pius VII, begun in 1809, had ended in January 1814, but he only reached Rome in May.) This letter from Quarantotti, distinguishing the two possible aspects of Catholic behaviour, was acceptable by many standards including, as has been seen, those of the English Catholic lay leaders. Nevertheless, when it arrived in England it 'set the Catholics of the United Kingdom by the ears', in the words of a nineteenth-century Catholic historian.[2]

On the one hand there was an understandable sensitivity among Catholics concerning the past history of subversion and even terrorism among their forebears. If the Popish Plot of 1678 was a fantasy, the Gunpowder Plot of 1605 was not, and stories of the reign of Queen Elizabeth – such as assassination plots theoretically accepted by the Pope, to say nothing of the martyrdoms carried out by her Catholic half-sister 'Bloody Mary' – belonged, rightly or wrongly, to English history. This historical dimension, coupled with more recent wars against Catholic foreign powers, should never be forgotten in the consideration of Anti-Catholicism in Britain. Certainly the ardent Catholic advocates of Emancipation, and other liberal advocates who were not Catholic, were concerned to make it clear that they were loyal patriots with absolutely no intention of 'evil artifices of whatever kind'.

On the other hand, any question which indicated a Veto over Catholic affairs from an explicitly non-Catholic source was already highly controversial before Quarantotti's bolt from the Vatican. It publicly divided the powerful Irish Catholic Church, for whom the uncompromising Bishop John Milner now acted, from the English, who prided themselves, by friendship and social class, on having some access to the monarch and the government.

The first question which needed to be solved was whether Monsignore Quarantotti had any actual right to send the Rescript. It was not his goodwill which was questioned, but his authority in the troubled situation caused by the Pope's prolonged absence from the Eternal City – not only absence, but obvious helplessness as a captive. The ins and outs of this authority remained dubious, but clearly the situation changed substantially with the return of Pius VII himself to Rome. Milner was present in Rome to argue the Irish case. Eventually a new Papal communication was sent at the end of 1814, which reached England in February the following year:

It concerned the Rescript 'issued and sent to you by our beloved son' – i.e. Quarantotti – 'during our absence and the dispersion of our venerable council'. This new communication was not what the pragmatists wanted. On the contrary: the whole matter was now being referred to the cardinals. In the meantime, 'We entreat you,' wrote the Pope to the Catholic Board, 'to be persuaded that in this important matter we shall most willingly comply with your wishes, so far as the dignity, the purity, and the integrity of the Catholic religion will allow.'[3] This was a victory for the Anti-Vetoists. Was it also a defeat for those who would secure Emancipation theoretically by the only possible means, that is, compromise?

The celebratory congress in London in June 1814 was a magnificent affair. Here were Czar Alexander of Russia, King Frederick William III of Prussia, Prince Metternich, Chancellor of the Austrian Empire, Field Marshal Blücher and other great men. A grand reception was held at Dover. After that entertainments were diverse, ranging from honorary degrees at Oxford to racing at Ascot, as well as a City of London banquet at the Guildhall; a naval review at Portsmouth, attended by the Prince Regent, concluded the festivities. In London itself there was a magnificent pageant, witnessed by one boy called Nicholas who, forty years later as Cardinal Wiseman, would be the first Archbishop of Westminster at the re-establishment of the Catholic hierarchy.

TOP: Lord George Gordon MP, leader of the Anti-Popery protests, encouraging the mob to enter the Houses of Parliament in June 1780; *left* The burning Catholic chapel of the Sardinian Embassy; *far left* Lord Stormont being assaulted in his coach for voting in favour of the recent Catholic Relief Bill. French engraving of the Gordon Riots (once in the collection of the Catholic writer Hilaire Belloc).

ABOVE: Plaque commemorating the Great Fire of London in 1666 put up on the house where it started in 1681, blaming the Catholics: 'Here by ye permission of heaven, hell broke loose upon this Protestant city from the malicious hearts of barbarous papists…'; taken down in the reign of the Catholic James II, then reinstated; now in the Museum of London.

ABOVE: The chapel at Lulworth Castle, Dorset, built by Thomas Weld in 1786 at a time when Catholic churches and chapels were technically illegal, so that most chapels were concealed within country houses. George III was said to have suggested with a wink to his friend Weld that it was actually a mausoleum which was taken by Weld to be 'a kind of sanction'.

Charles 11th Duke of Norfolk by Thomas Gainsborough. A flamboyant character, he was ostensibly a Protestant despite being the head of the leading Catholic family of Howard, on the grounds that he wanted to take his seat in Parliament: 'I cannot be a good Catholic... if a man is to go to the devil, he may as well go thither from the House of Lords...'.

King George III, 1810–15, by Edward Bird.

Robert Edward 9th Baron Petre. A Catholic grandee, famously benevolent, who was an early advocate of Emancipation. He was also able to be Grand Master of the Masonic Order in the days before Catholics were forbidden to be Freemasons. Cardinal Manning later observed that the Catholic Church was built on the foundations of Lord Petre as well as St Peter.

A Great Man at his Private Devotion.

'A Great Man at his Private Devotion', 1780. George III, who assented to the Catholic Relief Bill, shown as a tonsured monk with the implication that he was a secret Catholic.

Cardinal Ercole Consalvi, who came to London from Rome for the Congress of 1814, the first official visit by a Cardinal since the sixteenth century; a man of great personal charm and culture, he enjoyed enormous social success, including with the Prince Regent who described Consalvi lightly as 'Cardinal Tempter'.

GRACE BEFORE MEAT or a Peep at Lord PETER'S

TOP: Thorndon Hall, Essex, seat of Lord Petre, where despite his Catholic religion he entertained King George and Queen Charlotte lavishly in October 1778, to demonstrate his loyalty. ABOVE: An imaginary scene at Thorndon during the visit, to satirize the royal presence in a Catholic household, with Grace being said by a priest standing at the head of the table. Subtitled 'a Peep at Lord Peter's'.

Maria Fitzherbert, the Catholic widow who won the love of the Prince of Wales, and went through a form of marriage with him which was not valid in English law under the Royal Marriages Act 1772.

Henry Grattan, the Irish Protestant MP who represented Dublin City in the British Parliament and campaigned actively for Emancipation.

The APOSTATES and the EXTINGUISHER — or — KISSING the POPE's TOE!!

'The Apostates and the Extinguisher', 1829. The Duke of Wellington kissing the Pope's toe. The Duke swears with all humility to 'conform to the will of your Holyness'; the Pope hands over his diadem (the Papal tiara) for the extinction of heresy in Britain so that 'our true Catholic faith shall again govern your country'.

LEFT: Bishop John Milner, a forceful character – he was noted for his 'asperity' – who denounced the idea of a 'Veto' by which the Protestant sovereign could ban the appointment of individual Catholic bishops. RIGHT: George IV, who finally succeeded as King on his father's death in 1820, having been Prince Regent since 1811, by Sir Thomas Lawrence. A suitably royal image in contrast to the mockery of the cartoonists.

TOP: The Coronation of King George IV in Westminster Abbey, 19 July 1821; he took the Oath which pledged 'a binding religious obligation' to maintain the Protestant religion that came to dominate his conscience. ABOVE LEFT: 'A Voluptuary under the horrors of digestion'. The self-indulgence of the Prince of Wales, later Regent and finally King, led to the early deterioration of his appearance from the handsome looks of his youth. James Gillray, 1792. ABOVE RIGHT: Elizabeth Marchioness Conyngham, the royal mistress. It was said that the King had never known what it was to be in love before: he was seen nodding and winking in her direction at the Coronation.

From the point of view of Catholic Emancipation, the important delegate arrived from Rome and stayed for nearly a month. This was Cardinal Ercole Consalvi, the first cardinal to set foot officially on British shores since Cardinal Reginald Pole in the sixteenth century.[4] He secured his passport from the British Ambassador in Paris; in doing so, he did not insist on any kind of diplomatic precedence, which in Europe would have rated him just below royalty. He began tactfully dressed in black (ecclesiastical dress was forbidden by law), but seems to have progressed sartorially to a more splendid scarlet in that the Prince Regent expressed personal curiosity about his red stockings, part of his regalia. Certainly the red stockings made their mark, leading Castlereagh for one, despite being a Catholic sympathizer on the subject of Emancipation, to hope that 'ostentation' would be avoided: 'the religionists in the country [Protestants and Dissenters] would be very likely to cry out if my friend Consalvi's red stockings were seen too often at Carlton House'.[5] All the same, Consalvi had arrived with a placatory letter from the Pope to the Prince Regent, thanking him for the support Britain had given in the war, before turning to Papal concerns for the future. And the people cheered him in the streets, as one who had suffered under Napoleon.

The Pope continued to send his advice to Consalvi, some of which was less palatable: for example, he should not forget 'the persecuted' while he was evidently having such a good time. But fundamentally Consalvi's personal success, particularly with the Prince Regent, was rightly seen as an asset. In the words of the Pope, Consalvi should continue to cultivate his royal benefactor: 'and you will see this little grain of mustard seed bring forth abundant fruits'.[6]

Cardinal Consalvi, aged fifty-seven in 1814, was a man who caught the eye regardless of his dress. Tall and thin, with manners that were both simple and dignified, it was, wrote the novelist Stendhal a few years later, 'impossible to be a more handsome man'. Others stressed his high and broad forehead, his distinguished grey hair and Roman nose, and as the perfect accompaniment his 'soft insinuating tone of voice'. It was scarcely surprising that as Consalvi's amicable relationship with the English court developed, Sir Thomas Lawrence was wanted to paint him.* It was also reported by the Catholic historian John Lingard that Lawrence called Consalvi's head 'the finest that God had ever made'. It was significant that Consalvi was actually a cardinal without being a priest, perfectly possible within the laws of the Catholic Church. This made sense of Napoleon's verdict: 'Yonder man, who would never become a priest, is the best priest of the lot.'[7]

His career hitherto had been as vivid and traumatic as the history of Europe itself during recent years. He had endured imprisonment by the French Revolutionary armies, and had been made Secretary of State by Pius VII in 1800. It was Consalvi who had negotiated the famous – or infamous – Concordat of 1801. Brought to Paris in 1810 on Napoleon's orders, he had been banished to Rheims (where he wrote his *Mémoires*). There had been a release and another banishment, before he was re-appointed Secretary of State in May 1814. However, during one conversation with Napoleon in 1810, he did manage to display the kind of impeccable suavity worthy of cardinals in fiction. 'Is it not true, Cardinal,' asked Bonaparte roguishly, 'that all Italians are thieves and liars?' Consalvi was not to be outdone: 'Oh, no, sire,' he replied, 'just the major part – *la buona parte.*'[8]

Furthermore, since his early years Consalvi had had an unusual connection to England. As a young man he had attended for over five years the college at Frascati in Tuscany just opened by the Stuart Prince known as Cardinal Henry of York, who inherited (but chose not to press) the Stuart claim to the British throne after the death of his brother Charles Edward. Thereafter the Cardinal of York acted as a benevolent patron to Consalvi. According to Nicholas Wiseman, 'it was rather by the ornamental than by the useful arts' that the future statesman 'captivated the good Duke-bishop's affections. It is said to have been his skill and grace in a musical performance that first attracted his notice.'[9] The artist developed many other skills. As the Cardinal's

---

* A portrait that today hangs in the Waterloo Chamber at Windsor Castle.

executor, Consalvi would be able to transmit to the Prince Regent those relics bequeathed to him by his benevolent Stuart relative.

Consalvi's interests remained many and various: they included architecture and gardening. In London he was enthusiastic about the newly landscaped St James's Park and the improvements to the city made by John Nash, as well as the Italian music shops in Soho selling sheet music and instruments. Consalvi had many admirers. Elizabeth Duchess of Devonshire had retired to Rome during her widowhood: she had married her long-term lover the Duke after the death of his celebrated first wife, Georgiana. She knew Consalvi well and she too stressed his profound love of the arts; he also wrote poetry. A different but equally attractive aspect of his character was his kindness to those who served him; and, perhaps the greatest compliment of all, he was an 'unalterable friend': in short, 'I think if there is a pure and angelic mind on earth now, it is his.'[10] This obvious adoration aroused rumours that Duchess Bess had converted to Catholicism, but she denied ever discussing religious matters with 'my friend the Cardinal', beyond the odd question on her part; in fact they shared an interest in the archaeology of Rome such as the excavations at St Peter's.

The whole atmosphere in Europe was now one of practical politics towards minority religions. And Europe itself was not, after all, a solid Catholic bloc. A few years before, the Regent's brother, William Duke of Clarence, had looked forward to the ultimate settlement of Europe, 'in which case the Prince Regent, the Emperor of Russia the King of Prussia and the Prince of Sweden who are *not* Catholics will have much to say in settling affairs.'[11] It had certainly never been true that the English King was the only monarch to deal with the problem of a small but important religious minority. Austria had had to deal with Protestants, Holland with Catholics, and above all France with Huguenots.

In 1775 Louis XVI had been faced with his own Coronation Oath crisis. His chief minister, Turgot, wanted the King to drop the King's pledge to extirpate heretics, which had actually been inserted in the thirteenth century to deal with the Albigensian heresy of the Cathars, but was now applied to Protestants. The French King replied: 'I think there are fewer drawbacks to leaving things as they are,' although in point of fact at the ceremony itself, in the words of his latest biographer, 'he simply mumbled the French equivalent of "rhubarb, rhubarb" '.[12] The events of the French Revolution, when Catholicism was abolished as the religion of the State, and Napoleon's subsequent complicated relationship with the Papacy – all this had tempered the original divisions. Belgium, for example, was annexed to the French republic and subjected to the same regime.

It was thus possible for Consalvi's visit to herald a new stage in the history of the Papacy, now back in Rome (but still the object of sympathy as having been Napoleon's victim), and also in Anglo-Papal relations. It was no part of Consalvi's policy to strike harsh attitudes. He developed a rapport with the Prince Regent which was not without its lighter moments as he depicted it: 'in our familiar intercourse, when gently and in season I turned the conversation on to certain religious questions which are very delicate to touch on, the Prince Regent, putting his hand to his mouth as though telling me to be silent, but in reality encouraging me to speak, would call out with an inimitable accent of affected fear, and in effect good humour: "Hush, hush, Cardinal Tempter: when listening to you I seem to see Henry VIII and his daughter Elizabeth following me as avenging spirits." '[13] On a sadder note, when the daughter of the Prince Regent, Princess Charlotte, died in childbirth, Consalvi was moved to write a personal letter of condolence to the man to whom he was 'so gratefully attached', in the words of Duchess Bess.

The presence of Cardinal Consalvi did much to soften the image of the dangerous foreign Popish bogeyman which had hovered in the vision of England for so long. Even the Duke of Clarence, in no way an Ultra-Tory, shared this preoccupation. Advocating that the friends of Emancipation should be 'mild and steady' a few years earlier, he had added with a certain royal optimism: 'the grand obstacle and danger after all is *the Pope*'.[14] Perhaps when the war in Europe was over the Catholics might be persuaded 'to do away with the Pope?'. Cardinal Consalvi was not going to do away with the Pope; but he did personify the new Papal diplomacy, no longer reminiscent of the 'Popish villains' of yesteryear.

It was remarked that Consalvi tactfully declined to discuss the controversial Rescript, saying that he knew nothing about it. Despite that gentle warning from Rome about favouring Britain too much, the Cardinal continued to pursue the path of reconciliation – or compromise. He had two interviews with the Foreign Secretary, Castlereagh. When John Lingard went with Lord Stourton to Rome in 1817, they were received and helped by Consalvi. Nicholas Wiseman, by now a student priest in Rome, paid tribute to Consalvi's support: how he would yield on 'unessentials' to gain progress for the larger Church issues at the same time as the Roman *zelanti* felt he was yielding too much.[15] The Cardinal was also a strong active supporter of the restoration of the English College in Rome, wrecked during the city's travails.

During the Congress of Vienna, which took place later in 1814 until June 1815, Consalvi actively pursued the issues which were supposed to hinder Emancipation in interviews with Castlereagh. In a long meeting on 11 October, Consalvi enlightened Castlereagh about Catholic doctrines such as Papal Infallibility (not yet defined as dogma).[16] They then discussed the three main issues from the point of view of Rome, at all times in that conciliatory spirit – how can we make this work? – which Consalvi believed was the best way forward. For example, he accepted the Coronation Oath with one slight modification. Where the bishops were concerned, there might be certificates of loyalty issued by the government before appointments were made by Rome. There were other suggestions, such as a Minister in Rome to smooth the way between the Pope and Britain. State stipends for Catholic clergy in Ireland was another issue on which Consalvi had practical suggestions to make.

The visible association of a Papal dignitary with the Prince Regent, coupled with the latter's presumed 'Catholic' sympathies, created an atmosphere of hope on the subject of Emancipation; after all, the poor mad old King was now eighty-six years old, surely not destined to live much longer. The marriage to the

Catholic Mrs Fitzherbert was in the past, and the Prince's marital troubles with the tempestuous Caroline Princess of Wales were of a very different order.

It was true that, both personally and politically, the fifty-year-old Prince Regent no longer resembled the handsome, ardent young Prince Florizel who had wooed Maria, and dallied with the Whigs, dazzled by the ever-seductive Charles Fox, now dead eight years. His appearance began to be the subject of witty – or cruel – attacks such as the anonymous rhyme actually written by Charles Lamb:

> Is he Regent of the Sea?
> By his bulk and by his size
> By his oily qualities
> This (or else my eyesight fails)
> This should be the Prince of Whales[17]

His latest mistress, Isabella Marchioness of Hertford, two years older than the Prince, commanded her lover as much by her powerful character as by her stately and ample beauty (she was known privately as the Sultana). One observer, Mrs Calvert, recorded in June 1807: 'Last night we went to a ball at Lady Hertford's. I think poor Mrs Fitzherbert much deserted by him now. He has taken into his head to fall desperately in love with Lady Hertford... without exception the most forbidding, haughty, unpleasant woman I ever saw.'[18]

Gone were the days of semi-domesticity with his Catholic 'wife' Maria Fitzherbert, her virtue protected by being married to the Prince in the eyes of her own Church, although the match had no legality under English law. She spent much time bringing up her adopted daughter Minnie Seymour, whom gossips inevitably but almost certainly wrongly accused of being a royal bastard.*[19] Isabella Hertford, who did not treat her predecessor

---

* As one biographer puts it, there is no evidence to prove she had children – none were certainly born to her two early marriages – but it is at the same time impossible to prove conclusively she did not.

kindly in social ways, was an earnest Protestant, read the Bible daily and was interested in the Methodists.

Always impressionable where women were concerned, the Prince was beginning to listen to the siren voice of Protestantism even if it was in the improbable form of his mistress and her family. Francis Marquess of Hertford was a nobleman of noticeably elegant appearance, but 'without one virtue that can grace a name', in the words of a satirical poem, who acted happily as Lord Chamberlain of the Royal Household from 1812 onwards.[20]

Yet the Prince's circle continued to include Catholics, and Catholic connections. One member in particular was Charles, the 11th Duke of Norfolk: he who had declared that if he was going to hell, he would prefer to go to hell in the House of Lords, and became a theoretical Protestant. While still styled Earl of Surrey as heir to the dukedom, and thus able to enter the Commons, he had in fact contested a parliamentary seat as a Protestant to enter Rockingham's administration. Duke Charles fitted into a particular category: a Catholic who preferred an ambivalent status which enabled him to partake in the government if he so wished, but also to act as a generous patron to fellow Catholics. He kept Catholic chapels open and maintained his father's stipends to Catholic priests.

Joviality was the keynote of much of this Duke's behaviour. Nicknames bestowed on him included not only 'the Protestant Duke' but 'the Drunken Duke': it was said of him that when he was drunk, he became a Catholic again. Physically huge, both muscular and stout, Duke Charles was described euphemistically by a contemporary: 'Nature which cast him in her coarsest mould, had not bestowed on him any of the external insignia of high descent'; put more bluntly, he might have been mistaken for a grazier or a farmer. Worn old clothes, a lack of hair powder and enormous whiskers completed a conspicuously unducal picture. As against this, he was a passionate bibliophile: he greatly augmented the collection at Arundel, and in 1800 created a new library for it, lined and vaulted in mahogany, over a hundred feet long.[21]

Nevertheless, the Protestant Duke was both the premier Duke

in England, as such by birth destined to be Earl Marshal at the Coronation, and also by birth the head of the leading Catholic house. The Norfolks had a long and colourful history, including executions for treason: Thomas Duke of Norfolk, who had raised a Northern rebellion on behalf of Mary Queen of Scots and Edward the 9th Duke, who had fought for the Stuarts in 1715 before he succeeded, but was subsequently reconciled; it was in his London house that George III had been born. There were also some previous episodes of conformity to the State Church, as well as other instances of what the leading historian of the family has described as 'a zealous papist'.[22] Duke Charles was extremely proud of the position of Earl Marshal, and always appeared formally with the Earl Marshal's staff of office – from his point of view it was regrettable that there happened to be no Coronation in his lifetime, that of George III having taken place before he succeeded to the title.

The other side to the Duke was that he had been a Foxite Whig in the latter's lifetime, following Fox into Opposition. He opposed the slave trade and advocated Parliamentary Reform. Freedom of worship for Catholics in Ireland was something he believed in. His private life was also in keeping with that of many Whigs, although in fact not entirely of his own making. His first wife died very soon in childbirth, and his second wife went mad, which left him unable to marry and beget lawful heirs; the solution was an official mistress, Mary Gibbon, by whom he had five children, two of whom, known as Howard-Gibbon, became Heralds.

It was true that 'the old toper', as the diarist Creevey peevishly described him in 1805, was not the kind of aristocrat likely to convince the Irish Catholic Church, as represented by Bishop John Milner, of the value of the Cisalpine English laity. At which point there was one of those reversals which will inevitably occur in systems based on hereditary succession. Duke Charles died in 1815, and owing to the failure of his two marriages to produce a legitimate son, his heir was his cousin from the Howard of Glossop branch, Bernard the 12th Duke, known as Barney or Twitch or Scroop. Barney, short in stature and rather slight in build, was in other ways as well the opposite of his cousin.[23]

Here was a 'zealous papist' for whom Catholic Emancipation was his main aim in life. What is more, he had a legitimate son and heir, Henry, known after 1815 as the Earl of Surrey. These two successive Dukes of Norfolk, the showcase title of Catholic England, one of whom performed the ultimate compromise of passing officially as a Protestant and the other a strong supporter of pure Catholicism, symbolized the split in the Catholic world. One faction believed in *laissez-faire*, the other in steadfast rigour; both hoped for Emancipation.

Duke Bernard's presence as an ardent Catholic did, however, nothing to solve the problem of the Veto: was it acceptable in any form as had sometimes seemed the case, or was 'Cardinal Tempter' an illusion? Was there to be no compromise at all? It was Castlereagh again who pointed to the fact that the Catholics themselves must find a means of 'putting their intentions and principles beyond dispute, if they desire to conciliate'.[24]

At the same time, these were the years which saw the rise of specifically Catholic publications in the press. The *Catholic Magazine* of 1801 was an early attempt and included poetry, such as this lament on the 'Miseries of Heresy':

> Of that pure church despoil'd in Henry's reign
> For union fam'd sad monuments remain;
> Amid whose crumbling ruins spread around
> How sad, how desolate, is Albion found!

The most serious effort was the *Orthodox Journal*. This was founded by William Eusebius Andrews in 1813. The title of the paper was intended to indicate that 'it could not belong to any party, as it would be on the side of the TRUTH, which ought to be the aim of all parties'.[25]

Andrews was born in Norwich, the child of Catholic converts, where he had progressed from apprentice to editor of the *Norfolk Chronicle*, a post he held for nearly fifteen years. In London he set about using the press to advance the Catholic cause – a very different avenue of approach to the charm of Cardinal Tempter and the relaxed joviality of Duke Charles, but practical and in theory capable of wider appeal. It was indeed Bishop Milner who supported Andrews in his endeavour, so that the *Orthodox Journal* and Milner stood in contrast to the Cisalpine Catholic Board.

For Milner, it was the organ of public opinion that he chose to write on the subject of the Veto, on which he continued to hold strong views. So strong were his views, and as usual the strength of his language equalled the strength of his views, that in the end an appeal was made to Rome – surely this ferocity was unsuitable in a bishop? – and Milner was forbidden to write further in the *Orthodox Journal*. His expulsion from the Catholic Board was another logical step following his robust denunciation of the Veto and anyone who supported it. He went with a fierce dignity: 'Gentlemen, you consider me unfit for your company on earth, may God make me fit for your company in Heaven.'[26]

While these internecine struggles hardly helped the cause, as Castlereagh pointed out, there was at the same time in England after 1815 a general atmosphere of relaxation towards the Catholic community, even if it was for the time being unaccompanied by any positive legal results. The Tory administration was now headed by Lord Liverpool, since the assassination of Spencer Perceval by a madman in 1812. Liverpool was well able to bear the embargo on the discussion of Catholic Emancipation in the Cabinet which had been accepted by Pitt on his return to office in 1806. A man in his forties, he was a regular attender of the Anglican Church; but as Mrs Arbuthnot, the wise observer who was also the confidante of Wellington, put it, he wanted to have nothing to do with the actual issue of toleration (or otherwise) of minority religions.

In his first public statement on the subject in 1805 Liverpool had declared that the King by virtue of the British constitution was in a special relationship with the Church of England, and so long as Roman Catholics refused to take the Oath of Supremacy, it was proper that they should be deprived of political power.

The day after Liverpool was made Prime Minister in 1812, he announced a policy of neither proposing nor opposing the question of Catholic Relief as a government, leaving all Members free to act as individuals.[27]

Henry Grattan's latest Bill for Emancipation of 1813 had ended with defeat, although it was supported by both Canning and Castlereagh. Grattan was at his best as he condemned the exclusion of Catholics from political power: 'Why should they be sentenced to utter and hopeless exclusion from all political power? ... If it is ambition, then was Magna Carta ambition – then was the Declaration of Rights ambition? Protection, not power is the request of the Catholics ... It is the Protestants who ask for power.' It was after all Catholics, pointed out Grattan, who wrote Magna Carta.[28] The Bill passed its second reading but was lost in committee. Grattan would try again.

In June 1815 no lesser person than the Duke of Sussex, brother of the Regent, presented the Petition of the Catholics in the County of Lancaster, which was couched in 'respectful language'. Although a debate in May had included language by MPs which was certainly disrespectful about Catholics, notably about O'Connell in Ireland – Charles Yorke MP chose to mock him for claiming descent from the ancient monarchs of Ireland – another MP, Sir Henry Parnell, hailed Grattan. Here was one whom every Catholic should revere, as their great deliverer 'from the most intense system of persecution that ever disgraced a government or aggrieved a people'.[29]

Despite the temporary setback of Napoleon's escape, ending in his final defeat at Waterloo in June 1815, wartime problems began to subside; there followed the less dramatic trials of peace. It would be premature to describe Whigs and Tories as solid political parties in the modern sense of the word, as the events of the next decade would demonstrate. But there was at the very least a tendency for the Whigs to be Pro-Emancipation, in keeping with their general feelings about personal liberty, whereas the Tories were inclined towards an Anti-Catholic patriotic fervour and a feeling for the Establishment as represented by the State Church. As usual, throughout the history of the British Isles,

Ireland remained the wild card in the pack – hopefully an ace in the hand for the English Pro-Catholics, but there could be no certainty about this: from time immemorial in its interaction with England, Ireland had been less like an ace than an unruly knave whose actions could not be foreseen.

Viscount Palmerston was a Tory MP who was Irish and thus eligible for the House of Commons despite his peerage; he was currently Secretary at War. In 1813 Palmerston had spoken lyrically on the subject of his native country – which he had first visited in 1808 when he was twenty-four, but for which he had natural empathy – and its Catholicism: 'It is in vain to think that by any human pressure, we can stop the spring which gushes from the earth. But it is for us to consider whether we will force it to spend its strength in secret and hidden courses, undermining our fences and corrupting our soil, or whether we shall, at once, turn the current into the open and spacious channel of honourable and constitutional ambition, converting it into the means of national prosperity and public wealth.'[30]

This was a splendid passage but O'Connell, actually present in Ireland, was not interested in gushing springs and secret and hidden courses. As it happened, 1815, which saw peace in Europe at least for the present, might well have seen an eternal rest for O'Connell. On 23 January he made a speech to the Catholic Board in Dublin in which he castigated the Dublin Corporation under the rule of the Protestant Ascendancy as 'beggarly'.[31]

John D'Esterre, a member of the Corporation, was a former Royal Marine who famously could snuff out a candle at nine yards with a pistol shot. His challenge to O'Connell for his speech was in part based on his dire personal finances, approaching bankruptcy, which convinced him that he was insulted by the word 'beggarly'. He was in any case a man of fiery temperament, spiced with courage. He had defied the mutineers of the Nore towards the end of the last century when tied up at the yardarm – 'Haul away, ye lubbers! Haul away and be damned. God save the King!' – after which they cut him down. But it is also likely that O'Connell's opponents saw in D'Esterre someone who could be manipulated to secure their enemy's destruction.

At the same time, O'Connell himself had a complicated history where duelling was concerned. When he was a law student in London in the 1790s, there had been a row over a young woman at a party which might have resulted in a duel but did not – conceivably to O'Connell's discredit. In 1813, in an actual duel with the opposing counsel in a case in Limerick, he had allowed a compromise to be struck on the field of action without shots being fired; this time O'Connell was a sufficiently prominent public figure to provoke unpleasant rumours of cowardice.

After a series of manoeuvres, a challenge was issued by O'Connell and D'Esterre accepted it. Snow was falling lightly when the two men met at the demesne of Lord Ponsonby in Co. Kildare. D'Esterre fired first – too low. O'Connell then wounded him – as it happened fatally, the bullet passing into the spine, and D'Esterre bled to death two days later. The financial ruin of his estate followed: it was an indication of O'Connell's absolute horror at what had transpired that he was inclined to wear a glove or wrap a handkerchief round the hand that had fired the fatal shot. Another story had O'Connell raising his hat and saying a prayer whenever he passed D'Esterre's house. He also paid an allowance for D'Esterre's daughter until his death (his widow declined the offer of an income).

O'Connell's reaction to Consalvi, on the other hand, and his treachery in giving way on the Veto – and Papal authority – in favour of the English nobility (as he saw it) displayed another kind of violence. This was the violence of rhetoric, which, unlike physical force, was the resistance he actually advocated. Although O'Connell's courage in defending himself against what was seen as the attack of a Protestant assassin impressed the Catholics, he himself was more troubled.

His language regarding Consalvi was parallel to that of the Papal zealots in Rome who tried to wreck the Cardinal's attempts at compromise. To him Consalvi was a 'perfidious minister' and 'the mere agent of the British government'.[32] O'Connell stressed the very fact which had touched Napoleon, but in very different terms: 'Though a Cardinal, this man is not a priest.' Instead he was a salesman, looking for bargains: 'right glad I presume to have so good a thing to sell as the religion of Ireland'. The exact amount of his price was sneeringly said to be 11,000 guineas. There was a similar reference to 'Quarantotti – the odious, the stupid Quarantotti'. Even Milner was given a roasting for his Vetoist past, before being forgiven in favour of his current 'anti-vetoistical principle'.

O'Connell ended this particular speech to a meeting of the laity on 29 August 1815 with a characteristic peroration: 'But the spirit, the genius of liberty survives. Man cannot, with the knowledge he has acquired, and the examples he beholds, continue in slavery... See within the last twenty years how we have risen from a horde of helots to a nation... Let [England] act as she has done by the Canadians; let her leave inviolate the religion which the chief and the people of Ireland possess; and' – in an allusion to the courage of the Irish soldiers – 'we will in return support her by our unbroken strength, and sustain her with our young blood, in every distress, and through every peril!' He sat down, as usual 'cheered by most rapturous applause'.

CHAPTER SIX

Grattan the Great

'...*he felt his heart melted with the public sorrow
and private regret with which he had followed
to his grave that great man*'.

William Plunket, MP, on Henry Grattan's death, 1820

'THERE NEVER WAS SUCH A BATTLE. Waterloo was nothing to it.' It was in these exuberant terms that Daniel O'Connell described the prospect of his next dramatic involvement with the law.[1] Reality was very different. All this occurred only a few months after the sadly lethal affair involving D'Esterre. O'Connell – in common with his contemporaries, it should be said – still regarded a duel as a possible feature, and what was more, a courageous and honourable feature, of the political scene. D'Esterre's death had saddened him, but not as yet ruled out duelling from his political options.

One should not forget the extraordinary number of leading politicians who were involved in duels around this time, whether resulting in physical damage or something more ritualized. These included the earlier Prime Minister Lord Shelburne, the younger Pitt, Castlereagh and Canning, and even Grattan, who had fought a duel with his fellow MP Isaac Corry over the passing of the

Act of Union, wounding him in the process. And other 'political'
duels lay ahead; including one particularly dramatic one at a crucial moment in British history, a decade into the future. The Irish
Catholic bishops officially condemned duels, but it was said that
Archbishop Murray, turning a blind eye to the circumstances,
had cried out with joy at O'Connell's survival over D'Esterre:
'Heaven be praised! Ireland is safe.' When Berenice, the heroine
of Maria Edgeworth's novel *Harrington*, declared that she had
resolved never to marry a man who had fought in a duel, she
was bravely voicing a surprising independence from current
opinion.[2] The kind of contemporary anecdote which was found
more to the general taste was that concerning Lt Col. Henry
Lawes Luttrell, a Cornish MP, who reportedly refused to accept
a challenge from his father on the grounds that it had not been
given by a gentleman.

In August 1815 Daniel O'Connell certainly did not fall into
that category of which a Berenice might approve. He had after
all recently killed a man in a duel. In spite of that, it seems that
he went out of his way to insult the Chief Secretary, Robert Peel
(of whom he had already spoken with contempt at the time of
the Magee trial). Peel had indeed criticized O'Connell recently
and publicly, but O'Connell's response was made in 'such a
goading and aggressive manner' that it was difficult to see it as
'anything other than a deliberate provocation', in the words of
his biographer.[3] O'Connell's words were certainly ripely insulting. Let the police informers who were present report back this
expression: 'Mr Peel would not DARE, in my presence, or in
any place where he was liable to personal account, use a single
expression derogatory to my interest, or my honour.' Here was
Peel, the mere 'champion of Orangeism, I have done with him
perhaps for ever'.

If O'Connell had his honour, as the recent disastrous duel
with D'Esterre had demonstrated, so did Peel. By the standards
of the time he had little choice, but in any case there was nothing
timorous about Peel. Sir Charles Saxton, MP for Cashel, was
enlisted as his potential second if O'Connell refused to retract.
O'Connell's designated second was George Lidwell, a barrister

but a Protestant. Somehow arrangements for the duel went awry: the result, ludicrous if it had not been dangerous, was for a duel between Saxton and Lidwell in which there was a ritual exchange of fire but no damage done. In the meantime, both parties were appealing to the press and issuing statements which did nothing to calm down the bubbling mixture of honour, grievance and insult which ensued.

The next duel – between the true contestants, Peel and O'Connell – was aborted dramatically. O'Connell's treasured wife Mary had been a young and penniless cousin whom he had married secretly in 1802, after a fairly raffish past of philandering adventure. In his impetuous way, O'Connell simply fell in love with the sweet girl, despite her lack of prospects and the wishes of his uncle 'Hunting Cap' that he should marry elsewhere – for money, not love. When Daniel declared himself to Mary he said that he would devote his life to making her happy. If this was not an exact prophecy about the future course of O'Connell's private life, he did remain loving and caring throughout the course of what proved a long marriage.

By 1815 Mary had already endured the inescapable problems of being married to a popular hero, in this case one devoted to causes such as the abolition of the Union in direct contradiction of the government of the day. O'Connell's problems, which were Mary's problems too, also included rising debts; much of his financial future depended on the intentions of 'Hunting Cap'. Mary was a pious Catholic who took seriously the Church's prohibition against duelling, quite apart from her fears for her husband's safety. Despite O'Connell's elaborate precautions to deceive his wife about his intentions – and his movements – Mary got wind of the truth. She informed the sheriff, causing her husband to be taken briefly into custody.

As many other duellists had done in the past, these deter-mined opponents, animated by a mixture of pride and hatred, now resorted to the expedient of meeting in Ostend. O'Connell remained confident: 'I cannot bring myself even to doubt success.' In fact, success in the crude sense of a fight and a victor was never put to the test. Police spies were everywhere. Determined as Peel and O'Connell might be, the government in London was equally sure that the consequences of such a fight would be disastrous from any angle. A series of arrests and threats meant that Lidwell, the second, was held in London. O'Connell was held at Dover. Only Peel managed to get abroad, but in the absence of O'Connell there could be no duel.

At the time O'Connell deplored his treatment: 'What a glorious opportunity have they deprived me of – of *living and dying*.' But he never actually fought another duel. Both Peel and O'Connell therefore lived to fight what was in effect a far bigger fight, in which the principle of religious freedom far outranked personal animosity, and which would come to an unexpected conclusion.

In London, the existence of a Parliament – denied since 1801 to Dublin – meant that words, not pistols, were the weapons of choice. 'A final and conciliatory judgment': this was the declared aim of Henry Grattan in May 1817, introducing a motion into the House of Commons. He asked for a committee to consider the laws affecting Roman Catholics in Britain and Ireland; in this way he hoped that they could achieve 'the peace and strength of the United Kingdom . . . the stability of the Protestant estate' and 'the general satisfaction of all classes of His Majesty's subjects'.[4] It was Grattan's first such effort since 1813. He was now in his early seventies, but still capable of the oratory with which he had been mastering parliamentary audiences for over forty years.

Grattan showed himself immediately to be a contented supporter of the Veto and all its implications, just as he remained in favour of the Union, for the sake of the 'stability' which it brought – so long as it was a Union combined with justice. 'There may be domestic nominations, there may be a veto – there may be both! Now you may command your own Securities, and therefore not let gentlemen say "we cannot accede to Catholic emancipation, because we have no Securities".' Under the circumstances, were they really willing to endanger their own (Protestant) Church in order to exclude the Catholics? They should, on the contrary, give to the Catholics all they required, while taking care that their own Church was properly protected.

A spirited debate followed, including some highly Anti-Catholic speeches from MPs such as John Leslie Foster, a barrister, son of an Irish Protestant bishop and currently representing Yarmouth. Leslie Foster's attack on Grattan's previous bill had been published as a pamphlet: now he weighed into the subject of Emancipation with a recitation of Ireland's long, sad and sadly violent history, suggesting that the Catholic Irish would much rather forgo Emancipation than agree to the Veto. Others quoted from a recent publication by the Catholic Dr Gandolphy entitled *A Defence of the Ancient Faith, or a Full Exposition of the Christian Religion*. Here Gandolphy had argued that Roman Catholicism was the only real Christian religion: as for the Reformation, that was 'the sinful deed of lust, avarice and pride'.[5] It was an equally intolerant view.

Both Castlereagh and Canning made speeches supporting the motion. Nevertheless, Grattan was defeated by a majority of twenty-four votes. Many felt that the speech which really contributed to Grattan's defeat – yet again – was that of Robert Peel, the Chief Secretary for Ireland (a post he continued to hold until 1818). Admirers of Peel, and even those who criticized his oratorical style, paid him tributes. Foster, for example, thought it better delivered than anything since Pitt's time.[6] There was a suggestion afterwards that the speech had swayed thirteen votes, which, if true, would have accounted for the majority.

Peel's main message was in direct contrast to that of Grattan. 'In all this,' he declared, 'I see nothing that can lead to harmony – nothing that can constitute a final and satisfactory settlement – nothing but a wild and irreconcilable contradiction of principles.' And he urged each member of his audience to weigh 'the substantial blessings which he knows to have been derived from the government that *is*', against all the speculative advantages which he is promised from 'the government that is *to be*'.

The whole tenor of his speech was indeed unashamedly against any kind of progress or change, and in favour of what was long established – and thus by inference sacrosanct. Where any advance of Catholic power was concerned, he prophesied woe in terms of national danger – to the Protestants, that is. The

Roman Catholics would never rest until they had become 'by far the most powerful body in Ireland'. There was an 'inviolable compact' between Great Britain and Ireland. And the essential part of that compact was that the Protestant religion – admittedly the religion of the minority – should be the established and favoured part of the State. In his summing-up, at a late hour, Grattan exclaimed in scorn against these views: how could the Catholic doctrine of Transubstantiation actually endanger the English monarchy, the House of Brunswick?

Peel's private feelings about Irish politics were less high-flown; they can be judged by his communication to his friend John Wilson Croker on the eve of his departure from the Emerald Isle: 'A fortnight hence I shall be free as air ... free from Orangemen; free from Ribbonmen ... free from the Lord Mayor and Sheriffs ... free from Catholics who become Protestants to get into Parliament ... free from perpetual converse about the Harbour of Howth and Dublin Bay haddock; and, lastly, free of the Company of Carvers and Guilders which I became this day in reward of my public services.'[7]

The tide of debate in the House of Commons flowed on sluggishly, but for all Grattan's efforts still it flowed with Peel. The motion was defeated.

Grattan's next attempt was in May 1819, when he presented several Petitions once again in favour of Emancipation. Grattan made a long speech which aimed at countering in advance all the possible arguments against it.[8] Such an Act would, for example, give 'strength' to the Protestant Church, the Act of Settlement and the Protestant Succession to the Crown. 'The Roman Catholic combination of Europe has ceased ... the race of the Pretender is extinct [the Cardinal of York had died in 1807] ... the dangerous power of the Pope is no more.' Not only were the supposedly threatening attachments of the Catholics gone, but all the objects to which there could be any such attachments had been annihilated.

Even more powerful was Grattan's sonorous invocation of the real Ruler of the Universe: 'The King who would interfere, puts himself in the place of his Maker, and attempts to jostle the

Almighty from his throne; he has no credentials from God and can have none from man.' Naturally Grattan did not end without the obligatory reference to the contribution of Catholic soldiers to the British cause in the recent wars: 'the battles won with Catholic blood'. Grattan also went into detailed arguments about the legal necessities which were or were not involved.

Once more John Leslie Foster came up with a highly Anti-Catholic speech in which the entire stress was placed upon the rights of the Protestants in England and Ireland: their dislike of the idea of Catholics voting was cited most emphatically as though it was a legal argument. The last speech was made by Lord Lowther, who similarly stressed that further concessions to the Catholics 'tended to weaken the Protestant establishment'.

Finally, the debate ended in the kind of confusion which seemed emblematic of the misfortune of mixing religion with politics. Cries were heard of 'Question! Question!', growing ever louder. The Speaker called on the Ayes and Noes in turn. He decided that the Noes had it. There was then a loud general cry of 'Divide! Divide!' According to custom, 'strangers', those who were not MPs, now had to leave the chamber. But some 'strangers' remained, under the impression that the debate would continue: given that speakers of the importance of Castlereagh, Canning and Peel were waiting to be called, it was a reasonable assumption. Meanwhile there was an argument that the Noes had already been declared the victors.

The Speaker would have none of it. A division took place and this time the Noes were indubitably if narrowly ahead by six votes. Even then, the objections were not over. John Croker, one of the tellers, complained that several MPs had illegally entered the chamber after the question had been put and the Noes pronounced the winners. As a result, Lord Worcester, heir to the Duke of Beaufort, and four others for the Noes were struck off. Lord Forbes was eliminated from the Ayes. The result was even closer, but the Noes still won by two votes: 243 to 241. Grattan was defeated. Catholic Emancipation, in the form of Petitions for Relief, was in effect rejected by the House of Commons once again. Petitions presented in the House of Lords in the following weeks in favour of Emancipation or partial Relief by Lords Donoughmore and Grey were similarly defeated.

Grattan died in June the next year, a month before his seventy-fourth birthday; the Protestant champion of the Catholics was buried in Westminster Abbey, close to Pitt and Fox, which, given Grattan's belief in the permanence of the Union of the two countries, seemed appropriate enough.* Daniel O'Connell, however, claiming him as 'the greatest man Ireland ever knew' at the by-election for his parliamentary seat which followed, believed strongly that he should have been buried in Ireland, blaming Grattan's family for the dereliction.[9]

William Conyngham Plunket, a determined and highly argumentative Irish lawyer, son of a Presbyterian minister in Enniskillen (a man once described as having an 'intensity of internal fire' which glowed like an iron stove), took over the baton of Emancipation in the British Parliament. The intensity was matched by his striking physical appearance: Macaulay called Plunket 'very ugly, but with a strong expression of intellect in his strong coarse features and massy forehead'. A Whig, just as Grattan had been, and the Member for Dublin University, he had shown his patriotism in 1816 when he had rebuked the Tory Speaker of the House of Commons for leaving out the contribution of Ireland, i.e. her soldiers, in congratulating Wellington on his victory at Waterloo.[10]

In February 1821 Plunket would move to consider Catholic Relief in a committee of the whole House, after presenting several Irish Catholic Petitions and paying tribute to his predecessor Grattan: 'he felt his heart melted with the public sorrow and private regret with which he had followed to his grave that great man', and Plunket unlike O'Connell praised the choice of Westminster Abbey: 'at his death, as during his life, he had been the bond between the two countries'. Even Peel found Plunket's speech 'the most powerful and eloquent ... I have ever heard in Parliament'.[11]

---

* There is a statue of Grattan in the Outer Lobby of the Palace of Westminster.

And, just as Peel was believed to have done previously for the opposite result, Plunket evidently swayed the House of Commons in favour of Relief. His basic theme was, crudely put: why pick on the Catholics? 'He might be an infidel, he might believe in Jupiter, in Osiris, the ape, the crocodile, in all the host of heaven, and all the creeping things of the earth, and [still] be admitted to all the privileges of the state.' For the first time since 1813 there was a victory for Emancipation in the Commons by six votes – and at the third reading by nineteen – only to be thrown out by the Lords. Plunket, like Grattan before him, was a contented Vetoist: the Pope's role was to be purely spiritual, and all appointments of bishops and clergy to be given to the Crown. The fact that the leading Catholic Bishop, Milner, continued to oppose any kind of 'securities' (controls exercised by the State over the Catholic Church) was consequently described by Plunket as 'an act of undeviating consistent bigotry'.

While the Parliament in London debated the issue of Emancipation publicly, but without success – from the Catholic point of view, that is, the Anti-Catholics taking a very different line about this heroic stand to hold off Popery – O'Connell in Dublin now began to play with a series of experimental Catholic organizations. He was able to use his immense personal popularity (to which his public acceptance of duelling had only contributed) for essentially peaceful, if contentious, ends. But there were problems. A profound disagreement between those who came to be known as 'Seceders' and 'Anti-Seceders' echoed the English arguments between Vetoists and Non-Vetoists. It was the basic question yet again of what 'securities' would be permitted, that is, non-Catholic interference with the Catholics' organization of their own Church in the interests of the Protestant State.

An early Catholic Association had been formed in 1815, before the Ostend debacle, which petered out two years later. An earlier Catholic Board had been ended, as contravening government rules of assembly. Now there were small, informal meetings in a drawing room in the house of the Earl of Fingall, which from their elegantly furnished surroundings took the luxurious name of 'Divan' meetings.

Lord Fingall, a man in his sixties, was far from being any kind of revolutionary figure. He was a man of great sweetness of character who found it easy to woo with courtesy, believing strongly in the kind of compromises which would bring about effective relief from disabilities for his fellow Catholics. He had, for example, headed a body of yeomen who had helped suppress the rebellion of 1798. A few years earlier he had secured the lifting of the ban on his Jacobite father: the previous Lord Fingall had been outlawed for adherence to James II, but since he had actually died before 1689, he could no longer be plausibly accused of the crime of supporting the Stuarts at that point. O'Connell and Fingall represented two opposing forces in the fight for Emancipation; not only that, but socially the hereditary aristocrat and the ambitious lawyer represented two sides of politically active Irish society at the time.

The Catholic Association had proved a disappointment. A new and, it was hoped, improved Catholic Board took its place in July 1817 with the hope of unity and action. But in the words of John O'Connell, Daniel's son, who edited his correspondence in 1846 after his death, this period was felt by O'Connell to be the nadir of his eventful campaigning life: 'a moral lethargy, a faint-hearted apathy hung over the country, and with the exception of himself, scarce anyone was in the field for Ireland'.[12] O'Connell himself remained a dedicated opponent of any kind of 'ecclesiastical' Veto, in direct opposition to the Irish Seceders. In the meantime, the English Parliament, in the shape of Robert Peel, had declared the issue of Emancipation 'irreconcilable'.

In one of his earlier, more violent perorations, O'Connell chose to quote from Byron's poem of 1812, *Childe Harold's Pilgrimage*:

> Hereditary bondsmen! Know ye not
> Who would be free themselves must strike the blow?

When the old King of England died on 29 January 1820, to be succeeded at last by his eldest son the Prince Regent, it would have been a bold prophet who foresaw the eventual fate of

Catholic Emancipation. Was it to be achieved by violence, as Byron's poem seemed to indicate? (Although O'Connell had arguably so far believed more in violent oratory than the violence of rebellion.) In both the English Parliament and the Irish governing class, there was a kind of stalemate.

Henry Grattan's reference to 'the Protestant Succession to the Crown' in his speech to Parliament nine months earlier was not without significance. The coming of a new King meant in turn the prospect of a new heir to the throne – or heirs. The Hanoverian Succession, which had enjoyed a period of orderly tranquillity, thanks to the high fertility of Queen Charlotte with her fifteen children, nine of them male, had become once more potentially complicated, if not in this generation, then the next one. Princess Charlotte, the only child of the Prince of Wales's ill-fated marriage to Caroline of Brunswick, had recently died in childbirth. The next male heirs in order of age were Frederick Duke of York and William Duke of Clarence.

Both the Duke of York and the Duke of Clarence had led rich private lives, with children galore, but all illegitimate and in consequence not in line for the throne. Then the Duke of Clarence was one of the two royal Dukes to be galvanized into making late (legal) marriages after the death of Princess Charlotte. His choice, Adelaide of Saxe-Meiningen, a widowed German princess with one child, had failed so far to produce a baby that survived. (Princess Elizabeth of Clarence was born and soon died at the beginning of the next reign.) In January 1820, therefore, the nearest existing legitimate grandchild of George III and Queen Charlotte to the throne was an eighteen-month-old princess called Victoria, the daughter of their fourth son, the Duke of Kent, who had died six days before his father. There were two other legitimate grandchildren at this time, both born in 1819 and both called George, one living in Hanover, sons of the fifth and seventh sons respectively; but little Victoria took precedence.

More to the immediate point was the fact that the Duke of York was now the heir presumptive to the throne occupied by George IV, now a corpulent and self-indulgent man approaching sixty. And York was a dedicated opponent of any reduction of the Penal Laws against the Catholics. His influence – and he was an eager, prolix speaker in the House of Lords – was a matter of reckoning. Ernest Duke of Cumberland was an equally malevolent opponent, but liberals, and even pragmatists, hoped that he would remain in Hanover. As against that another Royal Duke, the sixth son, Augustus, Duke of Sussex – although his lowly position in the vast family made his succession unlikely compared to that of the Duke of York – had presented Petitions on behalf of Catholics.

In the meantime the reigning mistress of George IV, Isabella Marchioness of Hertford, had been succeeded by Elizabeth Marchioness Conyngham; or, as the private despatch of a foreign minister seen by the Duke of Wellington had it: 'The Prince Regent aged 70 [actually fifty-eight] has left the Marchioness of Hertford aged 70 [actually sixty], to become wildly in love with the Marchioness Conyngham, aged 50.'[13] It was true that, like her predecessors, Elizabeth Conyngham was not young – she was indeed fifty in 1819 when she probably became the mistress of the then Prince Regent. A portrait by Thomas Lawrence of Elizabeth in her early thirties shows a voluptuous beauty of the type that appealed to the Prince. His devotion was generally remarked; her own devotion was generally felt to be to the financial advancement of her family.

On the other hand, she was by nature more of a Whig than a Tory, and as time would show shared the Whiggish predilection for Emancipation on practical, if not religious grounds. Her husband (raised from Earl to Marquess in 1816) came from the Anglo-Irish Conyngham family who therefore had that practical knowledge of the circumstances of Irish life, which, while it did not always persuade its possessors to support Emancipation – Protestant Ascendancy remained Ascendancy – was at least more realistic than condemning three-quarters of a nation as hopelessly barbarian.

Lady Conyngham was certainly installed by the time of the King's Coronation on 19 July 1821 when he was seen nodding and winking in her direction, sighing and making eyes at her, at one point taking off a diamond brooch from his breast and kissing it with his besotted gaze fixed upon her, whereupon she did the same to a diamond ring. Mrs Arbuthnot gave it as her opinion that the King had never known what it was to be in love before: strong words given the many attempts he had evidently made to find out.[14]

The Coronation of George IV when it came – complicated by his attempt to divorce the woman now officially Queen Caroline – has been described by Roy Strong in his study of the subject as 'the most extravagant in history'.[15] That was the impression which lingered with varying effect: short-term admiration from those who liked such wonders and revulsion from those contrasting such extravagance with the social needs of the less fortunate. The pathetic or grotesque attempt – once again, according to individual sympathies – of Queen Caroline to gain access to the Abbey was another feature of the event; especially since it would be followed shortly afterwards by her death.

Several Catholic peers were present, although unable to take their seats in the House of Lords; the hereditary Earl Marshal, the Catholic Duke of Norfolk, who should have organized the whole magnificent event, was obliged to depute his office. The banquet alone cost over £25,000 (nearly £2 million in today's money) and roughly £150,000 (over £11 million) went on jewels, plate and the various uniforms and costumes deemed essential to the national celebration. The nation, far from being grateful, was outraged by the expense; but curtailment thereof would be a decision for the next sovereign to make, whoever he or she was. George IV had waited for his moment and was determined to suffuse it with splendour.

However, he himself cut a figure 'more like the Victim than the Hero of the fête' owing to his now vast physical proportions, including his fifty-inch waist and wobbling fleshy face, all this enhanced rather than disguised by the lavish velvet and jewels with which he was optimistically adorned. The judgement was that of Lady Palmerston, who added that several times the new King was 'at the last gasp', but a cheering look from Lady Conyngham 'revived him like Magic or Ether'.[16] Naturally a Coronation entailed a Coronation Oath: in Westminster Abbey

King George IV swore in front of the Archbishop of Canterbury almost exactly the same oath as his father had taken sixty years earlier. The difference was not religious: it lay quite simply in the inclusion of the words 'and Ireland', inserted twice in recognition of the Union in 1800; after 'this United Kingdom of Britain' and 'the Church of England'.

This oath was that 'binding religious obligation' developed by 'the wisdom of our forefathers' which had caused the senior King such agony of conscience in 1801 that he convinced his Prime Minister Pitt that it had led to his madness.[17] In the future it would be a question of the significance attached to this oath by the son of George III – was it mere flummery or a profound personal and spiritual engagement? If there was any alteration in the state of religion in the United Kingdom, would the King, in the combative words of Henry Grattan, really interfere, putting himself in the place of his Maker and attempting to jostle the Almighty from his throne?

PART TWO

THE ABOMINABLE QUESTION

'The abominable Cath. Quest. which is now mixed up with everything we eat or drink or see or think'

The Bishop of Oxford to Robert Peel,
14 August 1827

CHAPTER SEVEN

Serving Ireland Royally

'I never felt sensations of more delight than since
I came to Ireland... Whenever an opportunity offers,
wherein I can serve Ireland, I will seize it with eagerness.
God bless you my friends.'

King George IV, Dun Laoghaire, 3 September 1821

W HEN GEORGE IV ARRIVED in Howth on 12 August 1821, he was the first reigning monarch to do so since Richard II in 1399. That visit had led directly to King Richard's ruin: 400 years later it was to be hoped that there would be better results. What was widely said at the time was that King George was the first English monarch who came in a spirit of conciliation to the country.*[1]

Certainly King George was greeted immediately with enormous enthusiasm by the Irish. This enthusiasm took many different forms: Mrs Arbuthnot learned that Castlereagh and Lord Sidmouth had been accosted on the day of the landing by a

---

* Although Queen Victoria was to visit Ireland four times, and King George V in 1911, there was then a 100-year gap until the visit of Queen Elizabeth II in April 2011, which received the same accolade as that of George IV.

street lady: 'A glorious day this for our country!' she cried. 'This night the King is to have all the fat women in Ireland!' (Was she perhaps influenced by the impressively ample appearance of Lady Conyngham, who was in attendance?) Lord Cloncurry, an actual witness, wrote later in his memoir that 'a strange madness seemed at that conjuncture to seize people of all ranks... Men and women of all classes and opinions joined in a shout of gladness.' There was no thought except of 'processions and feasting and loyalty – boiling over loyalty'.[2]

Among those who demonstrated loyalty was Daniel O'Connell, who employed all his fabled oratorical art – to say nothing of his imagination – in his welcome: 'In sorrow and bitterness, I have for the last fifteen years laboured for my unhappy country. It is said of St Patrick that he banished venomous reptiles from our isle, but his Majesty has performed a greater moral miracle. The announcement of his approach has allayed the dissensions of centuries.'[3] With language like this, it is easy to understand the verdict of the lively young Catholic lawyer and political activist from Waterford Richard Lalor Sheil, whose *Sketches of the Irish Bar* were published in *The New Monthly Magazine* from 1822 onwards: 'The Irish appeared drunk with joy, and rattled their chains as if proud of them.'[4]

King George arrived in the late afternoon of his fifty-ninth birthday. The journey had been delayed by news of the illness and death of Queen Caroline, which had led to a stay en route with the Marquess of Anglesey at Holyhead. During the onward journey, however, the King was in somewhat tasteless good spirits at this unexpected delivery from his enemy (it was with difficulty that he was persuaded to wear mourning for the departed). In fact the Countess of Glengall described him as 'dead DRUNK' from wine and whiskey punch when he landed.[5] Despite the lack of a formal reception due to the Queen's demise, the news had spread. People began to amass, as the King greeted the Earl of Kingston in an access of geniality not diminished by the whiskey punch: 'Kingston, Kingston, you black-whiskered, good-natured fellow! I am happy to see you in this friendly country.'[6]

He was then driven to the Viceregal Lodge in Phoenix Park,

surrounded by an admiring pack of Irishmen, some of them on horseback, 2,000 of them on foot. Once in Phoenix Park, King George kept up the level of geniality, urging the crowds to follow him right up to the house itself, where he made 'a short but hearty speech'. Throughout the King stressed his long-held desire to visit Ireland, the country which he swore that he had loved since birth. 'My heart has always been Irish. From the day it beat. I have loved Ireland.' In a subsequent dismissal which cannot have displeased the huge crowd, he urged them to go and drink his health as he would drink theirs (or perhaps had already done so), 'in a bumper of Irish whiskey punch'. After which he shook all the hands he could possibly reach, a gesture which went down particularly well.

Of course there were dissentient voices, and being Irish they were eloquent ones. One witness described Ireland as kneeling like a bastinadoed elephant to receive a paltry rider in the course of his visit. Hamilton Rowan, who had been the secretary of the Dublin Society of the United Irishmen and done time in prison, expressed great surprise at the shocking physical appearance of the King: 'Until I saw George the Fourth, I never met a person who in features, contour and general mien outdid their caricature!'[7]

The present incumbent of the Viceregal Lodge was Charles Earl Talbot, who had been appointed Lord Lieutenant of Ireland in 1817 at the age of forty. Talbot, a Tory, was a known opponent of Catholic Emancipation, but in other respects regarded as a man of integrity in Dublin circles. The Lord Lieutenant had wide-reaching powers; it was a role unique in the British Union in that it had no parallel in Scotland, let alone Wales.[8] Thus the post served to emphasize the separateness of Ireland rather than the new Union. Catholics were debarred: since 1690, Viceroys had consisted of a series of English Protestant aristocrats, including two future Prime Ministers in the previous century, Lord Hartington and the Duke of Portland.

Executive power nowadays tended to be exercised by the Chief Secretary – the post Robert Peel had recently held. Nevertheless, as time would show, the potential influence of a Viceroy could not be underestimated; nor the potential difficulty when a Viceroy seemed to prefer the interests of the people he governed to those of the King he nominally represented.*

The Viceroy – and his wife, the Vicereine – were of course the natural centre of Ireland as focused on Dublin. Although Dublin Castle was the official residence, Phoenix Lodge had come to replace it practically, as being more salubrious. Given that the couple had fourteen children, the last born while Talbot was in office, the choice is understandable. In 1821 Viceregal Society echoed the law and Catholic lack of privilege in that it was by custom predominantly Protestant; many owed their position to land notoriously acquired from previously Irish owners.

King George IV was, nevertheless, greeted by all classes. And the genuine friendliness and charm – seen in the hand-shaking – which were also part of his character, along with the fantasy and self-indulgence, were exercised to good effect. One comment by an old man – 'he's a real King, and asks us how we are' – prefigured the way royalty would go in future, slowly altering from figure of power to benevolent figurehead.[9] That last stage, however, lay far in the future. This was a man who still possessed extraordinary hereditary power, even if its exact practical extent might be arguable.

A quick period of seclusion to mark the death of Queen Caroline was followed by a magnificent procession into Dublin itself. One report suggested that there was at least a mile of carriages. The King wore the Order of St Patrick over his regimental dress, and waved a hat decorated with a huge bunch of shamrock. There was no mistaking his message: this was 'just the day he wished for'. The events which celebrated his stay included a review in the Park, and a Drawing-Room at which the dresses of a thousand ladies were satisfyingly 'rich and [in] good taste'. (This must have gratifying to the patriotic, since 'Irish manufacture to be worn' had been specified on the invitations.) At

---

* The office of Lord Lieutenant of Ireland survived until 1922; the last holder was in fact the one and only Catholic, Viscount Fitzalan of Derwent, a younger son of the Duke of Norfolk.

a banquet given at Trinity College, the King displayed further public jollity during the singing of 'Rule Britannia' by beating time vigorously with his hand on the table.

Only at the Lord Mayor's feast was a note of chill struck, indicative of the deep divisions which existed within this high-spirited gathering. When a toast was given to William III of 'glorious, pious and immortal memory' – the very name 'a kind of password to insult fellow (Catholic) citizens', as it was later described – Lord Cloncurry turned down his glass and remained seated, as did Lord Talbot of Malahide. On the other hand, the King did receive among several addresses one from the Catholic bishops, which was felt by the disapproving John Wilson Croker to talk too much of politics 'in an unseemly tone'.[10] The King also witnessed the installation of the Earl of Fingall, appropriately enough, as the first Catholic member of the Order of St Patrick.

News of King George's ultra-gracious behaviour and the consequent enthusiasm reached England. There were snorts of disapproval: the King 'seems to have behaved not like a sovereign coming in state and pomp to visit a part of dominions,' said Lord Dudley, 'but like a popular candidate come down upon an electioneering trip'. Although such was not Dudley's intention, he had in fact confirmed the success of the King's mission to charm and please, even if the expected result would not be his election to Parliament.

George IV also needed to indulge himself: that was part of his character.[11] For this he betook himself to the Irish residence of the Marquess and Marchioness Conyngham, Slane Castle overlooking the River Boyne in Co. Meath. There, presumably, he resumed those leisured activities with his mistress commemorated in a ballad of the time:

> 'Tis pleasant at seasons to see how they sit
> First cracking their nuts, then cracking their wit,
> Then quaffing their claret – then mingling their lips...

The next line less delightfully suggested that they also tickled the fat 'about each other's hips'.[12]

Slane Castle was, incidentally, not far from the site of the famous – or infamous – Battle of the Boyne, in which William III had put an end to the bid of James II to regain his throne. This was not the occasion to commemorate such battles. The King was now 'a most determined Irishman' who 'raved' about Ireland, according to Castlereagh. With continuing bonhomie he declared that he would like to stay in Ireland and have Lord Talbot go as his representative to England. In taking up residence there, he presumably had the comforts of Slane Castle in mind.

It was perfectly true that George as Prince of Wales had shown a natural affinity for Irishmen, just as he enjoyed the company of Catholics (including his 'wife' Maria Fitzherbert). This affinity included those who might elegantly advocate Irish nationalism along the way. One interesting example was his taste for the novels of the Protestant Irishwoman Sydney Owenson, Lady Morgan, who has been described as the first Irish nineteenth-century writer to give expression to the Anglo-Irish movement in favour of nationalism.[13] She was included in his favourites, led by Jane Austen and Sir Walter Scott. In this he followed his father: George III in his time was said to have praised the novels of another Protestant Irishwoman, Maria Edgeworth; after reading *Castle Rackrent*, published in 1800, he exclaimed: 'I know something now of my Irish subjects.'[14]

The remarkable Lady Morgan was a poet and novelist with a strong romantic feeling for the history of Ireland and its innate independence. She had begun life as Sydney Owenson in comparative poverty; her father being an Irish Catholic actor who had married a Protestant Englishwoman. For Sydney Owenson, existence as a governess to the Featherstones, a Westmeath family living in a castle, only encouraged her natural zeal for writing; later she married Sir Thomas Morgan, surgeon to the household of the Marquess of Abercorn, where she also acted as a governess.

In 1806 *The Wild Irish Girl* made her name with its wonderful heroine Glorvina in a book which has been described as 'an appeal to liberal principles combined with aristocratic sentiments'.[15] It preached a message whereby 'the English [*sic*] landholder' was openly to appear in the midst of his Irish peasantry, 'with an eye beaming complacency... show them you do not distrust them, and they will not betray you'. By working for the so-called English Irish, that is the now beaming landholders, the source of Irish poverty would be dried up and 'the miseries that flowed from it shall be forgotten'.[16] The book went through seven editions in two years.

A series of novels followed, as a result of which Lady Morgan found herself involved in a feud with the caustic critic John Wilson Croker in the *Quarterly Review* (he who had successfully demolished, as he believed, a young poet called John Keats in 1818). When Croker denounced her novel *Florence Macarthy*, Lady Morgan riposted with an insulting portrait of a certain reviewer she called Con Crawley in her next book. Her own 'little Red Riding Hood' figure, as she put it, tiny and dark-haired, pale-skinned, ever animated and witty, became a feature of society. There was no doubt on whose side George IV found himself: he attacked Croker for his insults as a 'damn blackguard'.[17]

The Morgans for their part ungratefully withdrew during the royal visit with a kind of social disdain. There were others who profoundly disagreed with it. Thomas Moore, the celebrated Irish nationalist poet now aged forty-two, had been born in Dublin where his father was a grocer. Tom was especially beloved of his mother, who, in his own words, made him at a very early age 'a sort of *show* child' due to his own natural talent for reciting and his mother's love of poetry; the fact that he was remarkably short as a grown-up meant that Tom retained some of this appearance of an eager child in later life.

Unlike Lady Morgan, Moore was a Catholic, but not a particularly religious one; it was the unfairness of the Catholic lot in Ireland which outraged him. As a Catholic student – one of the earliest intake – at Trinity College, he was insulted by the fact that he could at last study there, but not receive prizes or scholarships. Graduating in 1795, Thomas Moore then moved to London to study law. He made his way into sophisticated

Whig Society, being received by the Prince of Wales himself while the latter was still an ostentatious Whig supporter; the Prince allowed Moore to dedicate his translations of *Anacreon* to him.[18] An early clash with Byron led to sincere friendship: it was to Moore that Byron addressed a poem as he left England in 1816:

> The libation I would pour
> Should be – peace with thine and mine,
> And a health to thee, Tom Moore.

It was Moore's publication of 1808, *Irish Melodies*, which brought him national fame, with songs like 'The Last Rose of Summer' and 'Believe Me, If All Those Endearing Young Charms'. While 'The Harp That Once Through Tara's Halls', the first number in the book, eloquently lamented the lack of liberty in the country compared to days gone by:

> No more to chiefs and ladies bright
> The harp of Tara swells ...
> Thus Freedom now so seldom wakes,
> The only throb she gives
> Is when some heart indignant breaks
> To show that she still lives.

From the first, Thomas Moore was certainly an ardent patriot who was friendly with Robert Emmet when he was young (although never an advocate of violence himself). On grounds of patriotism, Moore was therefore a sympathizer with the movement for Catholic Emancipation as a cure for Ireland's woes, while being inclined to dismiss O'Connell as a rough type of demagogue. He certainly poured scorn on the latter's tactics of conciliation towards George IV. O'Connell himself showed more generosity in hailing the effect of *Irish Melodies* at a meeting of the Dublin Political Union: 'I attribute much of the present state of feeling, and the desire for liberty in Ireland to that immortal man – he has brought patriotism into the private circles of domestic life.'[19]

None of this affected the enthusiasm of the public for George IV and the hopes of their masters. The King departed from Dun Laoghaire on 3 September, which was renamed Kingstown. A 'most determined Irishman', in the King's own phrase, Daniel O'Connell, presented him with a laurel wreath. George IV replied with yet another handshake and an address to the crowds on the shore in the usual grandiloquent language: 'My friends! When I arrived in this beautiful country my heart overflowed with joy – it is now depressed with sincere sorrow. I never felt sensations of more delight than since I came to Ireland – I cannot expect to feel any superior nor many equal till I have the happiness of seeing you again. Whenever an opportunity offers wherein I can serve Ireland, I shall seize on it with eagerness.'[20]

There would of course be an obvious opportunity for the King of Ireland to serve Ireland in his encouragement, or at any rate lack of discouragement, for the campaign for Catholic Emancipation. At the time Daniel O'Connell, in keeping with his general belief in peaceful methods (duels were a matter of personal honour and different), believed that the olive branch in the shape of the laurel wreath was the best way of serving Ireland himself.

Once the King was back in England, the question was: what was to come of all this? In his diary on 5 December 1821 John Lewis Mallet, a civil servant, Secretary of the Audit Board, wrote that the visit left 'the Catholics elated with extravagant hopes – the Protestant party, or rather Orange faction, reproved and humbled without being weakened or made wiser ... such a country as Ireland cannot be pacified by fair words'.[21] Lord Redesdale, former Speaker of the House of Commons and Lord Chancellor of Ireland, described it in similar terms to another former Speaker, Lord Colchester, as 'that unfortunate journey'.[22]

It was Richard Marquess Wellesley, elder brother of the Duke of Wellington, and shortly to become a major player in this politico-religious drama, who made the important point. The King's behaviour in 1821 at the Irish visit was 'most injudicious' if he meant to oppose Catholic claims afterwards. The Catholics now believed that he was 'secretly friendly to their admission [to political power]'.[23] Yet the Whig grandee Lord Holland knew differently, from the private testimony of Louis-Philippe, Duc d'Orléans. The latter heard directly from the then Prince Regent of his secretly Anti-Catholic views: if the Catholics were admitted to political power, how could they be excluded from the Crown? Then his own family would no longer be legitimate. There was obviously considerable room for misapprehension here on the subject of Emancipation.

The situation in the government in London still concentrated power in the hands of the Tories under Lord Liverpool, who had now been Prime Minister for nearly ten years. A formidable ally had joined the government in late 1818, also in the House of Lords: this was Arthur Wellesley, Duke of Wellington, whose post was that of Secretary of the Ordinance. This was not his first political appearance: as Arthur Wellesley he had been in the House of Commons at an earlier date, quite apart from his long and varied military career involving, among other things, prolonged service in India. But now, inevitably and gloriously, he brought with him all the *réclame* of the victor of Waterloo.

Wellington was now in his fifties, seven years younger than the Prince he served. At a superficial level, it mattered in practical terms that he was deaf – and became deafer. He also had difficulty with his elocution, having lost his back teeth during his military service. As his elder brother Richard bluntly put it: 'Arthur can't speak the English language intelligibly.' None of this could dim the brilliance of the natural authority he exerted against the sombre background of recent events, in a country distressed with post-war unrest, quite apart from the Catholic Question. At a deeper level, he had a dislike of what he called 'factiousness', believing that 'a factious opposition to the government is highly injurious to the interests of the country'.[24] Such an instinctive reaction to unproductive argument – as he saw it – was perfectly comprehensible in a great general. This was, however, no longer the all-encompassing military sphere of the recent decade. It remained to be seen how such a dislike of the essence of a democratic constitution – opposition – would play out in the rough parliamentary world.

Richard Wellesley was appointed Viceroy of Ireland in place

of Lord Talbot in December 1821. Richard Wellesley had progressed through various titles: Viscount Wellesley, then Earl of Mornington, inherited from his father, before reaching that of an Irish Marquess in 1799. Physically the two brothers were not unalike, in that Richard shared the fine head and long nose, if the latter's was not quite so formidable as Arthur's much-caricatured prow; Richard was also shorter.

As characters, the brothers were very different. Richard Wellesley was the elder by nine years and had had a long diplomatic and political career after a shaky start when he was expelled from Harrow School and found a welcome in the rival Eton College.* He had been an Irish MP, then Ambassador to Spain; but the formative experience was surely his seven years as Governor-General of India at the turn of the century, where, in the words of Lord Cloncurry, he acquired 'habits of dominion'. It certainly led to arrogance and has inspired one historian to compare him to the similarly vain twentieth-century Indian Viceroy, the Marquess of Curzon, who, after he returned home, always walked 'as if accompanied by elephants'.[25] Wellesley liked to present himself with a flourish, his painted lips and rouged cheeks visible in his portrait by Thomas Lawrence.

Macaulay pronounced his verdict on Richard Wellesley later: 'a great and splendid figure in history and his weaknesses, though they make his character less worthy of respect, make it more interesting as a study'. Certainly Wellesley's private life was complicated. His brother Wellington brusquely referred to him as 'whoring', more tactfully described as indiscreet sex.[26] Wellesley had a long affair, producing five children, with the French actress of Irish descent Hyacinthe Roland, one who described herself as having 'quicksilver' in her veins, before marrying her in 1794. She died in 1816, leaving him, however, without a legitimate heir.

In short, Wellesley after India was a man of imperious behaviour, with liberal views; or, as the Prince Regent put it less kindly, here was a Spanish grandee grafted on an Irish potato.[27]

---

* A welcome in death as in life: Richard Marquess Wellesley is buried in Eton Chapel, with a handsome bust in the North Porch.

He became Foreign Secretary in Perceval's government, resigning however in 1812 over the issue of Catholic Emancipation. Here his Irish background led him to identify himself with the claims of the Irish Catholics, not so much in the idealistic cause of religious freedom, but believing that the political results of persecution would be eventually disastrous in his native land.

His appointment as Viceroy in late 1821 was consequently seen as Pro-Catholic and attacked as a result. The Tory MP George Bankes wrote in disgust to Lord Colchester: 'I can augur nothing good [from it]... Vanity, dissipation, want of private and unsteadiness of public character... and a strong predilection for the Roman Catholic cause, are not the component parts which ought to constitute the Chief Governor for such a country in such times as these.' For Bankes believed that many parts of Ireland were in 'as disturbed a condition as they have ever been', except during the rebellion of 1798.[28]

Wellesley's early actions as Viceroy confirmed this prejudice. As before, it concerned the historical figure of William III, who, whatever he might have done for the Whig aristocracy in 1688, survived to act as a symbolic troublemaker, whether as hero or villain, in Ireland. As Lord Redesdale put it: 'Every Protestant who enjoys property feels that if James II had won the Battle of the Boyne, his ancestor would have been executed as a traitor.'[29]

In July 1822 the Viceroy forbade the Protestants to take part in their traditional celebration of the battle, by which the statue of William III was garlanded and saluted in a special ceremony. A proclamation by the Lord Mayor of Dublin in October prohibited decoration of the statue in the future. The Protestants showed their disgust publicly. At a performance at the theatre in December 1822, a quart bottle was thrown at the Viceroy in his box by a person in the upper gallery. Magnificently, the Viceroy simply stepped to the front of the box, hand to heart, and gazed upward in the direction of the would-be 'assassin' (as the *Dublin Evening Post* termed him).

The dismissal of William Saurin in January 1822 was similarly interpreted as Pro-Catholic. Saurin, who had been Attorney-General for the last fourteen years, was that extreme Protestant

Ascendancy man who had been disgusted by O'Connell's defence of John Magee at his trial. For Saurin the Catholics were the main source of Ireland's evils; there could be no two ways about it, regardless of the fact that they constituted the majority of the population. Supporters of Emancipation in Ireland – not necessarily all Catholics themselves – had therefore reasons for hope.

In England, to the optimistic there appeared to be the same kind of movement. The Tory Prime Minister, Lord Liverpool, supported Catholics in the higher ranks of the army and the magistracies, even if he remained opposed to them actually being in Parliament. But the number of friends of Emancipation within the Commons was swelling. George Canning, for example, made Foreign Secretary in September 1822 after the death of Castlereagh, had long followed his mentor Pitt in supporting Emancipation, for the crucial reason of Irish security. Earlier in 1822, when he believed he was on his way to being appointed Governor of India, he had made an attempt to argue that historically Catholics could be members of the House of Lords.

It was an able, well-researched speech, belying Canning's own claim to speak 'with much trepidation and anxiety'. Although it began with the now habitual mockery of those on the other side – longing for *more* disabilities not fewer, how upset they must be by the Acts of 1778 and 1791, and so on! – he passed on to history. This was definitely not 'an insidious attempt' to get a partial solution to 'what is called the Catholic Question'. On the contrary, Canning concentrated on events in 1678 under Charles II, when the real intention had been to exclude the future James II, then Duke of York and the Catholic heir presumptive to the throne – not Catholic peers. He also cited the Popish Plot and the false testimony of Titus Oates which had led to the execution of the Catholic Lord Stafford, subsequently declared innocent.[30]

Nearer home, he referred to the events of the recent Coronation in which Catholic peers, notably the Duke of Norfolk, the Premier Peer, and Lord Clifford, with his long-reaching ancestry, had featured conspicuously as part of the magnificent pageantry. Were they now to be dismissed, 'as if called forth and furnished for the occasion ... their importance faded with the importance of the hour?'

Canning's speech was met by a forceful one from the opposing point of view delivered by Robert Peel. For Peel in private, this was support for Catholic Emancipation in a 'new and, I think, extraordinary and objectionable shape', as he described it to Saurin. In the House of Commons, however, he came forward with what he chose to call 'cold reasoning and sober views of the question'. He stressed the impossibility of separating the two Houses plausibly – admission of Catholics to the Commons having been firmly denied by Parliament at the time of William Plunket's Bill the previous year. 'Upon no constitutional ground, upon no ground of policy, could he see the propriety of such a measure.' And he dealt with the whole awkward subject of the Popish Plot by quoting Dryden in his political satire of 1681, *Absalom and Achitophel*:

> Some truth there was, but dashed and brewed with lies,
> To please the fools and puzzle all the wise;
> Succeeding times will equal folly call,
> Believing nothing or believing all.

Peel's conclusion was that 'the measure before them would not be final; and he doubted very much whether it would be conciliatory'. In short, the whole issue of 'securities' (State controls) should be reconsidered first.

Canning's attempt passed the Commons on the third reading by five votes, only to be flung out by the Lords once more. It represented the growing emphasis on the safety or otherwise of Ireland itself as a leading element in the fight for Emancipation. It was similar to the attitude of the new Viceroy, Richard Wellesley, with nothing innately idealistic about it, but a great deal to do with the best interests of England.

The issue of security in Ireland was after all something which could never be ignored by a Protestant administration, likened in some respects to a garrison. There was, as there had always been, another side to Catholic Ireland, that side characterized by travellers (and many English) as barbarous, but in fact owing a great deal to the appalling social conditions of the peasantry. This genuine potential for some kind of rebellion – it was only twenty-odd years since the desperate dash for freedom of Robert Emmet – coexisted with the romantic nationalist literature of Thomas Moore and Sydney Morgan. King George had declared himself on arrival to be eager to serve Ireland. That left open the question of how England itself would feel best served in this situation.

CHAPTER EIGHT

Millstone

'The Irish ... will ever be a millstone hung to the necks of the English Catholics. It is our obvious policy therefore to keep ourselves as separate as possible from the Irish Catholics.'

Robert, Lord Petre

'I AM NOT DISPOSED to incur the Penalties of *Praemunire*' (which in theory included death). In these terms George Canning wrote to Lord Eldon on 20 November 1823. He was referring to the seemingly innocuous letter by which the new Pope Leo XII officially announced his election to the British monarch; it came first into Canning's hands as Foreign Secretary.[1]

Canning was consulting the Lord Chancellor on the propriety of passing the letter on to King George IV, after which there would in theory be an equally formal reply. Eldon was the deeply Anti-Catholic Lord Chancellor of many years' standing, now in his seventies. A Tory of humble Northern origins (rudely known as 'Old Bags' by the Royal Family), he was a man whose power-ful intellect was matched by a dominating character. Eldon's answer was negative: 'this letter from the Pope is not such as ... should be offered to His Majesty'.

Praemunire had its origins as a fourteenth-century statute, taking its name from the Latin meaning 'to forewarn'. Its purpose was to prohibit the assertion or maintenance of Papal jurisdiction, and offending against it was treason, followed by the death penalty; a notorious example of its use being the indictment of Cardinal Wolsey in 1530. Three hundred years later, the caution of Canning, himself a declared advocate of Catholic Emancipation, in contacting the King had now been backed by Eldon's interpretation of the law. This was a King who had received Cardinal Consalvi with something approaching enthusiasm, and numbered aristocratic Catholics among his personal friends, leaving aside the relationship with Mrs Fitzherbert. It was a warning that in England there might be a further obstacle to granting Emancipation quite apart from parliamentary voting: the weight of history as interpreted by various Anti-Catholic types, many of whom felt themselves to be defending that national treasure, the constitution.

The strong Protestant historical view of the Roman Catholic Church as a tyrannous enemy of liberty spilled over into the energetic protests of many people calling for liberty themselves, including poets. Wordsworth admired Liverpool's ministry, as he made clear in a letter in 1813: 'I much prefer the course of their Policy to that of the Opposition'; of the two points close to his heart, the second was 'their adherence to the principles of the British constitution in withholding Political Power from the Roman Catholics'. Five years later, when John Keats called at Rydal during a walking tour of the Lake District, he was disappointed to find that Wordsworth was not there: he was supporting the interest of the Tory (and Anti-Catholic) Lord Lowther, his patron.[2]

The case of Lord Byron was more complicated. In 1812 he had spoken up for the Catholic religion in the House of Lords in a speech which put the reasonable liberal contemporary view very well.[3] All are 'advocates of Church and State', said Byron, 'the Church of Christ and the State of Great Britain; but not a State of exclusion and despotism, not an intolerant Church; not a Church militant, which renders itself liable to the very objection urged against the Romish communion'. He quoted 'the great Lord Peterborough' in the House of Lords a hundred years earlier: 'he was for a parliamentary king and a parliamentary constitution, but not a parliamentary God and a parliamentary religion'. Provocatively, Byron then introduced the subject of the Irish peasantry and compared their lot unfavourably to the black slaves who had been emancipated without any petitions. 'I pity the Irish peasantry for not having been born black.' Pointing to the history of Ireland and its appalling poverty, he had no hesitation in blaming the Ascendancy: 'Can you not relieve the beggar when your fathers have made him such?' he asked its representatives in the House of Lords.

At the same time Byron also attacked the European Catholics, Britain's 'Popish allies' in Spain and Portugal. Here Byron's feelings for justice put him in the other camp, which condemned the Catholic Church on the basis of its past history. The shadow of the iniquitous Spanish Inquisition – might it return? – was ever present. Byron therefore was typical of many English liberals who experienced a conflict between the political cause of Emancipation and the actual doctrines of the real Catholic Church.

Coleridge, on the other hand, moved from romantic feelings about Transubstantiation in 1802 – 'the beautiful Fuel of the Fire of Faith' – to fiery articles in *The Courier* under the pseudonym of 'Irish Protestant' denouncing the spirit of 'Catholic Jacobinism'.[4] In his *Lay Sermons* of 1817 he parodied Byron's invocation of the black slaves in comparison to the Irish by lumping together all superstitious peoples such as Papists, Muslims and Hindus: 'amulets, bead-rolls, periapts, fetisches, and like pedlary, on pilgrimages to Loretto, Mecca, or the temple of Juggernaut, arm in arm with sensuality on one side and self-torture on the other, followed by a motley group of friars, pardoners, faqirs, gamesters, flagellants, mountebanks and harlots'. He described Catholic Emancipation as an invitation to 'this Dragon' and 'miscreated shape' to enter the heart of government. It was not an attitude which held fast in Coleridge, but symbolized once again the ugly split between the liberal principles of Emancipation and the apparently illiberal Church it would promote.

In 1807, when he was in his thirties, Robert Southey made it clear that he looked at the subject of Emancipation from the point of view of the tyranny of the Catholic Church. He said of himself: 'on the Catholic Question I am as stiffly against them as his Majesty himself' (this was following the period when George III in effect outlawed the mention of Emancipation to him by his government). Southey's projected *Book of the Church* was, as he wrote from Keswick in 1811, 'A picture of popery and the evil from which the Reformation delivered us'. Five years later he denounced the mere idea of solving the problem of order in Ireland by such a method: 'As for conciliating the Wild Irish by such concessions, the notion is so preposterous that when I know a man of understanding can entertain such an opinion, it makes me sick at heart to think upon what sandy foundations every political fabric seems to rest.'[5]

Southey was, however, prepared to extend a grudging welcome to convents. Perhaps their existence was essential in Catholic Ireland, in which case, 'I would let them found convents', only restricting the nuns 'to taking the vows till after a certain age', as had been practised in Russia. 'The good would be, that they would get the country cultivated, and serve as good inns, and gradually civilise it.' Even Southey had to admit: 'As the island unluckily is theirs, and there is no getting the Devil to remove it anywhere else, we had better employ the Pope (represented by his nuns) to set it to rights.'[6]

In direct opposition to such myths – if that was what they were – a new, more nuanced Catholic interpretation of English history was being developed by John Lingard, a priest-cum-historian.[7] Lingard, who was now in his early fifties, had been born in Lancashire into a working-class family; his father was a Catholic convert. A bright boy, he got a scholarship to Douai College; he managed to make an adventurous escape at the time of the French Revolution in charge of the schoolboy William Stourton, the fifteen-year-old heir to Lord Stourton, who was being educated there (the less fortunate college printer was hanged). He was ordained at the Bar Convent, York, in 1795, ending up in a quiet mission at the tiny village of Hornby near

Lancaster. The connection with the Stourton family remained; hence his visit to Cardinal Consalvi with Stourton in 1817.

Lingard's philosophy was summed up as a wish to write history which included rather than excluded Catholics from their own national story, and as he wrote in a letter, good was to be done by writing a book which Protestants would read. He numbered Dissenters – Unitarians – among his friends, as well as the great reforming lawyer and future Lord Chancellor Henry Brougham, who used to visit him. Lingard's work, published in 1817, ostensibly on the laws and ordinances of Catholic countries concerning their non-Catholic citizens, took the line that the civil power was separate. He commended, for example, the new United States of America, where 'the Catholic clergy perform their sacred functions, and exercise their spiritual authority without molestation. The government meddles not with the appointment of their bishops, or their correspondence with foreign prelates.'[8] Furthermore, if a Catholic bishop got an order from Rome affecting civil interests, not only would he be unable to fulfil it because he had no relevant jurisdiction, but also he 'would not since the Pope had no civil authority, either directly or indirectly in this realm'. Perhaps it was not surprising that Lingard was denounced by the Anti-Vetoist Bishop Milner for such Cisalpine views.

Based on primary sources, including documents in Paris, Lingard's fine *History of England*, the first volume of which was published in 1819, marked the summit of his ambition. (Ultimately Lingard was able to build a chapel out of its proceeds which he named 'Harry the Eighth's Chapel'.) In his *History*, the Papal Bull against 'Harry' was denounced as vindictive. And conversely the Catholic Mary Tudor, 'Bloody Mary' of Protestant tradition, was also critically treated. Lingard described the executions of Protestants during her reign as being 'the foulest blot on the character of the Queen', but pointed with justice to attitudes of the time: 'it being her misfortune, rather than her fault, that she was not more enlightened than the wisest of her contemporaries'. He defended Mary Queen of Scots on the grounds that her guilt (over the murder of Darnley) was 'unprovable'. On the other hand, he accepted the guilt of the Gunpowder Plotters, while attempting to arouse sympathy for them on the grounds that their 'bigoted zeal' had led them astray. Moderate in his treatment of Charles I – a lesson to royalty to mediate its pretensions in conformity with the reasonable desires of its subjects – it was only in the case of Oliver Cromwell and Ireland that Lingard let fly: the conquerors of Drogheda and Wexford were 'ruthless barbarians'. Lingard continued the patriotic tradition of Joseph Berington in 1780 who, in *The State and Behaviour of English Catholics*, decried the conduct of some Popes in the past, while pointing out that modern Popes had neither horns nor cloven feet.[9]

Personal details about Lingard indicate a man of benevolence and whimsicality. As fame in his own field came to him, an Associate of the Royal Society of Literature and Corresponding Member of the French Academy, so did fame's awkward kinsman, public attention. In order to elude publicity, he placed his dog Etna (a poodle) in his window to fool observers, wearing his spectacles and a coat so that travellers could see 'Dr Lingard at work on his *History*'.* The Anglican vicar living opposite Lingard trusted him sufficiently to ask him to care for his pets on his death.

Yet the unparliamentary obstacle – the continued rift in the attitudes of the various types of Catholics – persisted, for all the spreading of a more tolerant warmth. In January 1823 Lord Redesdale, a Protestant, declared he could not see how anyone of good sense would think that Catholic Emancipation would produce peace in Ireland.[10] In one sense Redesdale was entitled to voice his opinion: a Tory politician and lawyer, he had been Speaker of the House of Commons and then Lord Chancellor of Ireland from 1802 to 1806, as well as Vice-Chancellor of Dublin University. The Irish Catholic Richard Lalor Sheil granted that he was a man of great learning and diligence, despite his obsession against Emancipation and his profound distrust of the Irish priesthood.

---

* A ruse which might not immediately occur to modern historians, but which gives rise to interesting possibilities.

Redesdale was able to quote the late Lord Petre (that grandee who had been George III's host at Thorndon Hall), who 'steadily held to the maxim of the English Catholics' to avoid all political connection with the Irish because the *views* of the two bodies were different. 'We,' Petre said, 'can have no *hope* of making England Catholic but the Irish still hope, and have ground for hope; and they will ever be a millstone hung to the necks of the English Catholics. It is our obvious policy therefore to keep ourselves as separate as possible from the Irish Catholics.'[11]

This view of Catholic Ireland as a millstone (including of course the 'barbarous' Irish peasantry) chimed with the kind of Anti-Papalism which existed not only in literary circles but even in the most liberal English environment. As has been seen, it had always been a strong element in Anti-Catholicism itself in the past, the Pope being regarded not without justice as an opponent in the reign of Elizabeth, and later as an easy target in times of stress such as the Popish Plot or the Gordon Riots. The tactful behaviour of the Papacy after the death of the last Stuart Pretender, Prince Charles Edward, and later his brother the Cardinal of York, eased the situation; its sufferings during the Napoleonic Wars aroused sympathy and tilted the balance further.

Nevertheless it was notable how even the most liberal Englishmen were capable of strong Anti-Papal reactions, even someone like the Whig grandee Lord Holland. 'The Pope,' he wrote on one occasion, 'is more and more bigoted and is in a dreadful state of indignation.' Lord Holland then alluded pointedly to Molière's hypocritical character Tartuffe.[12] Holland was referring to the new, highly conservative Leo XII and his rumoured edict against vaccination, which he apparently believed to be a dreadful interference with the will of Heaven. Yet Holland was undoubtedly a fervent Whig supporter of Catholic Emancipation. For many English people the Pope remained what in a modern catchphrase might be called the elephant in the room.

Coexistent with Redesdale's doleful prediction and this continuing stream of Anti-Papal consciousness, there was an actual development in Ireland which told a very different story. The winter of 1822 was especially harsh there, with the usual painful consequence of famine – and that in turn followed by angry disruption from starving, rebellious peasants. Habeas Corpus was suspended (as it had been in England in 1817 over industrial unrest). January and February of 1823 were compared by Wellesley to 'the Russian year' of 1813. The situation was of sufficient threat for the Viceroy to install palisades of cannon around Dublin at several entrances to the city.

It was in the aftermath of this cruel winter that Daniel O'Connell took a step that was not intended to be publicly radical – but was to have radical consequences. There was a private dinner on 8 February in the snowy mountains at Glencullen in Wicklow at the house of T. O'Mara.[13] Henry White, a Protestant now in his early thirties, was the son of a self-made Dublin man who had made his money as a bookseller and purchased the large Luttrellstown estate as a result; he himself had served in the 14th Light Dragoons in the Peninsular War, earning medals in the Battles of Badajoz and Salamanca. The wealthy bookseller had four sons, in fact, but when there was a vacancy in the winter of 1822, Henry White was deliberately chosen as candidate over his brothers because he was considered to be the Catholics' friend, receiving a hearty endorsement from Daniel O'Connell.

It was White who had publicly proposed a toast to the Pro-Catholic Viceroy Wellesley in January. He was now elected to the House of Commons for Co. Dublin over a strong Tory candidate of considerable landed interests. As O'Connell told his wife, no popular triumph was ever half so great. It provided an impetus. The decision was taken. A new Catholic Association was to be formed. But this was to be an association with a difference. From the first, O'Connell intended to involve the Catholic peasantry, via their parishes.[14]

The importance lay in the founding text of the lawyer Richard Lalor Sheil: they must avoid every semblance of illegality or enmity to the established order yet kindle 'the smouldering passions of an infuriated and oppressed people'. The vital words were in the first proviso. This was not a representative or delegated body, in order to avoid prosecution under the Convention Act of 1793. The crucial meeting was held in Richard Coyne's bookshop in Sackville Street,* with Coyne himself standing at the door in welcome; a figure of old-fashioned elegance, his silvery hair matched by his silver shoe buckles, with his frilly shirt and knee breeches. Subscription was to be one guinea (nearly £100 today) for full members, and one shilling for associates, per year.

About thirty-five people were originally present, with the Chairman, Lord Killeen, heir of the Earl of Fingall, representing at thirty-two the rising generation. To a certain extent the company was socially mixed, because it included not only members of the nobility and gentry, barristers and physicians but also merchants and traders. That encompassing aspect of the Catholic Association O'Connell now decided to take further by including within it the Catholic clergy – who after some debate were admitted without payment. In this way the Bishop of Kildare and Leighlin, James Warren Doyle, was able to join. The question of what was known as Catholic Rent was then raised: in essence these were financial contributions, not necessarily very large ones, to the cause of Catholic Relief in Ireland.

O'Connell first raised the subject of a small subscription which would enable all Catholics, however poor, to feel themselves part of the same movement, in January. It was an idea first propounded in the 1780s and O'Connell himself had put it forward in a limited way in 1812. Now the time for what was described as 'the grand, the wise, the noble plan' had come. The socially beneficial side of the Rent was stressed – support for Catholic education – so as to give it an innocuous flavour. The idea was to raise £50,000. In fact, so successful was the scheme that by December 1823 Catholic Rent was producing £1,000 a week (£75,000 today), with half a million associates paying a penny a month.

In all this O'Connell was careful to stress that this new Catholic Association was not and did not intend to be a sectarian body. It was open to Catholics and Protestants: Henry White, the new MP, became a member in October. O'Connell's aims were manifold: to meet parliamentary and legal expenses, assist propaganda in the press, protect the privileges of the Catholics and prosecute

* Renamed O'Connell Street in 1924.

aggressors. He fully expected, as he wrote at the end of December 1824, that the Catholic Rent 'will surely emancipate us'. But while urging that it should be pressed 'as much forward as possible', he was careful to add that 'a repetition of small payments is better than a large one'.[15]

In one parish in Co. Cavan, for example, contributors included a miller, a publican, a baker, a wheelwright and the son of a labourer, as well as farmers whose holdings ranged from four to thirty-four acres. Popular rhymes were quick to celebrate the event, as was reported to Robert Peel:

> One penny each month, is your just due
> Collected by some faithful brother
> Then why should Patrick's friends refuse
> In this grand plan to assist each other.[16]

1824 saw the publication (anonymously) of a new work by Tom Moore: *The Memoirs of Captain Rock*.[17] This prodigious bestseller gave a voice to an altogether less placid part of the Catholic population of Great Britain. The mysterious character of Captain Rock was encountered by Moore during a tour of southern Ireland. 'Captain Rock' was the name which signed actual threatening letters of a Robin Hood type against landlords and agents, possessing also something of the contrasting malevolence of the Sheriff of Nottingham. There were warnings against paying tithes to certain individuals, and if the warnings went unheeded, a violent night attack might follow. The winter of 1822 saw a peak of such attacks.

In the imagination of Tom Moore, Captain Rock took on a new life. He personified Ireland's struggle for justice for the majority at the hands of the minority. So long as that struggle lasted, Captain Rock would flourish:

> While Thousands proudly turn away
> And to the Millions answer 'Nay',
> So long the merry reign shall be
> Of Captain Rock and his Family[18]

There was something almost poetic about the fictional Captain Rock's eventual fate at the age of sixty. On one of his night-time escapades he is captured, without the authorities being aware of his identity. No one comes forward to testify against him. On the other hand, Captain Rock cannot give an account of himself: his crime therefore is to be 'out in the open air by moonlight'. And this is a transportable offence. Thus Captain Rock is sentenced to transportation to Botany Bay and that distant country where so many lads 'who love the moon' have preceded him. 'I may safely, I think, reckon upon the continuance of the Rock Dynasty,' concludes Moore. Where Lingard wove his tapestry of subtle reconciliation, Tom Moore spoke up for a more romantic, more dashing – and ultimately more violent – attitude to Catholic justice in the future.

The Earl Marshal's Bill of 1824, like Lingard's *History*, indicated the softer mood in England – at least for the aristocracy. Like the history of Captain Rock, it was a symbolic point, and in this case a highly visible one. The question concerned the organization of future Coronations and the hereditary right of the Dukes of Norfolk, recently exercised by a Protestant deputy; nor was it necessarily a matter of pure theory, given the age and shaky health of the present monarch. Why should not the Duke of Norfolk exercise his hereditary right to conduct a Coronation? Unlike the cousin from whom he inherited, the full-blooded previous Duke, who had adopted Protestantism, Duke Bernard was a proud Catholic in the tradition of his ancestors; as such he supported Emancipation, and saw no reason why he should not enjoy his hereditary post even before this was attained. The Duke arranged for a Private Members' Bill to be introduced to the House of Lords. During the debate, on 18 June, it was Lord Holland who pointed to the coincidence of the date: while Waterloo was being fought, 'how could it be supposed that there was any more danger to the church from the stick of the Earl Marshal than from the sword of the army and navy?'[19]

Another lofty aristocrat, the Duke of Newcastle, took a very different line in the Lords. Newcastle had succeeded to the title when he was ten, and become Lord Lieutenant of

Nottinghamshire in his early twenties. Supported by the Earl of Abingdon, he made a speech that left little room for doubt about his deeply conservative principles (with an artless preliminary admission that he was very little used to speaking in public).

He had already protested against Emancipation in 1821 in a pamphlet addressed to Lord Liverpool, and would go on to be an energetic lobbyer against any kind of change to what he saw as the sacred established order; in other words he became what was termed an Ultra-Tory. The Bill violated the constitution by enabling 'a Papist to hold high office near the person of a Protestant King', dispensing with the Oath of Supremacy. This was his creed – and creed seems the appropriate word for such a rigorous statement: 'On general principles, I object to any concession to the Roman Catholics, either collectively or individually.'

The Duke of York, heir presumptive to the throne as the King's next brother, was also of course strongly against it, as he was against anything at all Pro-Catholic. An attack of dropsy made speculation about the future of George IV and the length of the reign an increasingly exciting topic. Creevey wrote: 'We are full of a battle that is to take place in the House of Lords between the Duke of York and our Scroop [Duke Bernard].' Creevey described how the Royal Prince was 'perfectly furious' and writing to every peer he knew, 'calling upon him to come and protect the Crown against the insidious Scroop'. The King himself was also said to be angry. At the prorogation of Parliament when he made the customary regal appearance, according to Lord Colchester he looked 'very heavy, languid, morbid and livid', with the crown 'pressing heavily on his brows'.[20]

Yet the Bill passed. The Duke needed to take no oath except the Oath of Allegiance and the Oath of Office.* Lord

---

* Scroop, a.k.a Bernard 12th Duke of Norfolk, was destined to be in charge at the next two Coronations and had himself painted wearing his parliamentary robes. These robes continued to be worn at Coronations by subsequent Dukes of Norfolk, including that of Queen Elizabeth II in 1953.

Colchester probably phrased the attitude of the more practical Anti-Catholics best when he declared: let the Catholics enjoy 'their mere *honours*' so long as they do not share in 'political *power etc*'. In 1824 it seemed to those English who were in a position to affect the decision that the English Catholics would very likely be satisfied with mere honours.

There remained the question of the millstone – Ireland. The men who loved the moon, in Tom Moore's eloquent phrase for the rebellious peasantry, were not the only threat. There was a general fear of an uprising. 'If we cannot get rid of the Catholic Association,' wrote the Duke of Wellington to Robert Peel in November 1824, 'we must look to civil war in Ireland sooner or later.'[21]

CHAPTER NINE

A Protestant King

*'Their Lordships must remember, that ours is a
Protestant King, who knows no mental reservation,
and whose situation is different from that of
any person in the country.'*

The Duke of York, House of Lords, 25 April 1825

On 16 december 1824 Daniel O'Connell addressed the
Catholic Association in a speech which caused an immediate sensation. This was because he invoked the name of Simón Bolívar,
the great Venezuelan leader hailed as *El Libertador*, from which
O'Connell would derive his own honorific, the Liberator. Essentially Bolívar had secured liberty for South America from the
Spanish by military force, becoming President of Gran Colombia,
which included much of modern Colombia, Ecuador, Panama
and Venezuela, in February 1819. Recently Bolívar had defeated
the Spanish cavalry in Peru at the Battle of Junín.

The recent surge of independence in South America had
caught O'Connell's imagination because of the obvious parallels
with Ireland.[1] 'He hoped that Ireland would be restored to her
rights,' said O'Connell, 'but if that day should arrive – if she
were driven mad by persecution, he wished that a new Bolívar

may be found – may arise – that the spirit of the Greeks and of the South Americans may animate the people of Ireland.' One of his nephews had been granted a commission in an Irish legion being raised to fight with Bolívar in Venezuela; this was followed by a commission for O'Connell's own fourteen-year-old son Morgan. (In the event the whole project of the Irish Legion proved unfortunate, but that lay in the future.) At the time, his adulatory letter for Bolívar, to be conveyed by the boy, spoke of 'that sacred cause which your talents, valour and virtue have gloriously sustained – I mean the cause of Liberty and national independence'. In response O'Connell was toasted by Bolívar as 'the most enlightened, the most independent, and the most patriotic man, not only in Great Britain but in all Europe'.

Bolívar represented the zeitgeist and its emphasis on national liberty in the way that O'Connell hoped to do himself: Bolívar was, after all, not only a leader, but a triumphant one. It was through his actions that the former Spanish colonies were recognized as independent, including by Britain; while for the United States the celebrated Monroe Doctrine, as it would come to be known, stated that 'the American continents, by the free and independent condition which they have assumed and maintain, are henceforth not to be considered as subjects for future colonization by any European powers'.

It was against this background that O'Connell's speech could be interpreted in two radically different ways. For the Irish who listened to him, it was inspirational in the cause of freedom; for the English government it constituted a deliberate threat of force. O'Connell's old adversary, Robert Peel, who had been appointed Home Secretary in 1822, three years after he left Ireland, was of the latter view.

Peel took a continuing interest in Ireland, reading the Irish newspapers, and at one point assured Richard Wellesley that he had 'the strongest attachment to Ireland and the sincerest desire to cooperate with you in the promotion of her welfare'.[2] This attachment did not, however, include the belief that Catholic Emancipation would help with that welfare, let alone gain the approval of its prominent advocates. Four days after making the speech, O'Connell was visited at home by an alderman and a police constable, to be told that he must appear at the next sessions in order to answer a charge of speaking seditious words at a meeting of the Catholic Association.

The prosecution of O'Connell failed because the newspaper reporters found themselves unable to substantiate the claims of the prosecution. The only obvious result was a renewed, if unsought, opportunity for O'Connell to demonstrate his huge popularity with the public as he left the courthouse. The question of both South and North America, and O'Connell's emotional allegiance to them, remained to vex Protestants in England. Three years later, Dean Henry Phillpotts, the strongly Anti-Catholic future Bishop of Exeter, complained to the Duke of Wellington that O'Connell had actually praised America as a country without a Church establishment.[3]

The next step was a government bill making all societies in Ireland unlawful, which of course included the Catholic Association. This was announced in the King's speech on 3 February 1825 as follows: in view of the general prosperity in which Ireland was sharing, it was all the more to be regretted that associations should exist in Ireland which had adopted proceedings irreconcilable with the spirit of the constitution, and calculated, 'by exciting alarm, and by exasperating animosities, to endanger the peace of Society and to retard the course of national improvement'. The Bill was then introduced into the House of Commons by Henry Goulburn, the Chief Secretary for Ireland. The Association immediately decided to send a deputation to Westminster to plead against it – a deputation which included an initially reluctant O'Connell. The reason for this reluctance was, however, more human than high-minded: O'Connell was unhappy at interrupting his lucrative career at the Irish Bar at the time of the spring circuit.

The Irish deputation's journey through England was not without its humorous moments, as recounted by Sheil, the Irish Catholic lawyer who had helped found the Catholic Association with O'Connell.[4] At Coventry the mistress of the inn asked who they were. Ironically, on being told her guests were Irish, she replied: 'Parliamentary folks, I suppose.' With a slight mental reservation, Sheil nodded assent.

Throughout the journey it was O'Connell as ever who attracted the public eye. He sat on the box of the barouche enveloped in a huge Irish mantle: 'his tall and ample figure ... and his open and manly physiognomy, rendered him a very conspicuous object'. At every stop O'Connell would call for a newspaper 'with an earnest and sonorous tone' – every cadence and gesture bearing 'unequivocal intimations of his country', in other words an Irish accent.

An attempt to visit Bishop Milner in Wolverhampton en route was not, however, a success. First, in an indication of English provincial attitudes, the young woman who directed them to his house reproached them sharply for using the term 'the Catholic Bishop' in their enquiry as to his whereabouts. 'If you had asked me for the Popish priest instead of the Catholic Bishop,' she said, 'I should have told you that he lived yonder.' Then the Bishop, once the scourge of the Vetoists, hardly seemed to know who they were, only reacting briefly with vigour to the name of his old Vetoist foe Butler. Milner, who died the next year in his mid-seventies, was clearly in decline.

The journey from Holyhead to London averaged about six days at that time. (Jonathan Swift once suggested that the reason the Irish Bishops were so villainous was because highwaymen managed to substitute themselves for bishops en route.)[5] Throughout, Sheil felt a sense of Ireland's material inferiority and the consequent necessity for his country to move from poverty and sorrow towards 'the splendid spectacle' of England's civilization. He was awestruck by the numerous ponderous vehicles on the roads, the rapid and continuous sweep of the carriages, the splendid villas which the poet Cowper had compared to 'the beads upon the neck of an Asiatic queen'. Sheil was also impressed by the signs of England's increasing industrialization: 'a thousand Etnas vomiting their eternal fires' in this volcanic region of manufacturers; while London itself was sited in an everlasting cloud of 'bituminous vapours'.

The deputation was in fact travelling through a country where the religious demographic was gradually changing, due to this very industrialization. The need for labour, combined with the sheer poverty of Ireland, inspired that despairing urge for emigration in search of a better life which is universal to history. St Patrick's Day began to be celebrated in Manchester. By 1821 there was said to be an Irish Catholic population in Liverpool of 12,000, which would rise to 60,000 in the next ten years. In 1825 the Bishop of Chester estimated that there were now about half a million Catholics in England, risen from 67,000 in 1750, while in Glasgow the figure had leaped from 300 to 25,000, almost entirely imported from Ireland.[6] None of this predisposed that young woman in Wolverhampton and her kind in favour of the Papists. Such casual but deep-rooted prejudices – seen in the blood and flames of the Gordon Riots – were of course spurred on by the increase in Irish immigrants, and the fact that they undercut English labour.

At the same time there were Catholic advances in society, such as the establishment of the Jesuit College, Stonyhurst.[7] Its history illustrated in microcosm the various phases of the English Catholic community. The origins of the College were in St Omer at the end of the sixteenth century, founded by Father Robert Persons SJ, under the patronage of Philip II of Spain, when Catholic education was totally forbidden in England. In the eighteenth century the school had to move first to Bruges, and then Liège, and was finally set up in Lancashire in 1794, part of the exodus caused by the French Revolution.

Ancient Catholic names were involved: the land was first leased then donated by Thomas Weld of Lulworth, who had inherited it from his cousin Mary Duchess of Norfolk and was himself a former pupil from the days when the school was in St Omer and Bruges. Cardinal Consalvi, the fêted star of the 1814 London congress, made helpful interventions in Rome. The position of the Society of Jesus in England was of course complicated (technically there were no English Jesuits in England until the restoration of the Society in 1802). However, by the next century Stonyhurst would be a flourishing Catholic college, with the Boer War Memorial recording the great number of old

Stonyhurst boys who in the same campaign 'left for all time an example of Catholic loyalty and service'. In the 1820s there was prejudice, but there was also progress.

The deputation of the Catholic Association was admitted to watch the proceedings in the House of Commons as permission was sought for it to plead its cause in front of the House. The Irishmen were directed by the Speaker to sit under the Gallery as spectators; whereupon every eye, according to Sheil, was fixed on O'Connell. Beneath the 'icy surface' of the House of Commons he saw the 'constant eddying' as the drama unfolded. The delegation failed in one sense: in the event it was not allowed to plead its cause, the motion to this effect being voted down. But the enterprise did bring the charismatic O'Connell back to London and enabled him to flourish in an atmosphere of prodigious social success among the grand Whigs. (At least this might atone in some measure for his loss of earnings.) His letters home to his wife Mary poke rueful fun at his own enjoyment at being lionized: 'You like to be thought the wife of *a great man*.'[8]

On one occasion, he told her, there were actually four dukes present, with the Duke of Norfolk as host, and the Dukes of Sussex, Devonshire and Leinster as guests; also four earls and six other peers plus a couple of baronets. As for the magnificent house: 'I had no notion of such splendour', it being incidentally the house where George III was born. There was a series of magnificent apartments, rich with crimson and fretted with gold in this seemingly endless mansion. Massive lamps hanging from embossed and gilded ceilings gave only shadowy illumination, although the great chamber was glowing with light.

On 7 March, wrote O'Connell, 'we had *only* one duke – of Norfolk – only two earls, Grey and Bessborough, but then we had a Marquess of Lansdowne', at which O'Connell pulled himself up short: 'Only think that earls are now become so familiar to me that I left out Earls Fitzwilliam and Sefton... We had members of the Commons like garnish to a dish to complete the table.'[9]

O'Connell ended one description of a glorious dinner, bedecked, naturally, with dukes: 'You cannot think how everybody says that it is I who am carrying Emancipation, that it will be carried this session I look on as nearly certain.' The idea of a huge public dinner for Catholics was abandoned as being unduly provocative; so a general meeting was called instead at the Freemasons' Hall.[10] One of the speakers was Lord Stourton, an embodiment in himself of recent Catholic upper-class history: the boy who had escaped from Douai at the time of the French Revolution had subsequently married Catherine Weld, daughter of Thomas Weld, the benefactor of Stonyhurst. The Protestant Earl Fitzwilliam, a peer with huge Irish estates who had been briefly Viceroy of Ireland before the Union, then declared that he wanted to live long enough to see the Emancipation of the Irish people. Fitzwilliam's liberal sympathies were indicated by the fact he had recently been dismissed as Lord Lieutenant of the West Riding of Yorkshire for condemning the Peterloo Massacre.

The 'stout, red-faced' Duke of Norfolk was in the chair: this was Bernard, the 12th Duke, continuing to assert the discreet mastery over the English Catholic world to which both his inherited position and his personal strong faith entitled him. He chaired, for example, the other Catholic Association in England, untouched by the law. This Association was able to convene with such ease and respectability that a forthcoming meeting at the Crown and Anchor Tavern in the Strand was advertised on the front page of *The Times*. The notice included the announcement that the 'Gentlemen of the Irish Association' would be present.[11]

Sheil also gave Norfolk much credit for effecting unity between English and Irish Catholics: hitherto the Irish had tried to make up with a certain 'bombastic' display of public confidence for the actual insecurity they felt in the face of these entrenched aristocrats. It was in this atmosphere of optimism – despite the fact that the Catholic Association in Ireland had now been suppressed – that the latest Bill for Catholic Relief was introduced into the House of Commons on 23 March 1825.

It was the work of Sir Francis Burdett, Baronet, a long-standing MP and a veteran of protest. Burdett, now in his mid-fifties, had begun early with his expulsion from Westminster School, and as a young man experienced the French Revolution first-hand during his Continental wanderings; thereafter his life was one of continued excitement, as well as engagement in the radical issues of the day. As he said of himself in 1798: 'The best part of my character is a strong feeling of indignation at injustice and oppression and a lively sympathy with the sufferings of my fellows.'[12] A streak of melancholia in his nature did not make his sympathy any less. His distinguished appearance – he had an aquiline nose to rival that of the Duke of Wellington and similarly delight cartoonists – coupled with a fine, clear speaking voice, made him a popular performer in any cause.

Burdett, who as a young man had had a notorious love affair with Lady Oxford, married the heiress Sophia Coutts in 1793.* In the House of Commons in 1796 he opposed the war with France. Later he had a spell of confinement in the Tower of London over a breach of Parliamentary Privilege, and another in the Marshalsea Prison, together with a heavy fine, following his own condem-nation of the Peterloo Massacre. His appearance was that of a country gentleman fond of field sports, summer and winter in a broad-brimmed hat, blue brass-buttoned coat and breeches with top boots; the expression on his delicately chiselled face – the eyes with 'no flash or splendour' – was unchanging.[13] Burdett's language on the other hand was always colourful as well as strong: on the Peterloo occasion not only had he chosen to remind the King of the revolution of 1688, but made a lethal comparison to the vicious Roman emperors of history with the phrase 'bloody Neroes'.

Parliamentary Reform was for Burdett the key to the regen-eration of society: he had in mind honest country gentlemen who would displace the corrupt borough-mongers and restore ancient liberties. Thomas Moore would later refer to Burdett's approach as an 'antiquarian justification for reform'.[14] Obviously Catholic Emancipation, being about the liberty of the individual, and a theoretically persecuted individual at that, constituted a natural cause for such a campaigner. Burdett's interest was deepened by touring Ireland itself, and a friendship with the Irish revolution-ary poet Arthur O'Connor.

---

* Their daughter Angela Burdett-Coutts would be the celebrated nineteenth-century philanthropist.

The new Bill was framed by the co-operation of O'Connell and William Plunket, as well as Burdett. It was buttressed by two 'wings' in the form of sets of 'securities' which were intended specifically to calm the fears of Protestants. One of these was the elimination of the Forty-shilling Freeholders. Curiously enough, the so-called Forty-shilling Freeholders would have constituted a real danger to Protestant interests. This was because the franchise had become widely spread among the Irish Catholic peasantry, granted by Acts of the Irish Parliament before the Union, while the coming of the Union itself had not altered it. The Irish system of tenure, different from that of England, meant that around 200,000 poor Catholic voters were involved; the Ascendancy was intended to be placated by their elimination. The second 'wing' consisted of provision for the payment of the Roman Catholic clergy from public funds, with the obvious opportunity for the government to influence appointments and conduct.

The involvement of O'Connell in the process of devising the Bill was a fact that Peel would mention with contempt and anger in the House of Commons as he denounced it.[15] He had read about O'Connell's contribution in the press, where it had not been denied, and yet here was a man who had been the leader of an association now suppressed. O'Connell came back to England for the second reading, attending the debates in the Commons. On this occasion the Bill passed in the Commons by 268 votes to 241, with George Canning, unlike Peel, speaking in favour of it. Leaning on a crutch to ameliorate the fearful pain of the gout which was increasingly debilitating him, Canning spoke shortly but powerfully – 'as becomes an elderly gentleman with a stick', as he put it – and in his own estimation, swung many loose votes in favour of the Bill.

O'Connell decided to swallow his pride. He had already accepted the 'wings' of the Bill. He now intended to make a more personal type of compromise. O'Connell apologized to Robert Peel for the events of the duel ten years earlier.[16] Peel did not respond, but news of the apology was made gradually public. O'Connell got a message to Peel's second that he blamed himself for the whole incident. While O'Connell's enemies accused him

of 'crouching' before Peel, out of self-interest, the correct interpretation was rather more favourable to O'Connell the politician:
this ability to adapt in a minor way for the prospect of major
good was an aspect of his character which the flamboyance of
his public image sometimes concealed.

On 18 April Brougham had presented a Petition in Parliament
from Great and Little Bolton in Lancaster, in favour of the Bill.[17]
'He spoke not of the Roman Catholics merely. He was of the
opinion that the pure doctrine of religious toleration ought to be
extended to all sects, as well as to Roman Catholics. Why did he
wish this? Because he felt that a man was no more answerable
to the tenets which he espoused in religion, than he was for any
peculiarity in his physical or mental constitution over which he
had no control.' Additionally Brougham pointed out that tests
were useless and simply encouraged people to become hypocrites
by masking their true feelings in order to pass them.

Surely all men of goodwill would be convinced by such good
sense? It was not to be. In contrast to this rational disquisition on
the practical need for toleration in the Commons, an astonishing
outburst of bigotry followed a week later in the House of Lords.
And it was the voice not of a government minister, among whom
there were varying opinions – notably Canning Pro and Peel Anti
– but the voice of the heir to the throne.

On 25 April the Duke of York presented a Petition of the
Dean and Canons of Windsor praying that no further conces-
sions be made to the Roman Catholics. Even the nature of the
Petitioners, representing senior clergymen of the Protestant
Church, indicated the heartland of opposition to Emancipation,
which existed in what would now be called the Establishment.
The Anglican bishops in the House of Lords had regularly voted
against Emancipation, with very rare exceptions.

The Duke of York rose to his feet. His audience saw a portly
but well set up and dignified man of sixty-two (he was almost
exactly a year younger than the King), with the characteristic
slightly bulging blue eyes of his family. Here was a Royal Duke,
known to be generous and good-hearted towards others, Catholics not excluded: he had in fact shown kindness to Franciscan

nuns from Bruges in the past when they settled at Taunton.[18] For two-thirds of his life he had been the next heir to the throne after his brother, the exception being the brief lifetime of his niece Princess Charlotte. Since George III's death the Duke of York was the actual heir to the throne.*

The life of the Duke of York up to this point had included its fair share of tumultuous episodes. His own marriage to a German princess had failed, and without leaving any children. Destined from early boyhood for a life in the army, he had been awarded a rising series of military appointments culminating in Commander-in-Chief; although the nature of his military competence in the Dutch War is commemorated, fairly or unfairly, in the famous nursery rhyme about the Grand Old Duke of York who had 10,000 men but did nothing much but march them up and down the hill. More creditably, he had been involved with the vital reorganization of the British Army during the Napoleonic Wars and the foundation of Sandhurst Military College. Less salubrious was a charge of corruption as a result of his mistress, Mary Anne Clarke, selling army commissions, which resulted in the Duke resigning his position as Commander-in-Chief in 1809, although he was later exonerated and reappointed.

Good-natured he might be, and a loyal friend, the Duke's importance at this point was as 'the bulwark of the Protestant cause', in the words of Mrs Arbuthnot. As the government began to show fissures in its attitude to Emancipation, the Duke of York presented himself as a rallying point for those who saw themselves as the true Tories. The Duke announced that he must be permitted to say 'a few words' before he moved that the Petition should be read. What followed was a long Anti-Catholic rant, verging at times on the hysterical, which was subsequently printed and circulated with a cover ornamented with gold.[19]

The Duke began with a clear declaration of his intentions.

---

* Theoretically he was the heir presumptive; the word 'presumptive' indicated that if the King managed to have another child lawfully begotten in some new marriage, the Duke would be displaced; but that, frankly, was not thought likely or even possible by anyone.

There were occasions when every man owed it to his country and to his station to declare his sentiments, and there could be no opportunity which required 'more imperiously' the frank avowal of these sentiments than the present one. In His Royal Highness's opinion, their lordships were being called upon 'to make a total change in the fundamental principle of the Constitution ... to strike at the very root of its existence'.

The Duke then made a reference to his father's madness, to which he ascribed the earlier Emancipation crisis, before returning to the appalling proposal placed before the members of the House of Lords. They were 'required to surrender every principle of the constitution, and to deliver us up, bound hand and foot, to the mercy and generosity of the Roman Catholics'. What was more, there was no guarantee that the Catholics would actually be satisfied with such fearful concessions. From here he passed to the fate of the Church of England, if Emancipation came about, and horror of horrors! Roman Catholics were admitted to Parliament. They might then legislate for the Church of England, while allowing no input into the legislation for their own Popish Church.

From the Protestant Church, the Duke of York moved, in a passage which would prove extremely significant, to its official head, King George IV. 'Their lordships must remember that ours is a Protestant King, who knows no mental reservation, and whose situation is different from that of any other person in this country.' Everyone else, including himself, could be released from their oath by an Act of Parliament, 'but the King could not'. The King was a third part of the State, without whose voluntary consent no act of the legislature could be valid, and he could not relieve himself of the obligation of his oath.

The Duke concluded by apologizing for the length and at times warmth of his speech, but he felt the whole subject 'most forcibly'; at which point he made a second and even more pointed reference to his father's 'severe illness and ten years of misery' which had been caused by a previous campaign. Thus the special personal position of the sovereign was heavily underlined by the heir to the throne, in a way that could not be missed

– either by the Lords or the sovereign himself, the Protestant King. Certainly that heir left no possible doubt about his own reaction in the event of his succession.

Yet O'Connell, not fully understanding perhaps the kind of calculations that were being made about the future, remained optimistic. The day after this climactic royal intervention, he made a mighty speech to the Midland Catholic Association (the English associations were still legal) and a few days later was ushered to the front of an anti-slavery meeting in London, when he was recognized.[20] O'Connell proceeded to give of his best: the newly independent blacks would soon rise to the top of society. And he praised the Liberator of South America yet again in lavish terms – 'glorious Bolívar' – for bringing them freedom, while remarking that such statements would have been dangerous in his native Ireland where he himself was 'a slave'.

It was however about the same time that, according to the Duke of York, his brother declared that he would never give his assent to a Relief Bill. In the event George IV was not asked to do so. The Bill won on its third reading in the Commons, a vote taken at five o'clock in the morning only to be defeated once again in the House of Lords. It is easy to understand why Charles Throckmorton, of the prominent Catholic family, younger brother of Sir George Throckmorton, had a wager on the subject in May: 'Betted yesterday with Dr. Fletcher one guinea that the [sic] Catholic Emancipation would not take place in my lifetime.'[21]

Lord Liverpool now announced a very different kind of measure: a general inquiry into the state of Ireland, which was not however to concern itself with what was generally called 'the Catholic Question'. The Whig reaction to this prohibition was one of indignation mixed with derision. As Lord Holland put it, this was like Shakespeare's Mark Antony, who gave licence to men's tongues to discuss his faults but not Cleopatra. In short, how could they discuss the disease but not the remedy? Yet the disagreements within the Tory government on the very subject of Catholic Emancipation meant that there was a real danger in the summer of 1825 of this long-lasting regime coming to an end; in which case it was difficult to see how the Whigs would be kept out of office. So the Catholic Question remained to bedevil English politics – as it had been doing so vigorously since 1801, when at the time of the Union the promise of Emancipation, if it was made, was never kept.

As for Ireland, the question of peaceful religious toleration for the majority of the population could never be far away. On 1 June O'Connell took part in a triumphal procession home in Dublin from Kingstown, named at the time for George IV with what must now have seemed a certain irony.*[22] The Irish activists needed to pick themselves up after the recent banning of the Catholic Association, and look for a new, and of course legal, way of combining to campaign.

On the surface of Dublin society, Wellesley as Viceroy continued his public policy of conciliation by receiving both Orangemen and Catholics, including bishops. O'Connell enjoyed being 'a Castle man' because it annoyed the Orangeists. The novelist Lady Morgan commented wryly of one private party at the Castle: thirty years ago, the roof would not have been safe which afforded shelter to both O'Connell and that 'roaring lion' Colonel Blacker, Grand Master of the Orange Lodge.[23]

In the autumn of 1825 the Viceroy gave a very public demonstration of Pro-Catholicism by marrying an actual Catholic, whom he described to Lord Liverpool as 'worthy of my heart and hand'. (Liverpool commented that he believed the bride had enough sense to govern Wellesley better than he governed himself.) What was more, Wellesley celebrated the union with a Mass held on the following Sunday within the Viceregal Lodge – a symbol of British dominion – performed by a Catholic archbishop.[24]

The bride was an American: Marianne Patterson. In descriptions of her, contemporary prejudices of all sorts jostled with each other for pride of place. To one she was 'a Yankee and a Papist, turned into a Vice-Queen', and to another she was very

---

* The name lasted just under a century: in 1920 it was renamed Dun Laoghaire.

handsome, with a noble air and 'not a shade of her mother country'. In fact Marianne, now aged about thirty-five, was the daughter of a Baltimore merchant; her two sisters had already married into the British aristocracy, being respectively Duchess of Leeds and Baroness Stafford; her former sister-in-law Betsy was married to Jerome Bonaparte, brother of the late Emperor. Sheil's estimate was as good as any, if not untouched by prejudice of sorts: Marianne was extremely dignified, nothing of the *bourgeoise parvenue* about her, even if, as an American, she did not have quite such a pure complexion as an Irish lady. Her composure in difficult circumstances certainly deserved respect. When adjured by her husband not to read the gutter press, she replied with a nice mixture of humility and reproof: 'My dearest Lord, I will obey you, dearest, and never look at a scandalous newspaper, and if possible never be annoyed by their attacks; but it is easier for one like you, of unquestionable superiority, to despise them, than for me, a woman and a stranger.'[25]

The Duke of Wellington, the younger but more famous brother in the government in London, was appalled by the outrageous news of the ceremony. Mrs Arbuthnot had never seen him more annoyed; there was perhaps some personal element here, as the Duke had also been linked to the seductive Mrs Patterson. He wrote to Peel: 'You see that the marriage in Dublin has been celebrated. Allow me to ask you, Is not the appearance of the Roman Catholic Archbishop *in pontificalibus* [in his formal religious robes] contrary to the law? It is at all events very improper.' Mrs Arbuthnot was even more explicit: 'He had *the Catholic Archbishop of Dublin* to perform the ceremony which I think is a scandal, as his assuming that title [Dublin] is contrary to law.' She proceeded to list, disdainfully, the old men who had recently got married (Wellesley was sixty-five), including Sir Harry Featherstonhaugh, who at seventy-six had married a kitchen maid of eighteen. Most explicit of all in his disgust was the King. On 11 November he fulminated to Peel: 'That house is as much my palace as the one I am in and in my palace Mass is not said.'[26]

There was, however, no doubting the Viceroy's sincere passion: the following spring the Earl of Mount Charles told the King's

Private Secretary, Sir William Knighton, that he had never seen a man so in love. More soberly the Prime Minister, Lord Liverpool, commented that 'it was a very strange and awkward event'.[27]

O'Connell's future meetings involving the Viceroy, on the other hand, in contrast to this allegedly strange and awkward event, were all carefully arranged 'for all purposes allowable by law'. They also involved the great majority of the Irish people – but in a deliberately peaceable way that was a political novelty. The New Catholic Association, for example, was specifically founded for purposes of public or private charity.*[28]

At the same time, there was a gratifying rise in support for Catholic Associations generally in other parts of the world, notably the new United States. American newspapers with Irish readerships were beginning to reprint material such as parliamentary debates and O'Connell's speeches on the subject of Emancipation. The *United Catholic Miscellany* demanded in strong terms for financial aid to be supplied: 'You will soon be called, fellow countrymen, for your assistance – you cannot – you must not refuse... no Irish man except a grovelling wretch, will refuse his contribution.'[29] The Friends of Ireland were constituted at a meeting in New York in July 1825 to support O'Connell's New Catholic Association, and chapters became widespread, often including as members United Irishmen, those who had taken part in the 1798 rebellion, or at any rate sympathized with it; the New York chapter would rise to 1,000 members.

John England, born in Ireland, was the Bishop of Charleston in the American South and strongly supported Emancipation. In 1823 he wrote to O'Connell as an 'expatriated bishop' who was once 'your fellow-agitator and your ghostly father'. He organized sympathizers in Augusta, Georgia, who sent an address back to Ireland.[30] Later George Washington Parke Custis, stepson of the late President, would remind the Friends of Ireland and Religious Liberty in Washington of the aid that Irish-born colonists had

---

* In a book published in the 1960s the Marxist historian Eric Hobsbawm made the point that this was the only Western nationalist movement organized in a coherent form, before 1848, genuinely based on the masses.

given in the Revolutionary War: 'it was Ireland who cheered you in the dark hour of your trial, Irish hearts, and Irish sinews were with you in your arduous struggle for independence'. Now was the time to come to the aid of 'poor Erin'. In February 1826 Irishmen in Baltimore issued a high-flown address, extolling their own freedom and suggesting that the voice of free America was already being heard on the dark Atlantic wave: 'every hedge in Ireland should be vocal' with the proud example of the land that had achieved independence.

In 1826, the hedges of Ireland would in fact be vocal with rather different sounds than the extolling of America. For this would be the year of a General Election throughout the United Kingdom.

CHAPTER TEN

Noise of No Popery

'A defeat [for Palmerston] will be a complete triumph
for the No Popery faction... and the noise of it will ring
through every corner of the kingdom'

The Rev. Adam Sedgwick on the Parliamentary Election,
Cambridge, 1826

DURING THE GENERAL ELECTION of 1826 in England cries
of 'No Popery' were heard in constituencies from north to south,
from Yorkshire to Cornwall.[1] The Catholic Question was turning
out to be the main point of argument, although the government's
rising support for adjustment of the Corn Laws also featured.

Raucous words did not preclude actual blows. Arguments
frequently turned to physical force: there were deaths at Carlisle
and Leicester, and serious riots and attacks at Lincoln, East
Retford and Northampton. In Caithness the defeated candidate
inspired a large mob to attack a freeholder who was believed to
have betrayed him. The Marquess of Blandford, heir to the Duke
of Marlborough, a rumbustious character at the best of times,
notoriously rioting as a schoolboy at Eton, was standing for the
local seat of New Woodstock; he joined zestfully in the street
fighting with his brother.

In the Cambridge University seat, Lord Palmerston stood again. His support for Emancipation had been consistent, remembering that lyrical evocation of his native Ireland in 1813 with its reference to the 'unstoppable spring which gushes from the earth'. Palmerston shared the point of view that times had inevitably changed, and the argument to history could not be sustained: what if Nelson, Fox and Burke had all happened to be Catholics by birth? Would it have been right to deprive the nation of their services? This support cast his victory in doubt as well as incurring Whig rather than Tory support. The Rev. Adam Sedgwick, one of Palmerston's supporters and a Fellow of Trinity College, wrote to John Hobhouse that a defeat for this candidate would be 'a complete triumph for the *No Popery* faction ... and the noise of it will ring thro' every corner of the kingdom'. Instead they must work to defeat his opponents, 'the County Parsons and the bigots who are at the moment dishonouring the land we live in'.[2]

'No Popery' protests were not necessarily the product of principled Anglican belief. On the contrary, a cynical campaign had been building up nationwide to benefit from the issue of Catholic Emancipation to the detriment of its supporters. In the borough of Taunton, for example, Anti-Catholic candidates successfully contested the seat against sitting Members who had supported Burdett's Bill for Catholic Relief the year before. In Coventry, two Pro-Catholic MPs were abandoned by their political agent; he advertised for two candidates who would pledge themselves to oppose Catholic Emancipation. At East Retford an Independent True Blue Club was formed with the specific aim of banning Pro-Catholic candidates. Anti-Catholicism, in short, supplied a convenient focus for opposition in the summer of 1826.

The situation in Windsor was especially galling from the Pro-Catholic point of view. The sitting MP, Sir Edward Cromwell Disbrowe, learned that the King had determined to withdraw his support from him at the coming election in consequence of his recent vote on the Catholic Question. Sir Edward, despite a middle name that indicated descent from the Protector's sister, came from a family of royal servants, his father having been Chamberlain to Queen Charlotte. A diplomat by profession, he had replaced his brother-in-law in 1823 as Member for Windsor in the court interest.

In true diplomatic fashion, he was now anxious that the King be informed via his powerful Private Secretary, Sir William Knighton, that it was all an unfortunate misunderstanding. He thought he was free to express 'his own individual sentiments', and if he had realized his vote could have been construed as committing His Majesty's opinion 'on so important a question', he would not have given it. Sir Edward humbly pointed out his endeavours 'to keep up the Court interest in the borough, in which he has not been sparing of time or expense'.[3] The King, however, was adamant; a new candidate was chosen for 1826 and Sir Edward duly returned to the practice of diplomacy, from which he had so regrettably lapsed in more ways than one.

The Pro-Catholic party as a whole favoured discretion, in contrast to their adversaries, if not the craven obeisance of Sir Edward Disbrowe (who was after all sitting for Windsor itself with the Castle looming both metaphorically and actually above his head). The Whig grandee Lord Althorp, of strongly liberal views, disapproved of a county meeting being held in Northamptonshire in February 1826, just in case Anti-Catholic feelings should be aroused.

The reasonable Protestant point of view held that the Catholics, treated benevolently, would behave in similar fashion. This was put most cogently by the Anglican clergyman Sydney Smith, with all the wise wit at his command. In a speech of 11 April 1825 to the Clergy of the Archdeaconry of the East Riding of Yorkshire he suggested that 'a Catholic layman who finds all the honours of the state open to him, will not, I think, run into treason and rebellion'. In his anonymous *Letters, on the Subject of Catholics, to my brother Abraham, who lives in the country, by Peter Plymley*, published shortly after the fall of the Ministry of All the Talents in 1806 (addressed to a fictional country clergyman), he had written in a similar vein: if the Catholics 'taste the honey of lawful power they will love the hive from whence they preserve it'.* The fictional Rev. Abraham, however, was granted very different views, based on the entrenched version of Anti-Catholic history – what Smith called the tradition of 'fire, faggot and bloody Mary'. Smith in his role of Peter Plymley expostulated: 'Are you aware that there were as many persons put to death under the mild Elizabeth as under the bloody Mary?'[4]

From the beginning of their imaginary correspondence, Smith sounded a mocking note: 'In the first place, my sweet Abraham, the Pope is not landed – nor are there any curates sent out after him – nor has he been hid at St Albans by the Dowager Lady Spencer – nor dined privately at Holland House – nor been seen near Dropmore.' Although it was true that if the Pope probably *was* hovering about the coast in a fishing-smack, there he would fall prey to English shipping. The Pope was indeed the bogeyman throughout their correspondence, with Peter Plymley demanding scornfully: 'I thought that the terror of the Pope had been confined to the limits of the nursery, and merely employed as a means to induce young master to enter into his small clothes with greater speed and eat his breakfast with greater attention to decorum. For these purposes, the name of the Pope is admirable, but why push it beyond?' Unfortunately, nearly ten years after the publication of *Peter Plymley*, Smith was protesting in a country where 'No Popery' was still the most popular election battle cry.[5]

There was another eloquent argument to history and tradition, less crude than the 'Bloody Mary' line of talk if equally unrealistic to the detached observer: the question of 'recovery' by Emancipated Catholics of the pre-Reformation Protestant churches which had once been their own. This was well expressed by Wordsworth in the series of sonnets in his *Ecclesiastical Sketches* of 1822.[6] Wordsworth himself suggested that the sequence derived from a view of the site of a new church his patron Lord Lowther was building in 1820: 'the Catholic

* Hesketh Pearson in his biography *The Smith of Smiths*, published in 1934, compared Smith to someone in the First World War declaring that Germans were gentlemen.

Question, which was agitated in Parliament about that time, kept my thoughts in the same course'.

He drew attention to the dread possibility of the 'recovery' in the event of Emancipation, in a story about the 'very clever R. C. lady' wife of the agent to the Duke of Norfolk. She was asked what would satisfy her. ' "That Church", replied she, pointing to a large parish Church in Sheffield where the conversation took place.' Wordsworth added: 'This, at the bottom of their hearts, is the feeling of them all.' Naturally Wordsworth supported the Anti-Catholic Lowther interest again in Westmorland, where Brougham challenged it for the third time in 1826.[7] He feared lest the law be changed, and this supposed terrible fundamental feeling at the heart of all the 'R. C.s' to roll back and thus destroy the noble Protestant heritage should prevail.

In terms of the future, the most significant episodes of the General Election of 1826 took place in Ireland. Once again there would be no Catholic candidates able to put themselves forward, despite their constituting the vast majority of the population. Around this time, Tom Moore satirized the flagrant disproportion of Protestants to Catholics in the population of the island, as also their lethal attitude to their compatriots:

> To the people of England, the humble petition
> Of Ireland's disconsolate Orangemen, showing
> That sad, very sad is our present condition ...
> That forming one seventh ...
> Of Ireland's seven millions of hot heads and hearts,
> We hold it the basest of all base transactions,
> To keep us from murd'ring the other six parts ...[8]

O'Connell at least was determined that the six million disconsolate Irish Catholic peasants should be discouraged from similar crimes.

In Ireland, violence – the violence of a suppressed and poverty-stricken people with little to lose, helped on by drink when possible – was endemic, not necessarily in a political cause. In counties like Galway and Kerry these kinds of conflict occurred during the election as they always had. But there were also significant and novel gains for the Catholic cause: pre-eminently that of Waterford. Here, in the words of Lord Duncannon, heir to great Irish estates, the election was not only a triumph for the Catholic cause, but it was conducted 'much to their credit with the most perfect order and regularity'. Furthermore, as Duncannon put it, 'the priests have tried their strength and succeeded against the landlords'.[9] Daniel O'Connell and his associates were actively involved in the whole process.

In Waterford it was decided to challenge the power of the local great family, the Beresfords, with their chief the Marquess of Waterford. The scion of the family who fought the election on this occasion was Lord George Beresford, son of the Marquess. Now in his mid-forties, he had been an MP since 1802 and held this seat since 1814. A soldier in his youth, he had been made Comptroller of the (Royal) Household in 1812 and a Privy Councillor. A vigorous opponent of Catholic Emancipation, a diehard generally in his social views, his arrogant attitude to the Catholics explains perhaps why opponents of the family resorted to calling them 'the Bloody Beresfords, alternatively the blood hounds or "Orange Blood-suckers"'.[10] More politely, the extent of the Beresford patronage over army, navy and Church in Ireland, where they were deemed to control a quarter of all the places, was summed up as 'nothing too high or too low for their grasp'.

Lord George told the local Catholics that they should be grateful to their 'natural protectors', the aristocrats. And he turned fiercely against the priests, whom he accused of profaning the Sabbath and polluting the altar. He also denounced 'a few itinerant orators, emanating from a scarcely legal body called the Catholic Association' who, aided by the priests, were trying to impose their views upon the legitimate electors of the county. His style of oratory often found him, according to reports, literally foaming with rage, so as to render him for better or for worse practically inaudible.

The man chosen to oppose him – a Protestant naturally, according to the law – also had local connections: Henry Villiers

Stuart, aged only twenty-two, owned estates in Waterford inherited from his maternal grandfather, having been born into the Scottish noble family of Bute. In the autumn of the previous year, he had offered publicly to step down from campaigning if Beresford would guarantee not to oppose Catholic claims, an offer which was duly treated with contempt by Beresford and his supporters.

As it was, the events of the election were to be a sad disillusionment to Lord George. The Catholic (freeholder) voters arrived in huge numbers prepared to vote against him. No longer was he to be comfortably returned by a mere show of hands. Indignantly Lord George demanded a poll, which according to the rules would last for a month, and necessitated a public declaration of each vote: surely the electors would quail before publicly defying the powerful Beresford faction? O'Connell had the answer. The Forty-shilling Freeholders were marshalled into the city of Waterford, accompanied by their families; temporary arrangements were made for their food and housing. Then, for six days, there were processions as singing and cheering voters decked out in the green ribbons of the Catholic Association, or carrying green branches, went to register their votes – for Villiers Stuart. In so doing they showed the courage to defy the power of the great landlords, and as tenants undoubtedly risked their own livelihoods.

As Thomas Wyse wrote in his 1829 account of the Catholic Association, they were supposed to be 'mere serfs' so far as exercising a free vote was concerned.[11] Wyse, an Irish Catholic landowner educated at Stonyhurst and Trinity College, Dublin, was a keen advocate of Emancipation. He had recently married Letizia Bonaparte, niece of the Emperor, when she was only sixteen. Letizia showed her allegiance, not with green branches but with Orange ribbons which she tied to the soles of her shoes, to make it clear she was symbolically trampling on the Orange faction.

At the end of the six days, Lord George Beresford retired from the contest when Villiers Stuart had polled 1,357 votes to his own 528. He announced that he would petition to have the election declared void on the grounds of intimidation by the Catholic clergy, who had 'applied the terrors of another world to the political concerns of this'. Beresford did not succeed, and Villiers Stuart went on to justify the confidence in himself by making his maiden speech in the House of Commons on the necessity of Catholic Emancipation, the present lack of which he contrasted with the more enlightened conditions in Canada and India.

Perhaps the most remarkable aspect of the whole Waterford election of 1826 was O'Connell's successful campaign to ban alcohol. The pork butchers of Waterford, for example, who had a reputation for serious roistering under normal circumstances, took a pledge to drink no whiskey till after the election. Instead they patrolled the city by night to make sure others imitated their own self-denial. The perfect order and regularity of which Duncannon spoke obviously owed a great deal to this self-imposed – or butcher-imposed – restraint.

Of course the power of the priesthood was not always exercised so peacefully as in Waterford. John Leslie Foster, the Anti-Catholic sitting Member for Louth, complained of 'a personal fury almost demoniacal' stirred up against him: 'Very many Protestants were forced to vote against me by the threats of assassination or having their houses burnt.'[12] The people he described as 'my voters' had to be locked up in enclosed yards to save their lives. Foster had refused to vote for Catholic Relief, on the grounds that Emancipation was against his 'conscience'; in particular he deplored the influence of the priesthood, but he was also prepared to contemplate practical measures such as 'a modification of the franchise', eliminating many Catholics for the sake of security.[13]

The families of the Protestant Ascendancy were not always united either in favour of or against the cause of Catholic Relief. Palmerston cited Hercules Pakenham, MP for Westmeath since 1806, as one who had once been 'most adverse' and then changed his mind. Pakenham, brother of the Earl of Longford, came of a classic Anglo-Irish Protestant family which had acquired its Westmeath estates when an ancestor came over in Cromwell's army in the seventeenth century; the Duke of Wellington had married Kitty Pakenham. Hercules was a veteran of the Peninsular War. He would be described by the official *History of Parliament* as a 'lax attender' at the House of Commons, with no interventions at all recorded in 1824. He had voted against Catholic Relief in 1821, and voted for the suppression of the Catholic Association.

At some point his attitude altered and he voted for Catholic Relief in 1825. Now he was able to identify with the plight of the Catholics. A man 'could scarce begin his career when he was checked, not by difficulties that might be overcome by daring spirit or patient resolution, but by a statute, that impenetrably barred his advance'. Could any man with common feeling and sympathies bear this state of things? Hercules could put his hand to his heart and confess that he did not think he could bear it.[14] Unfortunately this led to Pakenham being discarded for the parliamentary seat of which his brother Longford (a strong opponent of Emancipation) was patron. This was said to be in 'the high Protestant interest'. The Catholic press was full of indignation that he was the victim of the positive vote he had given the year before.

Gustavus Rochfort was chosen instead after a gruelling contest, a soldier from a large, poverty-stricken family in Westmeath. Rochfort justified the Protestant faith in him: soon he was presenting Petitions against Catholic Relief in Parliament, and voting with the consistency of a thoroughgoing member of the Ascendancy – that consistency which Hercules Pakenham had felt moved to abandon. However, the second Member elected for Westmeath (which was a two-Member constituency) illustrated the fluid nature of the election: Hugh Morgan Tuite was also a Westmeath local, and offered himself specifically because he was Pro-Catholic. After a struggle, he won the second seat by twenty-four votes, although he then had to endure many months of Petitions against him, alleging electoral improprieties committed by his supporters.

Nothing could gainsay the fact that at Waterford the great landlords had been defied, and defied successfully; furthermore, it was O'Connell who had helped achieve the victory. 'The

Beresfords are gone! Gone for ever!' cackled the *Dublin Evening Post*. Of course the Beresfords were not gone. But the Protestant Ascendancy had had a notable and very public defeat.

Of the 380 constituencies in the election, just under a third were contested, and most of the results were known by the end of June.* A recent 'realistic assessment' puts the net gain overall for the Anti-Catholics as thirteen seats. In England,[15] Cambridge University was not, however, one of the Protestant gains: Palmerston came second in the poll to the Tory Sir John Singleton Copley, beating the Anti-Catholics Bankes and Goulburn, and was thus one of the two elected Members. He now reckoned that the 'No Popery' cry had been tried in many places and not succeeded after all: 'there does *not* exist among the people of England that bigoted prejudice on this point' of which the Anti-Catholics accused them.[16]

The new session in Parliament would test the truth of Palmerston's judgement. George IV, according to custom, opened it in a speech from the throne on 21 November. Canning, as Foreign Secretary, wrote to the King that night with due respect, 'humbly' hoping that he had not suffered any inconvenient fatigue. But his basic message was a gloomy one: 'Mr Canning is sorry to say that he thinks he sees indications of rather a troublesome Session. But he especially fears that the subject of *Ireland* will be forced early into the discussion.'[17]

The government reassembled under the premiership of Lord Liverpool. He remained an opponent of Catholic Emancipation, on grounds of the monarch's special relationship with the Church of England. Equally, his Cabinet remained mixed on the subject, with Canning notably in favour and Peel equally prominently against. By now, however, the subject of Emancipation was so far merged into Canning's 'gloomy message' of Ireland that security issues could never be wholly divorced from it. Liverpool himself was certainly willing to admit that certain measures were necessary, even if his basic opposition remained.

---

* Before 1918 General Elections did not occur on a single day and polling could be spread over several weeks.

All of this was troubling enough to the King, not in the best of health, as Canning feared. But he had at the same time a personal concern which was very likely to meld into the political. This was also to do with health: the rapidly degenerating health of his brother, the rabidly Anti-Catholic Frederick Duke of York, whose succession to the throne had been so much dreaded by the supporters of Emancipation. For the Pro-Catholics, indeed, the most succinct reaction to the Duke's 'speech of terror' in 1821 was that of the liberal peer Lord Ashburton. He simply wanted to call out meaningfully in reference to the Duke of York's possible succession: '*Long* Live the King.'[18]

Now the younger brother seemed increasingly likely to predecease George IV, with consequences which could not be reliably foreseen. William Duke of Clarence was next in line, generally believed to be a more liberal figure altogether. Actual influence over the emotionally pliable monarch such as Frederick exerted, was a different matter; for lower down in the vast family of George III there lurked the sinister figure of Ernest Augustus Duke of Cumberland.

Already in June the King had written a distraught letter to his brother York in which concern for the future of the Crown was implied.[19] Frederick must pay 'the absolutely necessary and requisite attention' to his general health according to the advice of his physicians. He owed it to himself but at the same time it was 'a positive *moral duty*' by which he was beholden to his brother and the country. 'For God's sake, for my sake, and for the sake of all those to whom you are so very dear, let me enjoin you, let me implore of you now,' he wrote, to persevere in the regime which had been prescribed until he was completely recovered. 'My heart is too full, to say much more at present... God bless you, D[eare]st Frederick'.

A libellous attack in Dublin by Richard Lalor Sheil on his 'Dearest Frederick' during the recent election sent the King into predictable spasms of rage. 'The late outrage by a barrister in Ireland against the character of His Royal Highness the Duke of York' was how the Viceroy described it. Peel as Home Secretary had already 'begged to assure' King George that something 'so revolting to every feeling of common decency and humanity' as Sheil's speeches had not escaped his attention.[20]

The Viceroy, Wellesley, hastened to assure the King that 'this unparalleled crime has excited universal disgust and horror in the breasts of all your Majesty's faithful and loyal subjects in Ireland', especially at a time when the Duke of York's health was in such a painful state, causing feelings of sorrow and 'fraternal grief' to the King. Wellesley referred further to 'the brutal disturbance of suffering hitherto deemed sacred by the common consent of civilised society'. Given that Sheil alluded to the colourful past of the Duke, including the corrupt business concerning his mistress Mary Anne Clarke, as well as reading aloud his private love letters (describing him as 'hot and reeking' from concubinage) in order to put 'his morality in comparison with his religion', this official indignation was easy to understand.[21] On the other hand, in view of the all-out nature of the Duke's attack on the Catholics, perhaps the Viceroy exaggerated slightly in his use of the words 'universal disgust' to describe the reaction in Ireland.*

Nor did the depredations of dropsy cause the Duke of York to cease in making such attacks. For better or for worse, he also maintained his lifestyle; he was witnessed by Prince Pückler-Muskau in late October drinking six bottles of claret at dinner with 'very little change in his countenance', although otherwise he was a shadow of the stately man he had once been.[22] In November he insisted on having a personal conversation with the Prime Minister, Liverpool, 'on the critical situation in which this country is at present placed'. The various points of discussion were then summarized and sent to the King, who had not been present.

The Duke's main fear was that the official neutrality – still maintained – of the government on the subject of Catholic Emancipation was putting the Protestant establishment in peril. Writing to his brother, Frederick ended: 'the great body of the British nation staunchly clings to the same principles, those principles in which we have gained honour and security since the year 1688'.

---

* The libel action, although mounted, was later dropped by Canning.

Such blatant interference of a public nature aroused disapproval even among the diehard Anti-Catholic members of the Cabinet; in fact Peel believed that the Duke regretted it later, 'although he said he was not ashamed of it'. But the Duke indicated a climbdown by blaming his illness for a possible element of exaggeration in his fears.[23]

On 5 January 1827 the voice of the Duke of York fell silent for ever. Charles Greville, the diarist, hoped to visit him as he was dying, having been 'the minister and associate of his pleasures and amusements for some years', one of those, unlike the Catholics, who paid tribute to his great kindness. He arrived too late but in time to pay his last respects: the Duke was sitting exactly as he had at the moment of his death, in his great armchair, dressed in his grey dressing gown, his head inclined against the side of the chair, his hands lying before him and looking as if he was in a deep and quiet sleep.[24] York's death brought fearful grief to the 'dear King brought up and educated with him', in the words of the younger brother Cumberland. The whole country was plunged into mourning, with black crêpe on hats and black gloves, black-edged writing paper and servants in black liveries.

Mrs Arbuthnot waxed sentimental in her *Journal*: 'We shall not look upon his like again in a Prince; kind-hearted, amiable, constant in his friendships, good natured to the greatest degree... *Publicly* too, he is the greatest loss, for he was the rallying point for the Tories and bulwark of the Protestant cause.' She did add that his illness dated from a chill he got from laying the first stone for the mausoleum of his mistress the Duchess of Rutland: a true Hanoverian fate, given that the pair of them were to be seen frequently canoodling in public despite their advanced years: 'It is very odd our Royal Family should take to being *si amoureux* after sixty years old,' as Mrs Arbuthnot put it.[25]

Other reactions varied from concern at the fate of the Liverpool government, which some believed owed its continuing existence to York's support, to outright rejoicing. As early as November John Campbell, a future Lord Chancellor, had predicted that his death would be 'a great public benefit'. Mrs Arbuthnot's hero Wellington believed that the Anti-Catholic speech of 1825 had given 'all the low, shabby people in Parliament a sort of standard [flag] to which they may rally'. In Dublin at a Catholic meeting, the attacks on the Duke of York were so vehement that O'Connell was moved to intervene. 'We war not with the dying or the grave. Our enmities are buried there. They expired with the individual.'[26]

In January 1827 it remained to be seen whether the noise of 'No Popery', heard throughout the recent General Election and so ardently proclaimed by the Duke of York, would show any signs of dying with its royal supporter.

CHAPTER ELEVEN

Mr Canning

'Mr Canning is dead. There is another blow to wretched Ireland. No man can become of importance to her but he is immediately snatched off by one fatal accident or the other.'

Daniel O'Connell to his wife, August 1827

THE FUNERAL OF Frederick Duke of York took place late in the evening, according to royal custom, on 20 January 1827. In St George's Chapel, Windsor, his body would join those of Henry VIII and Charles I. Both of them, as it happened, were also second sons who, unlike Frederick, had succeeded to the throne, although with very different results. The worrying question of Frederick's own possible accession to the throne was now for ever solved.

The weather was icy: this freezing temperature, or rather the lack of provision for it where a number of elderly men were concerned, would have important consequences. According to Greville, 'nothing could be managed worse than [the funeral] was'.[1] Except for the appearance of the soldiers in the chapel, the spectacle was not particularly imposing and the cold was intense. There was a delay of nearly two hours before the coffin was brought in, while the congregation waited. The matting in the aisles, which might have alleviated the damp chill of the chapel, had been removed; among others Lord Eldon, who had been Lord Chancellor more or less continuously since 1801 and was now in his late seventies, was left to stand there on the stone for two hours. Canning made a dour joke on the subject afterwards to Wellington: whoever removed the matting must have had bets against the lives of the Cabinet. It was a joke he might regret.[2]

Afterwards both the Duke of Sussex, younger brother of the dead man, and the Duke of Wellington got severe colds as a result of the exposure. Greville believed that the Bishop of Lincoln died of it. Then all the common soldiers were rumoured to have fallen sick. Ominously, it was Canning himself who was most severely struck down; he was still unwell several weeks later. Severe rheumatic pains in his head, added to a continuous painful condition thought to be gout, caused him agonies.

There was more to come. The Prime Minister, Lord Liverpool, had the good fortune to miss the funeral because he was convalescing at Bath from an illness which had struck him down before Christmas. Seemingly, he recovered and was back in London in February, while it was Canning who was now recuperating at Brighton with his wife. Here Canning and George IV, in residence at Brighton Pavilion, exchanged gifts: the Cannings received healing royal fruit and happily responded with some wild pig which had been presented to them, since the King was known to have a passion for it. On 17 February Lord Liverpool was found lying unconscious on the floor of his London house; ironically, he was actually holding a letter in his hand giving a worrying report on the state of Canning's health.

The immediate question – who was now to serve as Prime Minister? – reflected on a small scale what one exasperated Anglican clergyman would call the 'Abominable' Question of the time. It was the Bishop of Oxford who told Robert Peel (the MP for the University) later in the year when discussing a new Chancellor for Oxford: 'the Abominable Cath. Quest ... is now mixed up with everything we eat or drink or see or think'.[3] Canning was the obvious choice of successor, at any rate in the opinion of Canning himself and quite a few others. But Canning was committed to the cause of Catholic Emancipation, a well-known source of madness in the previous monarch, and various hysterical outbursts in the present one. Also Peel, the Home Secretary, was likely to refuse to serve under him, due to this very commitment on the part of Canning.

Meanwhile the politics of dispute did not stand still. On 5 March Sir Francis Burdett brought in yet another Bill for Catholic Relief.[4] He chose to emphasize, among other signs of hope for the cause, the King's visit to Ireland in August 1821. This showed how seriously George IV's signs of favour had been taken then, with his apparently heartfelt declaration on departure that whenever an opportunity offered to serve Ireland, he would seize it 'with eagerness'. Burdett pointed out that 'most ardent hopes had been raised' – and if that was not the intended message, why should the ministers have advised the King to make the visit to 'that unfortunate country' with all the pomp and circumstance of royalty? The King had been received as 'the Messiah bringing healing on his wings', and he was of course the first English sovereign who arrived as a harbinger of peace, not war.

Burdett also alluded, like many other supporters of Emancipation, to the military valour of Irish soldiers in the English cause in the past: historic names like Crécy and Agincourt were thrown in, as well as Waterloo. 'They never failed us in the hour of peril and combat,' he declared. The next speaker, although he disagreed with Burdett, was moved to congratulate him on his eloquence.

For all that eloquence, Catholic Relief was defeated by four votes in the House of Commons. This reversal – the first defeat on the subject of Emancipation in the Commons (as opposed to the Lords) since 1819 – can probably be attributed to the slight swing against Catholicism in the recent 'No Popery' General Election.[5]

There was talk, not for the first time, of possible trouble in Ireland as a result of the defeat: five million rounds of musket-ball cartridge were believed to have been ordered for garrisons all around the country. Thomas Moore celebrated the news in cynical style:[6]

I have found out a gift for my Erin
A gift that will surely content her;–
Sweet pledge of a love so endearing!–
Five millions of bullets I've sent her.

She ask'd me for freedom and right
But ill she her wants understood;–
Ball-cartridges, morning and night,
Is a dose that will do her more good.

Liverpool's collapse proved to be due to a severe cerebral haemorrhage, leading to partial paralysis, and he resigned officially in April.* During the weeks which followed his initial collapse and preceded this resignation, the wheeler-dealing among Pro- and Anti-Catholics, also between Whigs and Tories, was dominated by the Abominable Question. All sorts of candidates were proposed, including the Duke of Wellington. Internal debates also took place as to whether the so-called 'open system' should continue in which Cabinet ministers were free to have their own views on Emancipation.

The Duke of Newcastle was that Ultra-Tory who had angrily opposed the restoration of the office of Earl Marshal to a Catholic, on the grounds that it violated the constitution to have 'a Papist' hold high office near the person of the King. On principle Newcastle objected to any concession whatsoever to the Papists and he paid a special visit to George IV on 24 March to hector him on the subject. He was rewarded with a long account of the history of Roman Catholicism from James II to the present, given to him by his sovereign, followed by the welcome announcement that the King professed himself 'a Protestant, heart and soul'. The Duke of Newcastle assured Lord Colchester in consequence that the King would never give his assent to any measures for Emancipation.[7]

---

* Liverpool did not actually die until December 1828 at the age of fifty-eight, having suffered another minor stroke in July 1827; but he was henceforth out of political life.

In spite of the King's manifest reluctance, it was Canning who was eventually invited to become Prime Minister on 10 April. There was a flurry of Anti-Catholic resignations, including that of the Lord Chancellor, Eldon. In the Lords Eldon spoke with emotion, eliciting at one point a rare interpolated comment from the official parliamentary report in Hansard: 'His lordship here became sensibly affected.'[8] It was the imputation that the ministers had all acted in concert to dictate to the King that distressed and angered Eldon.

Most prominently, Peel and Wellington resigned. Peel gave a clear explanation of his reason for doing so in a speech to the House of Commons three weeks later in order, as he put it, to vindicate himself against charges of disloyalty to both sovereign and government.[9] He focused entirely on the subject of Catholic Emancipation. For eighteen years, Peel said, he had pursued one undeviating course, offering 'an uncompromising, but a temperate, a fair, and, as I believe, a constitutional resistance to the making of any further concessions to the Roman Catholics'. For fourteen of those eighteen years he had been in office, and for eleven of the fourteen, closely involved with the issue.

Most emphatically, Peel stated that he regarded the removal of barriers to Roman Catholic power as inconsistent with the constitution. How could he then remain in a government of which the new head believed the exact opposite? A junior minister who resigned also on Anti-Catholic grounds was George Dawson, an Irish MP from the north, Peel's friend from Oxford days, who was married to his sister Mary. The two men were close: Peel had made him his Private Secretary in Ireland, and later his Under-Secretary at the Home Office.

The Duke of Wellington withdrew not only from the government but from the post of Commander-in-Chief of the Army, to which he had only just been appointed on the death of the Duke of York. His implied contempt for the new administration might seem to justify Byron's description of him as:

> Proud Wellington with eagle beak so curled
> That nose the hook where he suspends the world.

Mrs Arbuthnot, however, had another, less lofty explanation. The Great Duke had, she wrote, acted in a huff. Daniel O'Connell, for one, must have been pleased by Wellington's resignation since he had exploded at the news of the appointment: Wellington, he said, deserved the execration of the people of Ireland, as he had won his title with Irish soldiers' blood, and then voted against 'the freedom of the Catholics of Ireland'.[10]

But the Duke's whole pattern of behaviour at this time seemed to many to demonstrate that declared hatred of 'factiousness' (otherwise, intrigue) which might prove a disadvantage to a practising politician. On the whole question of withdrawal from the government, the Duke spoke at length in the House of Lords, a somewhat confused speech which led one observer, Prince Pückler-Muskau, to remark that the Duke was no orator, since he conducted his defence 'like an accused person'. It was noticeable that Wellington explicitly ruled himself out as Prime Minister with the words: 'I am sensible I am not qualified', as well as warding off charges of disloyalty for deserting his sovereign.[11]

Once again opposition to Catholic Emancipation was given as the prime reason. Wellington's resignation, like that of Peel, was because the new head of the government disagreed with him – and the King – on the matter of Catholic Relief. According to Mrs Arbuthnot, there was loud cheering at the time in the House of Lords, but here was material indeed for his enemies should circumstances ever dictate a very different public reaction to the whole subject. (The same could be said about Peel; but then any recantation by Peel on Catholic Relief was surely unthinkable.)

In private George IV made his own continuing opposition to Emancipation furiously clear in a heavily underlined letter to the Archbishop of Canterbury.[12] The King was infuriated by news-paper reports of Lord Mansfield's speech in the House of Lords. * Mansfield had denounced Canning as 'a constant, zealous and most able advocate' of a measure which the late King George III had detested.

---

* Great-nephew of the very different Lord Mansfield sympathetic to the Catholics in 1780.

The King was appalled. Because Canning was his Prime Minister, this implied 'a direct calumny' upon his own Protestant Faith, as opposed to his father's, and upon his honour. 'This I do not choose to pass unnoticed... I do not deserve as King of this country, this wicked attempt to misinterpret and falsify both my principles and conduct to my Protestant subjects.' The Archbishop of Canterbury was to make Lord Mansfield aware of the royal displeasure.[13]

Obviously Canning would now face considerable difficulties in forming a new Cabinet. The Abominable Question haunted everything, and among the Tories there were now, roughly speaking, four groups where Catholic Relief was concerned. Canning and his supporters had always been liberal on the matter, not so much on religious grounds as practical considerations to do with Ireland. There were others, lukewarm on the subject but now prepared to agree with him. Wellington and Peel had both declared themselves publicly dead against. A fourth group of Ultra-Tories, symbolized by the Duke of Newcastle, were against reform of any sort.

Nor were the Whigs in much better array, even though they were regarded as in principle in favour of Emancipation: Lord Eldon pointed out that the Whigs of former days had been constant advocates of a Protestant King, a Protestant government and a Protestant Parliament. 'The present race of Whigs, through the issue of their loins had totally lost sight of their original distinctive characteristic.' Nowadays it was more complicated. The Abominable Question was at the forefront of discussion at the parties of the formidable Lady Holland in her stately mansion, Holland House. Lord Holland himself had told Lord Grey as long ago as 1810 that 'the Catholic claims should be a *sine qua non* to the acceptance of office'. Lady Holland, who according to her critics needed a padlock on her tongue, complained after Liverpool's stroke that 'this confounded division' of the country into Pro-Protestants and Pro-Catholics was making the King as powerful as ever Henry VIII had been. And she was hostile to Canning.[14]

Fortunately, the new Henry VIII's mood now swung temporarily in Canning's favour, due to the secession of so many

Anti-Catholics from the Cabinet – disloyal by his standards, whatever might be said by them in self-defence in Parliament. For the time being, Canning intended to maintain the system of Lord Liverpool by which Catholic Emancipation was an open question. Two other major contentious questions, concerning the Corn Laws and Parliamentary Reform, were also to be left open. However, the Whig Lord Lansdowne, of whom the Hollands approved, became Home Secretary.

But the future for Catholic Relief remained uncertain. George IV's approval of Canning was evidently not matched by any change in his attitude to the constitution and his own position within it. The King specifically told the Marquess of Londonderry (half-brother of the late Castlereagh) on 13 April that he was bound by his Coronation Oath to resist Emancipation. Two of the most prominent Anglican clergymen, the Archbishop of Canterbury and the Bishop of London, were personally assured that he was an even stronger Anti-Catholic than his father.[15] Perhaps the King hoped by these manoeuvres to make it easy for the Anti-Catholics to remain in his government. The ploy did not succeed.

Canning's Cabinet contained in fact only three known Anti-Catholics. There was Lord Bexley, who alone among the Anti-Catholics had chosen not to resign from the previous Cabinet, and John Copley, now transformed into Lord Chancellor under the name of Lord Lyndhurst; fiercely Anti-Catholic, he was a brilliant lawyer, compared to Mephistopheles for 'the rich, melodious tone of his voice'.[16] Thirdly, there was the Marquess of Anglesey, known as 'One-Leg' after his injury at Waterloo commanding the cavalry of the Anglo-Belgian Army, a politically impetuous character, currently opposed to Emancipation.

Now there was the question of the Whigs joining with the Pro-Catholic Tories to support Canning's government. There were powerful Whigs headed by Lord Grey who refused to join the government unless it was specifically promised that the Catholic measure would be introduced. There was an additional factor in Canning's personal unpopularity with certain Whigs. This was attested by the noble reformer Lord Grey's disdainful remarks on the subject of his parentage, which by modern standards at least lacked taste: he could not *de facto* join a government, he said, headed by the son of an actress.[17]

These were the Whigs who believed the time for compromise was over, the time for outright Emancipation had come. Other Whigs were less dedicated on the issue and entered into talks with Canning: these, however, eventually broke down. It seemed that the long, long rule of the Tories – over fifty years with a short break in 1806 – was not yet over despite the increasingly splintered nature of the party.

Unfortunately, Canning's health had never really recovered from that fatal ordeal of the royal funeral in January. His sardonic remark to the Duke of Wellington on the subject of the lives of the Cabinet was now acquiring a horrible ring of truth; or perhaps the poisonously Anti-Papist Duke of York was enjoying revenge from beyond the grave. During July, Canning's health grew perceptibly worse and at Windsor it was noted that he looked dreadfully ill. The Duke of Devonshire generously loaned the Prime Minister Chiswick House on 20 July in order to help his recovery. But the pains grew worse, with inflammation of liver and lungs; hope faded and on 8 August George Canning died there at the age of fifty-seven, by a melancholy coincidence in the same room as had another politician widely thought to have died too soon: Charles James Fox. He had been Prime Minister for a mere 119 days.*

The King duly appointed what would be his third Tory Prime Minister in under a year: forty-five-year-old Viscount Goderich. Wellington had entertained some hopes, according to his correspondence with Mrs Arbuthnot. In that way that politicians have always behaved, a mixture of arrogance and humility, he took care during this period of uncertainty to be found always 'At Home', in case the call to office came. But for George IV it was to be Goderich, a member of the Liverpool administration, lukewarm perhaps on the subject of Emancipation but who had not felt inspired to resign. The time had not yet arrived to

---

* This remains the shortest period of office for any Prime Minister of the United Kingdom.

tackle what from the Anti-Catholic point of view was described as all the mischief Canning had done: 'as much in four months, as it was possible for a Man to do. God knows how it is to be remedied', in the words of Wellington.[18]

Born Frederick Robinson, Goderich had been given his peerage by Liverpool shortly before the latter's collapse; he had asked for it himself, on the sympathetic grounds that his eleven-year-old daughter had died, and being in the Lords made it easier to spend the evenings with his sorrowing wife. Goderich was the younger son of Lord Grantham, progressing from Harrow and Cambridge to a seat in the House of Commons at the age of twenty-four and from there via various government posts to being Chancellor of the Exchequer in 1823.

Although basically liberal, voting against slavery for example, he was not seen as a man of very strong political convictions – something which might be construed as an advantage in the present situation. On the other hand, a certain nervosity, a propensity to go to pieces under stress, even a tendency to weep during the making of a speech – not helped by the death of his child – was more dangerous when there were so many big political beasts around. (Lord Grey had a nasty habit of referring to him as 'Lady Goderich'.) During the autumn of 1827, as Goderich failed to provide the King with the stability he required, the latter came to describe him as 'a damned, snivelling, blubbering blockhead'.[19] This was not only cruel but unfair: the confusion of English politics at this time, among Whigs as well as Tories, with no generally viable solution to the Abominable Question in sight, would have tried a Machiavelli or a Metternich. Goderich was neither.

Throughout this time, O'Connell in Ireland let his political actions and speeches be guided by one thing only: what was potentially good for Emancipation. That is to say, at the death of the Duke of York at the turn of the year he had expressed hopes for a better future with the new heir to the throne: William Duke of Clarence. He had even sent a message of encouragement to be passed on to the Duke's entourage: 'In plain English, the Duke can command Ireland heart, hand and soul if he pleases.'[20] He was quoting once again the widely held belief that Clarence had liberal sympathies, unlike his brother Cumberland.

Thereafter O'Connell sent a series of messages to Eneas MacDonnell, an activist lawyer and former newspaper editor now in London as the agent to the Catholic Association – or, as he was embracingly described, agent to 'the Catholics of Ireland'. Members of Parliament for the Irish counties were to be instructed that every man was to be regarded as an 'actual enemy' [sic] who did not support Canning against Peel and the Anti-Catholics. Burdett's defeat in March found O'Connell full of public indignation: a meeting was called at which opponents of Emancipation were declared anathema, to receive no support at the next General Election.

Nevertheless, O'Connell was for good reason devastated by the cruel news in August. He wrote to his wife in despair: 'My heart's darling, Mr Canning is dead. There is another blow to wretched Ireland. No man can become of importance to her but he is immediately snatched off by one fatal accident or the other.'[21]

That Irish novelist approved by George IV, Lady Morgan, believed that Canning's absorbing idea had been to become the Atlas of England, 'to raise her on his shoulders'. Such a man would be sadly missed at this awesome moment. O'Connell cheered himself with the assurance that at least under the circumstances it was 'impossible to form a No-Popery administration', hoping for the Whig Lord Lansdowne. Nor did he immediately reject the idea of Goderich, although by the end of September he was privately doubting that the new administration had enough good sense and courage to act honestly by Ireland.[22] There were some individuals 'perfectly free from guile', others such as Henry Joy, the new Attorney-General and 'a virulent Anti-Catholic partisan', for whom he had angry contempt.

Whatever the developments in England, it was in Ireland that the Catholic Association was able to tap into the true and intimate concerns of the people. Hence the furore raised in the autumn on the subject of Catholic burial grounds. Like the lack of Catholic chaplains in Dublin's Newgate Prison, it was an issue which struck at the emotions as well as the intellect. The matter was raised with energy at a meeting of the Association in September by the Rev. William L'Estrange. By an Act passed in 1824, clergy who were not Protestants and thus not part of the Established Church were allowed to officiate at burials in Protestant churchyards, provided that the local clergyman (of the Church of Ireland) gave permission; if he refused, he had to give his reasons in writing. There also needed to be payment of a burial fee. Obviously this system, connected to such a serious and emotional moment in any family's life, was subject to possible abuse. In fact it had always been customary for Catholic clergy to officiate at Catholic burials in a predominantly Catholic country – only, as with so much of Catholic daily life, it had been technically illegal.

Now a subcommittee was formed to procure free Catholic burial grounds as part of the Association's campaign to make legal what had long been popular practice. O'Connell had already given an opinion on 'Rights of Sepulture' four years earlier: that the praying for the dead by a Catholic priest at a funeral or in a churchyard was emphatically not against common law. The Catholic religion had its existence in the common law before the Reformation, so that praying for the dead could not now be prohibited at funerals, in churchyards or elsewhere. On the contrary, it was a common-law part of the duty of the priest that he was bound to perform. O'Connell now wrote at length along the same lines to L'Estrange: it was perfectly legal for any sect of Christians, such as the Quakers, to have separate burial grounds.[23]

O'Connell reiterated his earlier argument about the Catholics' historic right. All this applied to enclosed as well as unenclosed churchyards, and it was obviously advisable to have a chapel adjacent for the sake of celebrating with 'suitable solemnity and religion'. He ended on a less high-minded note which referred to the burial fees charged by the Protestants: 'This measure will take away a large quantity of plunder from a very vile class, the parsons of the [Established] Church.'

On a different level, O'Connell's emphasis on industrious but peaceful political activity was maintained. Personally, he was haunted by debts, which the inheritance from his late relative 'Hunting Cap' had failed to wipe out. In public things were very different: the Catholic Rent continued to be collected in an orderly fashion. Contacts and local alliances were being made which might be useful one day when battle was once more openly joined, as it had been at the time of the General Election in 1826.

In England throughout the autumn, the confused administration of Goderich, Tory but including Whigs, did not flourish, nor was it growing in favour with the King. By mid-December, as Charles Greville put it, Prime Minister and monarch 'had been going on ill together for some time'. He also recorded what he had heard from Lord Mount Charles, the eldest son of the King's mistress Lady Conyngham – a good source for information about the royal mood: 'the King is quite mad upon the Catholic question... his real desire is to get rid of the Whigs, take back the Duke of Wellington and make an Anti-Catholic Government'.[24]

Viscount Lowther, in a letter to the King's Secretary, Sir William Knighton, on 6 January 1828, reported that there was much talk of changes in the ministry. From all he heard, the general wish was for the King to decide in favour of a ministry which was either exclusively Tory or exclusively Whig. 'The majority of the *John Bulls* like a plain downright straightforward course and are already quite nauseated with the twistings and patchings of the middle Party.' They saw that there was no force or energy in the government, hence all their plans were weakened and 'drivelled away' by the necessity of compromise. Nor was the verdict much better from the Whig side. In the New Year the leading Whig, Lord Holland, dismissed Goderich in a letter to his son as having behaved with 'irresolution, levity and *pour trancher le mot* [let's say the word] incapacity', even if he had no bad design for anybody. All the same Holland personally could not 'prudently or creditably' accept a post in his government.[25]

Goderich's term as Prime Minister ended on 8 January 1828, over a clash between his Chancellor and his Colonial Secretary, but it was as much dismissal as resignation. It was said that he wept and had to be handed the royal handkerchief. Early in the

morning the Duke of Wellington received a visit from the new
Lord Chancellor, Lord Lyndhurst, to break it to him that he was
wanted at Windsor. There he found the King still in bed, still in
his night-clothes including a night-turban, announcing that the
Cabinet was defunct. Wellington was invited to form a government.

He agreed, although still unsure whether the role of Prime
Minister accorded with that of Commander-in-Chief – which
represented the monarch's own view. George IV for his part,
his assurance as a monarch having grown with the confused
autumn, had two prime conditions for his government. Catholic
Emancipation must remain an open question, and the Cabinet
must contain both Pro- and Anti-Catholics. In short there was
to be absolutely no official governmental support for further
Catholic Relief (which he had taken up again under Goderich).
The uncompromising resistance of which Peel had openly spoken
in May was still discernible in the mentality of the monarch. He
also pettishly insisted that Lord Grey was not to form part of
the administration – a veto based on a personal clash over a lady
long ago.[26]

At the time this did not seem a particularly auspicious opening
to the New Year for the Catholics or their supporters. Thomas
Spring Rice, an Irish MP in favour of Emancipation and Under-
Secretary for the Home Office, quit his post. He told O'Connell
that a 'Tory and exclusive government' certainly could not claim
any sympathy from him 'should such a *monster* be formed', as
he thought most probable.[27] There were a host of angry Catholic
Petitions in January which seemed at the time to be utterly in
vain. Yet 1828 was in fact to prove the turning point in the
struggle for Catholic Emancipation.

PART THREE

====================

THE DUKE
AND THE
DEMAGOGUES

'We find the influence of these demagogues
paralysing the royal authority itself'

The Duke of Wellington, Memorandum, August 1828

CHAPTER TWELVE

O'Connell's Boldest Step

'The setting-up for Clare was the most daring,
and the boldest step which this man ever took, or ever
will take. Were he to live a century, he could do nothing
which would show so much of daring and
intrepid talent.'

Richard Lalor Sheil on Daniel O'Connell,
Sketches of the Irish Bar

THE DUKE OF WELLINGTON held a dinner for his new
Cabinet at his splendid London residence, Apsley House, on 22
January 1828. Lord Ellenborough, who was present as Lord
Privy Seal, described the mood of the evening as guarded at best:
'the courtesy was that of men who had just fought a duel'. Given
the fractured state of the government during the past year, there
had been no decisive victors in the various political duels, unless
it be the Duke himself, the great general now taking charge of
his country – or countries. At least he was flourishing under
the strain: his wife Kitty confided to her sister: 'Thank God the
Duke's strength seems to increase, his powers to rise as they are
called for, and his popularity with those who were of the party
adverse to him in politics is wonderful.'[1]

The Duke was now nearly sixty. Physically, his formidable appearance, which the public and the caricaturists loved equally if for different reasons, was undiminished. His public speaking style, which deteriorated further as his deafness increased, remained a weak point: O'Connell would refer with a malign flourish (but no fear of contradiction) to a 'stuttering, confused, unintelligible speaker'.[2] But a perceived lack of formal oratorical skill by his enemies had never held the Great Duke back from giving sharp practical orders which expected and received obedience: and that was surely the point of government, as he saw it.

In the current government the general desire now was for some kind of cohesion, in contrast to the Goderich administration. In spite of this, the Whig Lord Lansdowne was known to be unwilling to serve under an Anti-Catholic Prime Minister, and that set the tone for other Whig lords to refuse. Charles Wetherell, MP for Bristol, was made Attorney-General; he had been an MP for various constituencies (including Oxford City) since 1812, and was previously Solicitor-General. This was a man whose eccentric appearance, like 'some untidy friar', belied his keen legal brain and taste for invective enlivened by 'happy sarcasms'.[3] Wetherell might look like a friar but he was in fact a ferocious opponent of friars' rights in the shape of Emancipation. Robert Peel returned as Home Secretary, as well as Leader of the House of Commons. Lord Lyndhurst remained as Lord Chancellor.

In the end it was reckoned that there were seven Pro-Catholics including William Huskisson, noted for his strong liberal views, and Palmerston. Against this there were six Anti-Catholics, headed by Wellington and Peel, and including Lyndhurst. But there was no declared policy on Emancipation. Wellington's memorandum on the subject read: 'Every member of the government is at liberty to take such part as he pleases respecting the Roman Catholic Question, whether in Parliament or elsewhere; but he acts upon this question in his individual capacity.'[4]

A new government meant that the transfer of the Viceroyalty of Ireland, organized by Canning during the brief summer of his premiership, now took a practical form. Canning had indicated to Wellesley that his time was over, and the Marquess of Anglesey was appointed, although Wellesley did succeed in remaining for the rest of the year. He pointed out that it was 'of the highest importance both to my interests and honour to remain here till January next ... To remove me before that period of time ... would bear all the appearance of a recall and would expose me to great inconvenience.'[5]

Returning to England, Wellesley was disappointed not to be offered a position in the Cabinet by his brother. On this fraternal failure to oblige, his American wife Marianne allowed herself to repeat a sardonic comment once made about the family: 'God made "Men, Women and Wellesleys."' She also felt that the Irish Catholics had not been sufficiently appreciative of his efforts: they abused him because he had not lent himself blindly to their party views. She had some justice on her side: the Viceroyalty of Wellesley had indeed marked a dilution in the atmosphere of Protestant Ascendancy, with Catholics freely entertained at the Viceregal dwelling (even before the appearance of a Catholic Vicereine in Marianne).

The new Viceroy was to be 'One-Leg', the Marquess of Anglesey, who had come into Canning's Cabinet the previous May as an Anti-Catholic. Perhaps George IV should have suspected a potentially dangerous transformation in his emissary when he bade him farewell on 21 February. 'God bless you, Anglesey,' said the King. 'I know you are a true Protestant.' 'Sir,' responded the new Viceroy, 'I will not be considered Protestant or Catholic; I go to Ireland determined to act impartially between them and without the least bias either one way or the other.'[6]

In February Lord John Russell, rising star of the Whigs, proposed a measure which directly touched on the principle of Catholic Emancipation: a repeal of the Test and Corporation Acts. Russell, who would be described as 'Lord John Reformer' by Sydney Smith, was a younger son of the Duke of Bedford, and a member of a celebrated Whig dynasty. Thanks to this privileged birth, Russell was elected as MP for the family seat of Tavistock in 1813 when he was twenty-one. Almost immediately he showed his own mettle. Physically Lord John was not impressive, very short but with a surprisingly big head, so that his tiny size sometimes caused amazement when he stood up. His voice was equally small, which annoyed the parliamentary reporters, and he frequently paused or stammered. On the other hand, he was intellectually brilliant and his aspirations for social changes such as Parliamentary Reform were immense.

Russell now proposed a new Sacramental Test Bill, as it was termed, of which the objective was to repeal the existing Test and Corporation Acts passed in the reign of Charles II.[7] This had required all government officials, including mayors, to take the sacrament of Communion according to the rites of the Church of England. In practice an annual Act of Indemnity had often been passed, so that Dissenters could hold office; but it clearly constituted an inferiority at law. Russell argued that liberty of conscience was the best safeguard for the Church of England rather than exclusion, and that in any case religion should not be dragged into purely secular concerns. 'I am opposed to religious tests of every kind,' he declared: the oath he would wish to see applied to persons taking seats in Parliament, and attached to all the offices of government or corporations was 'a simple provision, that they should be called upon only to swear allegiance to the King'.

The new government supported the bill, once a deal was struck by Peel, that loyal Protestant. A declaration was to be included in the bill in which individuals promised never to use office to 'injure or weaken the Protestant Church'. Peel successfully introduced this in the House of Commons on 18 March, although the Ultra-Tory Lord Winchilsea did attempt vainly to substitute a belief in the divinity of Jesus Christ (which would have eliminated some Dissenters once again).[8] After it passed in the Commons by forty-four votes Peel also persuaded the leading archbishops and bishops in the House of Lords to support the bill.

When the Act was passed, Lord Holland was quick to see the relevance to the cause of Emancipation. On 10 April he wrote that it was 'the greatest victory over the *principle* of persecution and exclusion yet obtained ... Catholic Emancipation when it comes will be a far more important measure, more immediate and more extensive in its effects – but *in principle* this is the greatest of them all as it explodes the real Tory doctrine that *Church & State are indivisible*.' He repeated his conviction to Anglesey, the new Irish Viceroy, a month later: this was just what George III had imagined he could not repeal because of his Coronation Oath.[9]

Lord John Russell was certainly much cheered by what he called Peel 'hauling down his colours' on the question of Dissent. Russell trusted that they could soon make Peel give up on the next proposition, that 'none but Protestants' could serve the State, that is, support Catholic rights, having granted them to Dissenters. Others were more dubious about the connection. There were those, equally sincere in their support of the Catholic cause, like William Huskisson and Palmerston, who drew back from this particular issue which they feared would actually slow down progress towards Emancipation; there would be a compromise, satisfying in practical ways to the Anglican establishment, which could then soldier on ignoring the Catholics, who would remain as before totally inferior at law. Protestant Nonconformists might turn against the Catholics once they had won their own case.

More practically encouraging from the point of view of Emancipation, the Act which had banned the meetings of the Catholic Association was not renewed in May by a decision of the Cabinet. It was decided that the Act had been 'ineffectual', and in any case things were quieter in Ireland. Sir Francis Burdett also introduced a new Catholic Bill on 8 May which led to a three-day debate in the House of Commons.[10]

In his speech Burdett stressed the 'undeviating loyalty and faithful adherence to their country and sovereign' of the Catholics of Ireland. He took the opportunity to compare this loyalty to that of Scotland, mentioning the rebellions of 1715 and 1745. And he magnanimously offered Prime Minister Wellington the possibility of yet another triumph: the Great Duke would add to his titles that of 'the pacificator of Ireland, the consolidator of the power of the English empire, the rewarder of those brave Catholics who fought under his banner' – that theme of gratitude for Irish military support stressed once again – 'adding another wreath to the laurel of victory'. The vote was won in the Commons by six, Peel for all his new pragmatism being among those who voted against.

In the House of Lords things went, as usual, much less well from the Catholic point of view. While Lord Wellesley, the former Viceroy, declared his increased conviction of the necessity of the measure, his brother the Prime Minister made his continued disagreement absolutely clear in language so courteous that it verged on sarcasm: 'My lords, I rise under extreme difficulty to address your lordships on this most important subject. I feel particular concern at being under the necessity of following my noble relative, and stating that I differ from him I so dearly love'. And the Great Duke voted Against.

There was, however, during this debate one speech from a close relative of the King from which hope could be derived. The Duke of Sussex was the sixth out of the nine sons of George III (chances of his succession were therefore remote, with the Dukes of Clarence, Kent and Cumberland above him), but he had been consistent in his Whig sympathies. Now he announced that he saw nothing to dread from 'the diffusion of light and knowledge'. On the contrary, he saw every reason for hope: for why should there be all this apprehension with regard to Rome? He voted for the bill as did another royal prince, his cousin the Duke of Gloucester. Once again, Lord Holland interpreted this favourably in a communication to Anglesey in Ireland. For the first time, he reported, Sussex had shown himself 'really good in argument and taste' as well as learning. 'We are a people strangely fond of Royalty,' he mused, like many commentators ever since. On the vexed subject of the Coronation Oath, 'the opinion of every branch of the Royal family is imagined to be of more consequence than [that of] other men'.[11]

Unfortunately, the presence at the King's side of another royal, the Duke of Cumberland, was a much less promising portent. Ernest Augustus Duke of Cumberland had arrived in March. He was now aged fifty-seven, nine years younger than the King. Tall and aggressively self-confident, as a young man he once boasted to George III: 'I am a man who can never go round about to do or get anything.' He knew that everyone would tell his father the same: Ernest's way was 'straightforward'.[12]

Certainly Ernest's Anti-Catholicism was straightforward enough. His declared purpose in coming to England from Germany was, in his own emphatic words, 'to take my seat [in the House of Lords] and give my *vote* in the Catholic question, especially as *unhappily* none of my brothers will do it and it is highly necessary that the *nation* which is not at all Catholic inclined should know that there is one of the family who is truly and honestly Protestant'. The prospect of the Duke of Cumberland taking his seat was in fact something Wellington had dreaded a year earlier, when he advised Knighton, the royal Private Secretary, against it. 'It is a great object for the King to keep himself quiet and without discussion on this question' – of Catholic Relief – he wrote; Cumberland's presence would make that impossible.[13]

Educated at the University of Göttingen with two of his brothers, Cumberland had chosen a military career and fought in the Hanoverian army against the French, gaining a reputation for courage and military cool – against which had to be put wounds leaving one eye useless and his once-handsome face badly scarred. He was now an awesome, half-comical, half-frightening figure of military bearing, bald but with a luxuriant white moustache and patriarchal white whiskers surrounding his angry face.

Cumberland's private life was less straightforward. Although the rumours which made him the incestuous father of his sister Sophia's child were almost certainly not true, they were plausible to many of his contemporaries.*[14] Other unsavoury scandals, involving his twice-widowed wife (and cousin) Frederica of Mecklenburg-Strelitz, and her earlier marriages, combined to make the Duke and Duchess of Cumberland unwelcome in English Society: Queen Charlotte, for example, had refused to receive the Duchess. They had resided in consequence mainly in

* Generally believed in fact to be the son of General Garth, whose surname the boy took, although the issue of possible incestuous abuse is less clear.

Berlin. Life abroad did nothing to dim his Ultra-Tory views: if anything it enhanced them.

The influence of Cumberland on his pliable brother certainly contributed to Lord Chancellor Lyndhurst's verdict in June: 'the King is the real difficulty'. At a Cabinet dinner held at Apsley House, the Duke of Wellington confessed that 'he did not see daylight' on the Catholic Question, although there was no one who desired the settlement of it more than himself.[15]

At this point, in the summer of 1828, there occurred one of those incidents, apparently of minor importance at the time – ever fascinating in retrospect to historians – which was to have dramatic consequences in the story of Emancipation. As so often in English history, the drama was rooted not in England itself, but in Ireland. In late May it was proposed that William Vesey Fitzgerald, the MP for Co. Clare, should take on the role of President of the Board of Trade, in the Cabinet, in place of William Huskisson. Fitzgerald, now in his forties, had sat in the House of Commons for various constituencies since 1808. He came from a family with prominent interests in Clare, who were generally speaking held to be benign landlords.

In the House of Commons, Fitzgerald was considered to be clever and capable, without being particularly popular. He had already held several government posts, including that of Irish Chancellor of the Exchequer, benefiting from a friendship with Robert Peel forged when the latter was Irish Secretary. (The two men had both been at Christ Church, Oxford, although not at the same time.) Apart from his parliamentary career, Fitzgerald had also occupied various diplomatic posts. It had been suggested earlier he might go to America as Ambassador, a prospect he dismissed as 'odious'; although in 1824 Vesey Fitzgerald had contemplated accepting an Irish peerage. This would have reconciled him to the odious New World, and at the same time removed him from Co. Clare where his life as an MP was becoming increasingly difficult due to Catholic agitation. In the event he remained an MP.

During the parliamentary rumpus of the spring of 1825, centred on the suppression of the Catholic Association, Vesey Fitzgerald had voted for the bill on the grounds that the Association had thrown 'the Protestant mind... into a state of panic which it would be difficult to describe'. Yet broadly speaking he supported Emancipation, voted for Catholic Relief in 1827 and presented Catholic Petitions from Co. Clare. Wellington's decision to offer him the Board of Trade was put down to Peel's influence.[16]

There was one small formality to be undergone before Vesey Fitzgerald could step into place. By the rules of the time, there had to be a by-election if a Member of Parliament was appointed to a new office. Thus Vesey Fitzgerald had to offer himself to Co. Clare for re-election.

Afterwards Peel wrote to Sir Walter Scott that he wished his friend had been present at the Clare by-election which duly followed: 'for no pen but yours could have done justice to that fearful exhibition of sobered and desperate enthusiasm'.[17] The first manifestation of these powerful but contradictory qualities at work was at the meeting of the Catholic Association. It was a question of opposing Vesey Fitzgerald and there was an intense debate on the subject. Then O'Gorman Mahon, a young Catholic landlord, was deputed to approach the wealthy Protestant William Nugent Macnamara, who had acted as second in O'Connell's lethal duel against D'Esterre and had interests in Co. Clare.

O'Connell was convinced that Macnamara would accept. The Corn Exchange, on Burgh Quay by the River Liffey, was the locality established by O'Connell where as many as a thousand people could meet. Conveniently the coal-porters' stand nearby provided loyal amateur guards, who boasted of being prepared to throw invading troublemakers into the river. It was here in a speech on 23 June, made in his usual flamboyant style, that O'Connell declared that 'if his friend had not offered himself, he [himself] would certainly have stood'. Whatever happened, Clare should not be without a candidate backed by the Association.

The next day, 24 June, the news was broken that Macnamara had indeed refused to stand. At a large Catholic meeting held on the same day also at the Corn Exchange, various names were suggested to replace Macnamara. But, in the words of the *Dublin Evening Post*, they were all drowned out by 'deafening cries of "Mr O'Connell! Mr O'Connell!"'[18]

The credit for this outpouring was claimed by David Roose, a stockbroker, and P.V. Fitzpatrick, a friend of O'Connell, who met in a Dublin bookshop and agreed that O'Connell should stand; Fitzpatrick then convinced the Liberator. But it has been pointed out that as early as January O'Connell had in fact indicated that he would stand one day, the obvious step on the road to liberty. Now the moment had indisputably come. And Clare itself was a propitious place since the Clare Liberal Club had been established the year before.[19]

When the great man himself was called upon to speak, he declared in that rich prose to which much of Ireland bowed in emotional obedience that he in his turn was ready to obey 'the voice of the nation'. In the assessment of O'Connell's colleague Sheil two years later, 'the setting-up for Clare was the most daring, and the boldest step which this man ever took, or ever will take. Were he to live a century, he could do nothing which would show so much of daring and intrepid talent.' Sheil went on to quote Voltaire: it was one of those steps that 'vulgar men would term rash, but great men would call bold'.[20]

The keynote of the campaign, which was to be of vital importance in the future, was struck by O'Connell when he announced that 'ours is a moral not a physical force'. This was a further development of the surprising tranquillity with which the fight against Lord George Beresford had been conducted in Waterford at the General Election of 1826. Thus the people of Clare were adjured to abstain from any kind of violence, which in view of the traditional rough handlings at any election – and not only Irish – remained an astonishing pronouncement for its time.

That was one challenge to unspoken traditional procedures. But the mighty gauntlet which O'Connell now flung in the face of the government concerned his religion, not the behaviour of his putative constituents. O'Connell was a Catholic and as such frequently held to be ineligible for the British Parliament. There was, however, no such specific law enacted. Nor was it true, as O'Connell had at first mistakenly believed, that, if elected, he would be fined £500 a day for non-attendance due to refusal of the Anti-Catholic oath.

O'Connell was quite clear on the subject in his electoral address, disseminated by the newspapers well in advance of his arrival in Clare: 'You will be told I am not qualified to be elected. The assertion, my friends, is untrue. I am qualified to be elected, and to be your representative. It is true that as a Catholic I cannot, and of course never will, take the oaths at present prescribed to members of Parliament.'[21]

O'Connell then proceeded to give details of the oath. He would be required to say 'That the sacrifice of the Mass and the invocation of the Blessed Virgin Mary and other saints, as now practised in the Church of Rome, are impious and idolatrous.' He commented: 'Of course, I will never stain my soul with such an oath. I leave that to my honourable opponent, Mr Vesey Fitzgerald. He has often taken that horrible oath. He is ready to take it again, and asks your votes to enable him so to swear. I would be rather torn limb from limb than take it.' This was the key point. Parliament, the authority which created these oaths, could also reject them. 'Return me to Parliament,' commanded O'Connell, 'and it is probable that such a blasphemous Oath will be abolished for ever.'

O'Connell went further. He suggested that the eyes of all Europe would be on the events in Clare, and if, having been duly elected, he was excluded (due to his unwillingness to take the oath), it would produce 'such a burst of contemptuous indignation against British bigotry' in every enlightened country in the world that the voice of all the great and good in England, Scotland and Ireland would join to the universal shout of the nations of the earth and overpower every opposition. No longer would Peel and Wellington be able to close the doors of the constitution against the Catholics of Ireland.

This was stirring stuff. These were also fighting words. In complete contrast was the exemplary behaviour of the Catholic forces in Co. Clare. According to Wellington's report to the King, no violence, disorder or even insult was committed. Supporting O'Connell were what Peel would later describe to Scott as 'tens of thousands of disciplined fanatics, abstaining from every excess and every indulgence, and concentrating every passion and feeling on one single object'.[22] This was symbolized by the pledge taken by the local Catholic Association to abstain from whiskey for the campaign, just as the butchers had volunteered to deny themselves in Waterford. (Modest wine, porter and cider were provided but these did not count; O'Connell himself stuck to water.) This was not seen as an empty pledge for display only. Those who were unwise enough to flourish the bottle notwithstanding got plunged in the river, and then kept there in the water for hours, with periodically renewed dunkings.

The local Catholic clergy were also now poised to take on a vital role. In Wellington's words, those of an experienced military campaigner, it was under the direction of their parish priest that the whole of 'the lower orders of the population', with the exception of a few Protestants, 'moved in regular military order ... to the election town'. There they remained till it was their turn to vote. At night they 'bivouacked' in an open space near the town or 'cantoned' in neighbourhood houses on rainy nights and paid for their lodgings.[23]

The appearance of O'Connell himself with his entourage at 11 a.m. on Monday, 30 June created a sensation. This was in Ennis (the name comes from the Irish *inis* for island), a busy market town through which flows the River Fergus near the Shannon Estuary in western Ireland. As the county town of Co. Clare, this was the designated voting place. The crowds, who had been waiting for him all night, surged impatiently in the streets until the hour of the nomination. *The Times* reporter wrote that it was impossible to describe 'the shouts, the tumultuous and deafening cheers' with which they were received as they came into the town.

The speech which followed has been estimated by his biographer as 'without doubt one of the greatest of his life'.[24] His adversary's previous support of Emancipation did not hold him back. Sheil recorded that Fitzgerald frequently muttered an interrogatory 'Is this fair?' when O'Connell used what he called 'some legitimate sophistication' against him. This included mocking Fitzgerald's tears at the mention of his dying father's name: 'I never shed tears in public,' said O'Connell. Defensively, Sheil admitted that sensitive persons might find this unduly harsh; but

Fitzgerald had made a very powerful speech and the effect had to be got rid of. 'In such a warfare a man must not pause in his selection of weapons, and Mr O'Connell is not the man to hesitate in the use of the rhetorical sabre.'

Lord Holland put it in another, less flattering way in his correspondence with the Viceroy Anglesey: O'Connell's 'first and main object is naturally to maintain the ascendancy he has got – if he can – in good fellowship with the Government and in real promotion of the Cause, but if not, in the teeth of the Govt. and at the risk of the cause'. Campaigning verses were equally simple – they might be political:

> Ask your Hearts if Vesey can be true
> At the same time to Wellington and you?

Or, more emphatic about O'Connell's perceived contest with Wellington, the man who had defeated Napoleon:

> Who will beat Wellington, thro' his own merits,
> And by the justice of his cause:
> O'CONNELL,
> Irishmen,
> If we beat the MINION of Wellington, in Clare,
> the Great Captain is himself defeated, and by whom?
> By the
> Great Catholic Leader
> DANIEL O'CONNELL

The latter was posted as a placard all over Clare. It went on:

> We tread the Land that bore us,
> Our Green Flag flutters o'er us;
> The FRIEND we've tried is by our side,
> And the FOE we hate before us.

Anglesey's ADC reported to him that people were saying locally: 'O'Connell be with you,' the name of the Liberator replacing that of God. Most eloquent of all was the banner which read quite shortly: 'Vote for your Religion.'[25]

Various slashes of O'Connell's rhetorical sabre included a stab at Fitzgerald's friendship with Peel, which led to Fitzgerald smiling when O'Connell denounced him. O'Connell then began to quote Hamlet on his uncle: 'A man may smile...' before letting his voice trail away. 'I will not use the word,' said O'Connell, implying but not pronouncing the rest of the quotation, which ended 'be a *villain*'. But he did manage to describe Fitzgerald as a smiling, gay deceiver. The finale of his speech, adapting Shakespeare again, was on a higher level: 'Romans, countrymen and lovers, I come here not on my own account but yours – I am not fighting my own but the Catholic cause. Let them make this their cry: "O'Connell, the Catholic cause and Old Ireland." '[26]

At the voting itself, the priests had a significant role to play, given that there was no such thing as a secret ballot at an election at this period: all preferences were made public in a way which could be threatening for the person concerned if he went against powerful local interests.* Tenants were naturally wary of offending their landlords. In this case there were scenes where priests ostentatiously embraced those who had voted the right way, and made a penitential – and possibly ominous – sign of the cross over those who had voted for 'the wrong side'. An empty coffin was carried through the streets, purporting to contain the body of a man who had died suddenly in consequence of having voted against Daniel O'Connell.[27]

Sheil gave a rich description of the Catholic priesthood in action – so very different, beginning with their appearance, from the Protestant parsons. Typically, the parson was marked by 'the mannerism of Ascendancy', wearing a broad-rimmed fire-shovel hat of smoothest and blackest material, stockings of glossy silk on 'finely swelling' leg, with his ruddy cheek and bright, authoritative eye above his well-fitted jerkin. Where Catholic priests were concerned, Sheil focused on Father Murphy of Corofin, tall, slender and emaciated in his long robes, with 'a

---

* The secret ballot was put into force in the Ballot Act of 1872.

peculiarly sacerdotal aspect'. He had long, skinny white hands, very thin, a long, sunken, cadaverous face but one that was illuminated by eyes blazing with all the fire of genius. Father Murphy first told his congregation that there would be no politics at Mass; then when Mass was over, he threw off his robes and called on the people *in Irish* to vote for O'Connell 'in the name of their country and their religion'. Inflamed by his emotion, he actually shook his fist as he grasped the altar with the other hand. After which Father Murphy marched them into Ennis, and to a man the tenantry of the Protestant Sir Edward O'Brien, who officially proposed Fitzgerald, voted for O'Connell.

The 'priesthood' was indeed widely seen by those who shuddered away from Catholic direct action as responsible for running – or ruining – the election; the fact that this was basically an Ascendancy point of view did not necessarily mean that it was wrong. All the Catholic priests, except two with specific Ascendancy connections, pledged their vote for 'the man of the people'.

Inevitably social distinctions played their part in this stratified society. The Irish novelist John Banim featured a scene in *The Anglo-Irish of the Nineteenth Century*, published in 1828, in which one character, Tom Steele, challenged another, William Smith O'Brien, to a duel, after the latter said that not a single gentleman supported O'Connell: this implied that he, Steele, was not a gentleman. The Catholic Forty-shilling Freeholders, granted the vote in 1793, who were suspected for good reason of being heavily in favour of O'Connell, were the targets of this kind of sneer. Sir Edward O'Brien pulled no punches when instructing his tenants to back his candidate: Ireland, he told them, would not be a fit place for a gentleman to live in if the results of the election demonstrated that property had lost its influence.[28]

As against this automatic display of Ascendancy condescension, the Catholic Association, in the provision of large sums of money through the Catholic Rent, which was collected monthly, demonstrated very different values. Catholic priests, too, were collecting money for the campaign at their churches, with a ready-made flock of potential donors in the members of their parish. The lesson here was that organization, including financial organization, provided a much surer path to victory than rowdiness shading on rebellion.

Voting, according to custom, took five days, beginning on Tuesday, 1 July. Over this period, the votes cast gradually tilted towards a clear winner, having favoured one man from the first (as with the ballot, there was no secrecy about the process). Many of the tenants of the Ascendancy were to be seen marching to vote, as though to battle, with a piper at their head. It was in this way that, at 11 a.m. on Saturday, 5 July 1828 in the courthouse of the town of Ennis, the sheriff made the dramatic announcement. The winner of the Co. Clare by-election by 22,027 to 982 votes was: Daniel O'Connell, a Roman Catholic.

It was a development that the Anglo-Irish Palmerston described in his journal as 'somewhat sublime'.*[29] The banquet which followed at nine o'clock that night with the new MP in the place of honour certainly justified the description.[30] There was beef, pork, mutton, turkey, tongues and fowl, and 100 tumblers of punch and sliced lemon. For a while there was no sound but that of 'hungry masticators'. Then the toasts began. Sheil's own speech was unashamedly belligerent: 'Protestants, awake to a sense of your condition. Look around you ... 7 million of Irish people are completely arrayed and organised.' And he ended with a clear threat: 'Annihilate us by concession; extinguish us with peace; disarray us by equality; instead of angry slaves make us contented citizens: if you do not, tremble for the result.'

O'Connell would be fifty-three in August. Physically he remained impressive. Prince Pückler-Muskau, who visited him at the end of September in Derrynane, found 'a tall, handsome man of cheerful and agreeable aspect' and, he added, with a touch of European prejudice, looking more like one of Napoleon's generals than a Dublin lawyer. John Banim gave a similar portrait of O'Connell in his novel which emphasized his good cheer: a 'tall,

---

* A towering Doric column surmounted by a cloaked figure with a raised hand was erected in Ennis in 1867, as a monument to Daniel O'Connell, on the site of the courthouse, demolished fifteen years earlier, where his victory was declared.

lusty gentleman, with the healthy, good-humoured face, he that walks so firm and stout'.[31]

In Ireland O'Connell's most daring and boldest step had resulted in triumph. The crucial question was now raised as to whether this firm and stout progress would take him into the British House of Commons, with the prospect of taking the Anti-Catholic Oath of Allegiance hovering over the entrance like a huge black cloud.

CHAPTER THIRTEEN

Brunswickers

*'Monday last was a glorious day... The hearts
of the Longford Protestants were revived and
a brighter day has risen upon them.'*

The Brunswick Club, Longford,
Westmeath Journal, 1828

THE CANDIDATE WHO had been so humiliatingly defeated by
Daniel O'Connell, William Vesey Fitzgerald, took the advice of
his friend Robert Peel. He delivered what has been described as
'an even tempered but occasionally tearful valedictory speech'
(showing once more that propensity for weeping on which
O'Connell had commented so derisively).[1] There were tears too
for O'Connell. These were tears of delirious, madcap joy – while
he remained in Ireland, at least.

When O'Connell questioned Prince Pückler-Muskau on his
visit to him at Derrynane whether he had been to the north
to admire the Giant's Causeway, his aristocratic guest replied
with a charming smile: 'Oh no, before I visit Ireland's Giant's
Causeway, I wish to see Ireland's Giants.'[2] But there was only
one giant in Ireland at this moment. Pückler-Muskau went on to
comment in his letter to his wife: 'Daniel O'Connell is indeed no

common man, though he is a man of the people.' With his power in Ireland, O'Connell could singlehandedly raise the banner of revolt, yet by legal, openly publicized means, he had created a power which was like that of a King. Although, added the Prince, with a swipe at the indulgent Hanoverians, it was odd to imagine George IV keeping 40,000 loyal Irish subjects from drinking whiskey for three days, as O'Connell had done in Co. Clare.

O'Connell's progress to Dublin from Clare, via Limerick, arriving on 10 July, was both ecstatic and triumphant. His escort was 60,000-strong. Where his progress towards Ennis had been illumined by the light of hope, this journey had the added element of joyous surprise at the successful turn of events. In one remarkable encounter, a young sergeant among the soldiers who were keeping a close watch on O'Connell's progress stepped out of line. He declared that he did so regardless of possible consequences, in order to have the satisfaction of shaking the hand of 'the father of my country'. Reports of this kind about men who were in fact soldiers in the British Army were, in O'Connell's opinion, likely to exercise an important influence on their Commander-in-Chief, Wellington.[3] The Irishman certainly took care to confide publicly in the *Dublin Evening Post* – for Wellington's ear – that 300 soldiers had thrown their caps in the air for him since he left Ennis.

O'Connell's arrival to address the Catholic Association at the familiar Corn Exchange was greeted with 'general exultation'; the men were standing and the ladies in the gallery waved their emblematic green silk handkerchiefs. Merrily, O'Connell told them to sit back and enjoy something they had never heard before: a speech by a Roman Catholic Member of Parliament. During the speech he emphasized that he had but one demand, and that was for 'unconditional, unqualified, free and unshackled Emancipation'.[4]

On that subject, there was a significant communication from Peel to Wellington on 11 August 1828. While Peel declared once again his uniform opposition to Catholic Emancipation – 'I wish I could say that my views upon it were materially changed' – he added that despite these views, 'I cannot deny that the state of

Ireland under existing circumstances is most unsatisfactory.' Peel was beginning to compare the actual danger from 'union and organization' of the Roman Catholic body with the 'prospective and apprehended dangers' to its constitution and religion. Put crudely, might there not be 'less evil' in settling the Catholic Question than leaving it open, with the country in a state of incessant agitation? Peel added that in the former case he would give any such settlement his full support, although he was careful to point out that, in the light of his known views, it would be better if he resigned and did so out of office.[5] The soft rustle of the wings of the angel – or demon – of pragmatism was beginning to be heard.

This was a private communication. One day later, on 12 August, in Londonderry there was a public dinner commemorating the raising of the Siege of Derry of 1689 (the first real victory for the cause of William III in Ireland over the Catholics).* Peel's brother-in-law, George Dawson, made a speech which shocked both the Irish and the English world and appalled many members of the Protestant Ascendancy. Greville wrote that he never remembered any occurrence which excited greater surprise. At the time, the speech, made on such a pre-eminently Protestant occasion, was greeted first with astonishment and then with a rising chorus of angry hisses. Greville also recorded the general impression that the speech was made with the Duke of Wellington's knowledge and concurrence, although he personally did not believe it.[6]

'Derry' Dawson came of a line of northern Irish MPs, having sat in Parliament for Londonderry himself since 1815. He was financially independent, having inherited £4,500 a year in rents from his father (over £300,000 a year today). Having resigned from his junior position in the government along with Peel the previous year, he had been reinstated when Wellington took office as Financial Secretary to the Treasury. Hitherto Dawson's 'violent Orangeist' credentials had been so marked as to cause one observer to comment that the colour orange was not strong

---

* Still commemorated on 12 August by the Apprentice Boys of Derry.

enough to describe him: it should be purple instead. Even a fellow Protestant had found him 'too acrimonious' towards the Catholic clergy, before adding snidely: 'though not beyond the truth'.[7] The Catholic Association, for example, was described by Dawson as 'wild, irresponsible and seditious'. Naturally he had voted regularly down the years against any form of Catholic Relief. Now Dawson argued publicly that the Catholics had a case. He expressed sympathy with their past sufferings, and he, the brother-in-law of Robert Peel, referred to the need for further concessions.

The Tory press howled with rage. O'Connell said publicly that nothing had ever pleased him more than the conduct of Mr Dawson, whose speech had done a great deal of good.[8] The *volte-face* was so striking that there was even a complicated theory that Peel and Wellington had deliberately put Dawson up to it in order to provoke Protestant fury, and thus justify once again defeating the cause of Emancipation. The reverse was the case. As Peel's private letter to Wellington of 11 August demonstrates, the Abominable (Catholic) Question was now being asked once again in certain important circles, but in a very different tone of voice. The discussions were also confidential. Under the circumstances, it was thought prudent to leave Dawson in his lesser government position so as not to call further attention to the episode.

Inevitably, the news of Dawson's untoward speech and the Protestant explosion which followed it reached the royal ears. The result was predictable. King George IV was furious, or, as Wellington put it, 'What was passing did not fail to have its effect upon the King's mind.' In any case, George IV's health was causing increasing concern, as the dropsy progressed and his painful gouty right hand was now 'as large as two hands'; Wellington thought he couldn't hold a pen if his kingdom depended on it.[9] As with his father, the two issues of health and Emancipation were beginning to mingle with George IV in a lethal combination.

Wellington, angry with Dawson but from the different angle of his delicate negotiations, reacted with his own explosion: 'Surely a man who does such things ought to be put in a straight waistcoat.' O'Connell would later refer to Dawson as the 'pilot balloon'. This was probably an accurate description if the word 'pilot' is omitted; in the sense that Dawson, as an Ultra-Tory but an Irishman, was expressing the growing feeling that there could be worse things than highly limited, security-bound Emancipation. But in August 1828 Wellington was not yet ready for anything as visible as a balloon (or Dawson). The Duke of Cumberland, from Hanover, was clear on the subject: 'that madman Dawson has *done* the government and the Duke in particular the greatest mischief, for it has shaken very much the opinion of the Protestants, as to the purity of his intentions'.[10]

It was not as if organized Protestant Anti-Catholic opinion was in any way quietening down in either England or Ireland. While Dawson's speech was laughed at by the Catholics, it was reviled in the bitterest terms by the new group, the so-called Brunswickers. In late June there had been meetings about a new Protestant Club to convene monthly during the parliamentary session. The name was changed to the loftier Brunswick Con-stitutional Club by Lord Eldon in July; it was an allusion to the origins of the dynasty currently on the British throne, syn-onymous with Protestant Ascendancy.

Naturally the Duke of Cumberland was an active patron, just as he was Grand Master of the Orange Lodges; he boasted to the Russian ambassadress Princess Lieven that he had started up the whole affair, and now had an organization ready to defeat the Catholic Association. (Wicked Ernest did not exclude other, less peaceful methods: he suggested to the King that he should put down O'Connell by force.) Although Cumberland now returned to Germany, he assured supporters and menaced opponents with a promise: 'the moment anything should occur in Parliament that interests Our Great Cause I shall not fail to be back on my post'.[11]

On 4 July the Marquess of Chandos was in the chair; the Dukes of Gordon and Newcastle, the Earl of Longford, Lords Farnham and Hotham and several commoners were present. Brunswick Clubs began to be founded in the country, all with the declared intention, as the name indicated, of protecting the constitution, which included of course the King's Coronation Oath and precluded Catholic Emancipation.

It was, however, in Ireland that the Brunswick Club found its truly fertile ground. The Irish Brunswick Club was founded by Wellington's brother-in-law, Thomas 2nd Earl of Longford, he who had withdrawn support from his own brother Hercules Pakenham at the 1826 General Election because the latter had conceded the need for Emancipation. It was as an Irish member of the British House of Lords that he had been present at the original July meeting in London: now he was on home ground.

The inaugural meeting was in Dublin on 14 August, two days after Dawson's speech in the north. O'Connell, with his usual touch for a lacerating phrase, referred to 'their ostentatious display of peerage strength'. It was perfectly true that the Irish Brunswick Club, apart from the Earl of Longford as President, had thirty-odd noblemen as Vice-Presidents. There was another acid comment on the new club, but from precisely the opposite point of view, by one who declined to join. These Irish Brunswickers were much too 'milk and water': they seemed to plan to put down the Catholic Association by 'Eating and Drinking'.[12]

Certainly, some of the letters in reply to the invitation sent by 'Brunswick Tom'* had a jovial touch, conveying the familiar close-knit network of the Anglo-Irish upper class – not so different perhaps from the close-knit network of the similar English Catholic group, except for the vital difference that the Brunswickers were determinedly preserving power, and English Catholics modestly hoping for a share in it. There was another basic difference: it is only fair to say that many of the Anglo-Irish Protestant grandees, including Brunswick Tom, had lived through the rebellion of 1798 and for this reason were inclined to see Catholic conspiracies everywhere. The safety of the English aristocrats was hopefully no longer an issue, unlike their legal status.

There was in fact nothing milk-and-water about the prospectus of the Irish Brunswick Club, printed in Dublin by J. Lennox Livingstone. Brunswick Tom believed it to be, incidentally, a

* As the 2nd Earl would come to be known in the family.

suitable gift from landlord to tenants, in their respective roles of 'Father and Children'; for it would teach them 'to Love and Venerate our [Protestant] Religion and Laws as Gloriously Constituted by the Wisdom, and Established by the Blood of our Forefathers in 1688'. The declared object of the club was the preservation of 'the integrity of our Protestant constitution', and the presentation address declared it to be in 'glorious and immortal memory of 1690'.

On the title page the words 'For King and Constitution' surmounted the Union Jack (and the Longford arms), with PROTESTANT ASCENDANCY unmissable in capitals. The text had a portrait of Brunswick Tom as its frontispiece, and was headed *No Surrender*, that watchword of the Siege of Derry standing for the Williamite defiance. It included outright abuse of those 'Noble Lords and Gentlemen' who had advocated the cause of Catholic Emancipation, and in so doing had encouraged the disaffected and seditious in 'this unhappy land'.

All of this was immensely appealing – to a small, but in their own estimation at least, powerful section of the population. The *Westmeath Journal* reported a subsequent meeting held in the actual town of Longford: 'Monday last was a glorious day... The hearts of the Longford Protestants were revived, and a brighter day has risen upon them.' Speeches, either replete with historical allusions or full of comic turns about O'Connell, were made respectively by the Rev. William Digby (nearly two hours of it) and the Rev. Richard St George ('called forth bursts of laughter').[13]

For his part, Wellington's reaction to the clubs in both countries was to shrug his shoulders. He told Peel that the Brunswick Clubs had a right to meet 'if they think it proper'. But it was a little too much to expect that the troops would be turned out beforehand to protect their meetings. The Irish Home Secretary, Lord Francis Leveson Gower, was instructed to ignore them in language rather less high-flown than that of the clubs themselves: 'They can do no harm except in the way of irritation and God knows there is no want of that ingredient in Ireland, whether Brunswick Clubs exist or not.' Privately Wellington was more brutal: to Mrs Arbuthnot he expressed the view that the lords, including his brother-in-law Longford, would not remain long in Ireland if there was 'a cutting of [Protestant] throats', thanks to the appearance of their clubs.[14]

O'Connell for his part interpreted the Brunswick Clubs firstly as part of the mission to terrify the Viceroy, Lord Anglesey, and his administration into Anti-Catholic action. O'Connell's second charge against the Brunswickers was that they encouraged 'the friends of bigotry in England'. As for the latter, O'Connell was quite clear in his own mind: 'It would be, indeed, quite idle to conceal from ourselves that the great enemy of the people of Ireland is his most sacred Majesty!!' Here was a King surrounded by 'pimps and parasites' who believed their power was connected to the continuation of abuses in Ireland.[15]

But O'Connell missed out one enormously important point about George IV's entourage. However bigoted, the King had, in addition to those around him, a Prime Minister in Wellington who was most emphatically neither a pimp nor a parasite. How far in fact was the attitude of the Great Duke softening towards Emancipation as a practical measure towards solving the crisis that was Ireland? This became the crucial internal query within the Catholic Question.

There are indications that by the autumn of 1828 Wellington's mind was far from being firmly set against any form of Catholic Relief, even if his recent public utterances might indicate that was so. Peel had put the choice succinctly in his letter of 11 August: was the government to continue to endure the practical consequences of its obstinacy in Ireland or attempt to solve the perpetual problem of the rebellious Emerald Isle by some form of concession?

It was helpful that the Whig high command for their part were not countering the Brunswick Clubs with new associations of their own. Richard Grosvenor, Viscount Belgrave, heir to the Marquess of Westminster and MP for Chester, did propose matching the Brunswickers, meeting for meeting, in a speech to the Cheshire Whig Club. Lord John Russell also suggested that the Pro-Catholics should form large petitioning meetings on the

Brunswick model. Lord Grey, on the other hand, opposed such moves when they were put forward, on the grounds that this would only stir up Anti-Catholic feeling. He had in fact just the same objection to Catholic clubs as he did to the Brunswick Clubs: they would embarrass the government. Lord Althorp agreed, believing that such schemes would arouse jealousy. Progress – unseen progress – was more likely to be effective.

Mrs Arbuthnot was becoming dubious about her hero's mindset. Her own attitude to recent events in Ireland had been mainstream Tory: 'the Catholics and their priesthood have driven Mr Vesey Fitzgerald out of the county of Clare'. As for O'Connell: 'he talks very big and very treasonably of coming over and storming the House of Commons and of putting an end to Tithes and the corrupt government of Wellington and Peel.' On 29 July she reported Wellington as racking his brains as to how to satisfy friends of Catholic Emancipation in England *and* check 'the Agitators' in Ireland.[16]

The government was paralysed by the fact that an Irish MP could not now be created a peer, because that would inevitably leave an empty seat in the House of Commons up for contest; then the hideous fiasco of the Clare by-election would happen all over again. Further aggressive Catholics would put their names forward and be elected. Wellington wrote a memo to that effect in early August. 'The influence of these demagogues is paralysing the royal authority itself.'[17] Ironically enough, the unabated vigorous protests by 'Irish landed Gentlemen' such as his brother-in-law Longford also helped convince the Duke that conciliation of the Catholics was the proper route to follow.

Mrs Arbuthnot's key assessment was, however, her description of Wellington as 'the only man who has considered the subject *practically*'.[18] It was that side of the Great Duke's character which did not flinch from taking unpopular action on the grounds that, in modern slang, somebody's got to do it. It is sometimes plausibly suggested, including by contemporaries, that the Clare election result was the decisive element which convinced Wellington (although O'Connell himself, as has been seen, ascribed the conversion to the behaviour of the Irish troops saluting him on his Ennis journey). Given his military genius, the ability to assess rapidly a change in the horizon of battle and act upon it, this makes perfect sense; from the Catholic point of view, it certainly justifies O'Connell's 'most daring and boldest step' in standing for Parliament in July 1828.

In contrast to this, Peel, who also saw the Clare election as a crossroads, was at this moment concerned with the effect it had on his own career: he was increasingly determined to resign, in order to go out amicably now, with his reputation for opposing Emancipation intact, and return as soon as a bill proposing Emancipation was passed. This of course would have left Wellington with the task of piloting the bill with all the implications of royal displeasure, while the integrity of Peel was carefully preserved.

Mrs Arbuthnot continued to chart the path of Wellington's progress – downward, as she saw it. By 9 October the Duke was no longer managing Ireland and the Catholic Question in a satisfactory fashion. 'I am afraid he has seemed not to take a sufficiently *Protestant* view of it.' In her opinion, he should have solved it by bolstering Protestant confidence. He should, for example, have recalled Lord Anglesey when he let his son and members of the Viceregal household go to Catholic Association meetings. Above all, Anglesey was guilty of the crime of being civil to Daniel O'Connell at the Viceregal court when the latter dared to wear – oh horrors! – his Liberator's medal, 'a harp *without a crown*'.

Wellington's practical plan of conciliation paid serious attention to the question of 'securities'. Effective administration rather than political clubs was the way to go. The Forty-shilling Freeholders would be raised to £5, thus eliminating a whole category of dissidents. There would be a grant from Parliament for the Catholic clergy, who were in turn to be licensed by the government. This would create a culture of dependency – on British, not foreign Papal authority. (There would be penalties for priests without licences.) Negotiations would be carried out for suspension of the oath which denounced Transubstantiation, and a possible substitute Oath of Allegiance. All of this was in essence practical, aimed at securing peace in Ireland, rather than taking into account religious feelings.

Unfortunately, King George IV showed no signs of relenting on the subject of Emancipation in the autumn, unlike his Prime Minister and – to a certain extent – his Home Secretary, Peel. It will be remembered that Catholic Emancipation was a subject which had been banned from being raised in Cabinet; that ban remained in force. The King's hyperactive mind was moving in quite a different direction. In a meeting with Wellington on 14 October, he wanted Lord Anglesey sacked for detailed offences including issuing proclamations without Privy Council authorization; he wanted the Ultra-Tory Lord Eldon made Lord President; above all he wanted to dissolve Parliament in order get in more Pro-Protestants – thus Anti-Catholics – at a new General Election.[19]

Wellington argued back against each one of these royal proposals as giving absolutely the wrong message at this particular time. He especially stressed 'the inconvenience and the evils' of an election. While Parliament continued to be so divided on the Catholic Question, it could not 'force Ireland to be tranquil'; an election would make things infinitely worse. The Duke issued the ominous words: 'There is no remedy for this state of things excepting by means of a consideration of the whole state of Ireland.' Sooner or later it would come to the same result, with or without a contest, 'after suffering the misery and distress and incurring great expense and running great risks'. Wellington ended by coolly apologizing: 'I am aware of the pain which I give your Majesty by stating these facts.'

A week later Charles Arbuthnot, who as Keeper of the Royal Parks and Gardens had court connections, told his wife that the King had been ill again and was 'frantic' about the Catholics. From his own point of view, George IV had a genuine grievance concerning Anglesey in Ireland; although the latter might argue that he was merely demonstrating that impartiality which he had promised in advance at his personal interview with the King. By November, Anglesey was being angrily described by the Ascendancy as 'a Papist' because of his perceived favour to the Catholics.[20]

The fact was that Anglesey, as an old soldier, was in a good position to assess the potential danger of Irish rebellion. He told the Cabinet shortly after the Clare election that neither the police nor the army in Ireland were truly dependable. There were even rumours of hostile intervention from the other side of the Atlantic. In August Maurice Fitzgerald, the Knight of Kerry, thought there might be an attempt to land arms. The Irish-American Bishop of Charleston, John England, was said to have organized a force of 40,000 men, headed by a general of Irish refugee descent, who would invade Ireland if Emancipation was not granted.[21] Orange and Catholic factions were apparently beginning to be formed within the ranks of the British Army. That old paradox was apparent again by which the so-called seditious Irish Catholic manhood formed a vital part of a Protestant regime's defence system.

In a letter to Peel of 23 September, copied by him to Wellington, Anglesey described the state of Ireland as 'alarming', with the continued assemblage of 'many thousands of persons, bearing flags, and moving by word of command' chiefly in Tipperary, Clare and Limerick. Peel agreed with Anglesey that a large disposable force – not less than three battalions and a regiment of cavalry or four battalions – should be kept within reach of Ireland 'on a very sudden call', with transport arrangements already in place.[22]

There had been an historic English disposition to believe in the hideous prospect of rebellion in Ireland. A few years earlier the poet Southey had been warned off visiting Limerick and its bishop by a friend, 'well informed of the state of things', who had told him: 'Pray do not think of going to Ireland. I would not insure any man's life for three months in that unhappy country. The populace are ready for rebellion and if their leaders should for their own purpose choose to have one, they have tomorrow a second edition of the Irish massacre.' As a true liberal, the Rev. Sydney Smith expressed his take on the situation in the *Edinburgh Review* in 1827: 'The moment the very name of Ireland is mentioned, the English seem to bid adieu to common feeling, common prudence and common sense'. In the House of Lords, as he denounced Canning's Bill for Catholic Relief, Lord Mansfield had voiced the perennial nightmare by which even seeming tranquillity was not to be trusted: the priests might advise their flocks to present for the time being a morbid and lethargic stillness, but always beware 'the serpent underneath'.[23]

This new official apprehension was quite different from that generic dread. Thirty years after the rising of the United Irishmen, wise observers like Anglesey were beginning to suggest that rebellion was an actual possibility. How close was Anglesey (and for that matter Southey's correspondent) to the truth? For the time being what mattered was not the truth, but what was believed to be true. The menacing last words of Richard Lalor Sheil at the triumphant banquet following O'Connell's victory at Ennis expressed the stuff of many Protestants' nightmares: instead of 'angry slaves', make of us Irish 'contented citizens' (by granting Emancipation); 'if you do not, tremble for the result.'

Was it actually possible that the angry slaves would turn on their masters, and if so, would it not now be better to take that action which would transform them into contented citizens? O'Connell himself in April had written to the Knight of Kerry about the results of the Burdett Catholic Relief Bill, not yet known: 'Believe me, there is an *underswell* in the Irish people which is more formidable than any sudden or *showy* exhibition of irritation. I have no doubt that if this present system is persevered in for 20 years, it will end in a separation brought about in blood and confiscation.'[24] Was O'Connell right? Were blood and confiscation – and separation – really moving nearer?

Meanwhile the jovial, confident Brunswickers in both countries stood for the enduring might of Anti-Catholicism in the higher echelons of society, thoroughly determined that the present system should prevail – not for twenty years but for ever.

CHAPTER FOURTEEN

Boot-and-Spur Work

*'How bootless then is this boot-and-spur work –
unless, indeed, pudding and beef be at the bottom
of the business – worthy motives, we grant,
for a ride to Penenden Heath.'*

The *Spectator*, autumn 1828

W HILE THE GREAT DUKE battled with the practicalities of
the Catholic Question, opposition took a highly visible form
on 24 October 1828. This was a huge protest meeting held at
Penenden Heath in Kent. There were those who saw shades of
the Gordon Riots nearly fifty years earlier and believed that the
spirit of Lord George Gordon had migrated into one of the leaders, the mesmerizing Lord Winchilsea. But there was a crucial
difference between the events of 1780 and those of 1828.

The eighteenth-century opponents of the modest Catholic
Relief agreed by Parliament had used flames and physical
destruction as their weapons of choice. In the third decade of
the nineteenth century, it was words not deeds. Dissenters and
Radicals were included. Furthermore, various Catholics were
present at what was essentially an Anti-Catholic meeting, and
the prominent Irish Catholic lawyer Richard Lalor Sheil, by dint

of purchasing a small landholding locally, was actually allowed to speak as a freeholder – if only for a short while. (But, as we shall see, Sheil had a solution to that.)[1]

Penenden Heath was a traditional place of assembly.[2] The name may have derived from the Saxon word 'to punish'. However, the heath had a somewhat mixed history as far as punishment was concerned. Wat Tyler had led a mob from there at the beginning of the Peasants' Revolt in 1381 and it was similarly used during Wyatt's Rebellion in the sixteenth century. On the other hand, public executions by hanging also took place on the heath, which included those suspected of being witches. More delightfully, Penenden Heath was the site of several early county cricket matches; in 1807 Kent 'punished' an All England XI, winning by 162 runs.*

The morning of 24 October was particularly fine and bright. Sheil quoted Goldsmith: the remnants of 'summer's lingering bloom' touched the immense and glorious prospect. Here was a long array of wagons moving slowly to the appointed place. Circumstances lent to Nature 'a sort of moral picturesque'. The rest of Sheil's description was understandably less approving. People sat in their wagons with 'a half-sturdy and half-fatuitous [sic] look of apathy' and in general appeared to be just about as dumb as the animals drawing the wagons. Placards bore the slogan 'Vote for Lord Winchilsea.'

The 10th Earl of Winchilsea was an Ultra-Tory whose style of oratory was quite as extreme as his political views – that is, verging on the apoplectic. A strong and open supporter of the Orange faction in the north, he was equally outspoken in his opposition to Catholic Relief of any description. He would be described later as addressing the House of Lords as though it were a mob on Penenden Heath; this was because, quite apart from presiding over it, his appearance there was certainly one of the pre-eminent features of the occasion.

Now in his mid-thirties, born plain George Finch-Hatton, he

---

* Penenden Heath is now a recreation ground on the outskirts of Maidstone.

had succeeded a cousin to the Winchilsea title two years earlier. As a landowner, he was noted for his method of dealing with poachers: they could either fight him or go directly to prison. Winchilsea's admirers called him a man of frank, kindly and generous character, but not wise. Tall and stout, his style was to leap about flourishing a white handkerchief as he first spoke, then shouted, finally roared – not for nothing had he been known in youth as 'Roaring Hatton' – and his last words were to call out 'God Save the King'. His 'bluff, rude and direct nautical bearing' reminded one observer of the quarterdeck, and left one to suppose that he might be the mate of a ship rather than a would-be counsellor to the Crown.

The *Spectator* had yawned in advance and disdained the idea of such a gathering. Why were people rushing to Kent? Why couldn't the same old Bill for Emancipation be passed yet again by the same old House of Commons only to be rejected yet again by the same old House of Lords? 'How bootless then is this boot-and-spur work – unless, indeed, pudding and beef be at the bottom of the business – worthy motives, we grant, for a ride to Penenden Heath.' It was true that there was a pudding-and-beef element to the crowds, as with any such mass meeting. But the speeches themselves were not by any means all rabble-rousing in the Winchilsea style.

Lord Camden, for example, who spoke in a very different, sonorous rather than booming, voice, condemned Catholic action, but he also condemned Protestant violence. Lord Darnley, who was Anglo-Irish, was hooted at for his origins: 'That there fellow is an Hirishman, Tim, put a potato down his damned Hirish jaw.' He was also told, as an absentee landlord, to get back to his estates.

Henry Roper-Curzon, 14th Lord Teynham, head of the ancient Roper family into which Sir Thomas More's daughter Margaret had married, possessed a Kentish property, Linsted Lodge: he was in favour of Emancipation but had abandoned the Catholic religion officially (thus he had been able to stand for Parliament in 1812). Unfortunately, when Teynham spoke he found his apostasy did not play well; there appeared to be a universal antipathy to a renegade and even the Brunswickers howled at him: 'That fellow's a going to shift his religion again!' and 'Oh my Lord, there's a man as says that what your Lordship's saying is all a damned Popish lie!' – reproaches from the Protestants which could be argued equally to be just or unjust.

When Mr Shea, an English Catholic gentleman, was called upon to speak by the sheriff, he made 'a bold and manly speech' despite the hootings of the Protestant party. But he did commit one fault, by the vociferous standards of the occasion: he dwelled too long on 'the pure blood of the English Catholics'. There was, however, a strong contemporary feeling that this pure blood of theirs should not stagnate quite so much in their veins and should circulate a little more rapidly. This at least was the judgement of the Irish Catholic Sheil. With their immense fortunes and a little more exertion, what might not these old English Catholics have accomplished? 'Excellent men in private life, they are not sufficiently ardent for politicians.' It was a verdict which expressed some of the truth – the social chasm between English and Irish Catholics – but not necessarily the whole truth.

When Sheil himself spoke, he was in effect brought down with 'a volley of execrations'. He was mocked for his slight stature and treated as a small, angry dog: 'How the little hanimal foams at the mouth! Take care of him, he'll bite for you! Off, Sheil, off!' Hardly any of his speech was actually heard while he 'stamped and fretted'. It was now that he smoothly got his revenge in what was a very advanced fashion for the time: he had already arranged for the whole text to be printed in the *Sun* newspaper that night. And a very fine speech it turned out to be, even if unheard, occupying three columns of text, and accompanied by rapturous if phantom applause.

Here were magniloquent references to Westminster Abbey, where heroes like Pitt, Burke and Fox were buried: 'If instead of counting votes in St Stephen's Chapel [the House of Commons] you were to count votes in the mausoleum beside it', the balance would be heavily in favour of those with the right to have the word *Emancipator* engraved on their tomb. 'Enter the aisles which contain the ashes of your greatest legislators, and ask yourselves as you pass how they felt and spoke.' Mrs Arbuthnot thoroughly disapproved of the speech being printed in the press in full, and in particular the way in which Sheil had thoughtfully interlarded his oratory in advance with satisfying words, not only *applause* but *cheers* and *immense cheering*.[3] All the same, once his speech had been recorded in the press, it could be argued that 'the little hanimal' had the last laugh even if he had had to copy it out himself.

Two Radicals, William Cobbett and Henry Hunt, both spoke. Cobbett was 'a rude and rough being' but there was a rigorous mind behind the rough countenance. Henry Hunt on the other hand had a melodious voice and a sweet, gentle aspect: he was known as 'the Gracchus of Manchester', an admiring sobriquet comparing him to the Gracchi, brothers and tribunes of the people who had attempted to redistribute land from the rich to the poor in second-century-BC Rome.

Methodists wore black and were easy to recognize from their 'lugubrious and dismal expression, even among many men in black'. It was true that Methodists were the most strongly Anti-Catholic among the Nonconformists.[4] Irish Methodists were known to speak at Brunswick Clubs, and there were Methodist preachers here. At Penenden Heath, however, Dr Jabez Bunting, a leading Methodist and one of the few who believed in Emancipation, deliberately chose to argue against the whole process of petitioning as a religious body.[5]

There was a great deal of the gross humour which goes down well at vast meetings. O'Connell, for example, was ridiculed for bending at the Clare election to receive the benediction of a bishop. As Sheil pointed out, that was 'hardly stranger' than for a duchess to print her beautiful lips on 'the black and bearded mouth of a coal heaver' – the reference was to the famous story of Georgiana Duchess of Devonshire exchanging a kiss for a vote for Charles James Fox at an election in 1784.* He might have pointed out further that a practising Catholic bowed down for a

---

* A butcher is normally ascribed the honour, rather than a coal heaver.

bishop to kiss his ring as a matter of course, which could hardly be said of duchesses and coal heavers.

The Anti-Catholic Petition which was the focus of this vast meeting – estimated by the Brunswickers to have been attended by at least 60,000 people – and was to be presented in Parliament, was acclaimed by all the Brunswickers.[6] They won the vote by a large majority. Now they all enthusiastically waved their hats in the air; parsons more soberly shook hands. Lord Winchilsea threw himself hither and thither, demonstrated 'almost insane exultation'. Just as the behaviour of Lord George Gordon had remained in the popular memory, it was his gyrating reincarnation as the Earl of Winchilsea that left the deepest impression fifty years later. Both men drew on the deep well of popular Anti-Catholicism in English (and Scottish) breasts. There were other meetings throughout the country, but this was undoubtedly the most outstanding.

All this enabled the Brunswickers to hail the occasion as a triumph for their cause. And yet the Catholics had secured an enormous amount of publicity in the press: not all of it unfavourable.[7] The best way to deal with the Roman Catholics might be to calm them with harmless concessions, rather than belay them and tear down their chapels in riots, however enjoyable a pastime – a commonsensical idea which was beginning to seep through. This relaxation – in some cases – of historical antipathy applied to Ireland as well as England.

In November the Anglo-Irish Whig Lord Duncannon wrote to Lord Grey of the situation in Ireland – he was in the habit of keeping him in touch – that there had been the 'most extraordinary alteration' among the 'lower orders' in the last eight months. 'They will think of nothing but this question, and the poorest person is now looking with the greatest anxiety to a settlement of it.' Wellington himself wrote to the Duke of Rutland at the beginning of December: 'matters are in a terrible state in Ireland and I think that quiet men begin to think that some effort ought to be made to settle the question'. On 28 December an Anglican Bishop, Charles Sumner of Winchester, wrote a memo to the Duke which took matters further:

there might be positive advantages to Emancipation – from the Protestant point of view. It was the 'jealousy of priests' which was actually preventing the spread of Protestantism. If Catholics were free to consider it, they would go for it: 'the Protestant religion would for the first time have fair play in Ireland' (although the power of the Forty-shilling Freeholders would have to be 'mortified').[8]

By now the quiet men of whom Wellington made mention included many in the Cabinet. But there were specific problems to be solved before further progress could be made, both linked to personalities. In the first place, the problem of the King, at this moment a King at war with his Viceroy, showed no signs of abating. In the second place, Robert Peel, while conceding the probable need for Emancipation, continued to hold to the view that he needed to resign from the Cabinet when it was brought before Parliament again.

In vain Wellington complained to the Viceroy, Anglesey, about the complication that his conciliatory attitude towards Catholics at the Viceregal court and elsewhere was causing for the real monarch of the real court in England. 'I cannot express to you adequately the extent of the difficulties which these and other occurrences in Ireland create in all discussions with his Majesty. He feels that in Ireland the public peace is violated every day with impunity by those whose duty it is to preserve it... [that] a formidable conspiracy exists.' How unfortunate under the circumstances that Anglesey had received O'Connell! Anglesey defended himself strongly; on the latter charge, O'Connell had asked for an audience and he had granted it. He had also told Peel, the Home Secretary, in advance.[9]

Then there was a question of Anglesey visiting Lord Cloncurry at Lyons House on his extensive estates in Kildare. Here was a leading Irish peer with a dubious record of involvement in the 1798 rebellion which had led to a period of imprisonment in the Tower of London; Cloncurry was known to favour Emancipation yet he had become one of Anglesey's informal counsellors. Once again Anglesey defended himself against the charges. First of all, he had stayed at Lyons House to attend the

Curragh Races – hardly a crime – and it was only there that he had learned of Cloncurry's back history of 'Jacobinism'. Even so, since Cloncurry had been liberated from the Tower without trial, surely Anglesey had the right to believe him 'without guilt'. None of this prevented the Duke from expostulating to Lord Bathurst: 'Lord Anglesey is gone mad. He is bit by a mad Papist; or instigated by love of popularity.'[10]

The King expressed equal indignation regarding his Viceroy. In a letter written by 'my own poor *enfeebled* hand', he described the latter's reaction to Wellington as 'nothing but a proud and pompous farrago of the most *outré* bombast, of eulogium upon himself'. If the Viceroy persisted in such conduct '*he must be removed by us* as shortly as possible'.[11] Finally things reached a pass where Anglesey's presence was clearly making a difficult situation – from the government's point of view – impossible.

On 24 December Wellington summoned the Cabinet and told them that relations between himself and Anglesey had reached a point of no return, and he informed the King the next day. He asked George IV to agree to the recall of Anglesey: 'no further time should be lost' in telling him he was to be removed, if the King agreed. The King did agree. Anglesey was to be recalled. Wellington wrote to him to that effect on 28 December. So far, so calm, at least on the surface. Real outrage against Anglesey, from government as well as King, followed, when first a private letter from Wellington to the leading Roman Catholic prelate in Ireland, and then the Viceroy's comment on this same letter, appeared in the press.

Dr Patrick Curtis, Primate of All Ireland, was now nearly ninety years old, a remarkable but still active link with the past, described as retaining 'episcopal vividness' even at his great age. He had been made Archbishop of Armagh by the Pope in 1819, but at the time of Wellington's peninsular campaigns Curtis had been Rector of the Irish College in Salamanca, where he was known as Don Patricio Cortés. In this capacity he had been able to supply Wellington with helpful intelligence. A British pension was granted to him after his return to Ireland. Such a connection was an example of Wellington's realistic approach to Roman

TOP: George IV in Sackville Street (now O'Connell Street), Dublin, amid cheering crowds, in August 1821. It was the first royal visit to Ireland since Richard II in 1399.

ABOVE, LEFT: Sydney Owenson Lady Morgan, the Protestant novelist, with a strong feeling for Irish nationalism; author of the bestseller *The Wild Irish Girl*, 1806.

ABOVE RIGHT: Richard Marquess Wellesley, elder brother of the Duke of Wellington, who married a Catholic as Viceroy of Ireland, in a ceremony performed by the Catholic Archbishop of Dublin to the disgust of George IV. His liberal sympathies for the Irish which resulted in great popularity, led to his eventual recall.

Daniel O'Connell in 1820 when he was forty-five; his dramatic appearance in his swirling cloak was an important part of his charisma.

Daniel O'Connell's house in Merrion Square, Dublin.

Holy Father
St Dominic
Immutable
Vicar of christ
Queen of Heaven
Power at loose
Keys of Heaven
Infallible
God on Earth
Power to bind
St Ursula
St Daniel
King of Kings
Keys of Hell

Maynooth   Stonyhurst
Jesuits   Dominicans
Dublin Lawyers - Apostates Priestcraft

'How to keep one's place.' British politicians, including Wellington, kneeling before the 'Holy Father' surrounded by saints, and offering him the crown; on the steps of the Pope's throne are significant Pro-Catholic words including Maynooth, Stonyhurst, Jesuits and Dublin Lawyers.

Brunswick Tom: Thomas 2nd Earl of Longford, a vigorous opponent of Emancipaton who founded the Irish Brunswick Club.

Bernard 12th Duke of Norfolk, a zealous Catholic. He was painted wearing his Parliamentary robes to celebrate the passing of the Act for Emancipation which enabled him as a Catholic to sit at last in the House of Lords.

Daniel O'Connell's statue erected in Ennis, Co. Clare, to mark his election for the British Parliament at the Clare by-election in the summer of 1828 (despite being a Catholic).

'The Field of Battersea': caricature of the duel fought there between the Duke of Wellington when Prime Minister, and the Marquess of Winchilsea, vociferous opponent of Emancipation, on 21 March 1829, shortly before the passing of the Act. The Duke reflects that he used to be a good shot but has been out of practice for years; Winchilsea decides to make himself small, fearing that if he is hit he may be tainted with some of Wellington's popery.

'The Battle of the Petitions'. Subtitled 'a Farce now performing with great applause at both Houses', 1829. Numerous petitions from the country, both Pro- and Anti-Catholic, were presented by MPs and peers to Parliament.

The Duke of Wellington is seen proffering a sickly John Bull with various objects including the Bill for Catholic Emancipation and Price List for Indulgences, a crucifix, rosary and a dagger, with Peel carrying the column put up to commemorate the alleged Papist origins of the Great Fire of 1666 and Eldon as a doctor. John Bull protests: 'I shall never be able to get this down – my Constitution is very much impaired…'.

'Leaving the House of Lords Through the Assembled Commons', 1829. Wellington gallops home triumphantly on leaving the House of Lords after a successful vote for Catholic Emancipation, while the mob yells, 'No popery – No Catholic ministers'.

Catholicism and the possible benefits it might offer. Certainly Curtis had shown himself conciliatory from the moment of his elevation. In a letter of thanks to the Foreign Secretary, Castlereagh, he promised to do his best to work for peace between the English and the Irish, and urged love and respect for 'our august Sovereign' George IV.[12]

On 4 December 1828 he wrote Wellington a long letter which began by apologizing – he had resolved never to intrude on His Grace's precious time and important occupations again, even to congratulate him on becoming Prime Minister, but the present situation necessitated it. There was general talk that the Catholic Question would be finally settled in the next session of Parliament, and at the same time there would be 'something in the shape of a Concordatum' concerning the Church in Ireland. Many of his own bishops and clergy, knowing of their previous connection, had urged their Primate to make contact: but he was in fact doing this privately.[13]

Archbishop Curtis proceeded to suggest a way of dealing with the ever-vexed question of 'securities'. In short, let Irish Catholic bishops and clergy be elected in the usual way, then 'approved and appreciated' by the Pope. At this point the new bishop would appear before a commission or a personage specially appointed by the government to present his credentials. After a certain number of days, the commission would either declare itself satisfied – or if not, then 'such bishop shall never obtain possession of, or govern, the diocese for which he was nominated, nor any other in Ireland'. The Archbishop believed that the Pope and all the bishops and clergy would 'cheerfully' acquiesce; the government would get the same or greater security than with the previously suggested Veto. Finally, Curtis pointed out that this was exactly what had been done in his own case, and at his own request, when Wellington had 'kindly condescended to take so active a part' in his own appointment in 1819.

Wellington responded on 11 December with a much shorter letter. But it contained a crucial declaration in the opening sentence. 'I am sincerely anxious to witness a settlement of the Roman Catholic question.' By 'benefiting the State', such a settlement 'would confer a benefit upon every individual belonging to it'. He did add: 'But I confess I see no prospect of such a settlement.' Wellington referred to the Party being mixed up with considerations of the question to such a degree, violence pervading every discussion, that it could not be considered dispassionately. 'If we could bury it in oblivion for a short time', then perhaps the manifold difficulties on all sides could be overcome.[14]

Oblivion did not seem a very likely prospect at the end of 1828, especially when the letter arrived in Ireland via the Irish postal service. It was stated by Curtis himself that before it reached him, the contents were already public knowledge, the letter having been surreptitiously opened, thanks to the fact that it had evidently been franked by the Duke himself: this alerted everyone to its importance.*[15] Consequently he felt obliged to show the Duke's letter to a few chosen friends, in defence of both Wellington and himself, lest the multitude fabricate 'some foolish and perhaps mischievous nonsense of their own'. Fortunately, continued the Archbishop smoothly, the contents could not fail to charm all parties: 'a consoling proof of your Grace's generous, upright and impartial benevolence' which he had long been endeavouring to impress on people's minds.[16]

Curtis went on to say that these friends, Protestants as well as Catholics, hailed Wellington's 'noble declaration' concerning the settlement of the Catholic Question with joy and gratitude. More flattery followed. But the real substance of his letter concerned Wellington's unique ability to effect the change: the bare intimation of the Duke's 'serious will' to remove Catholic disadvantages would cause the difficulties to 'fly and sink into nought'. In a few days' time all the opponents of Emancipation would think no more of the concessions than they did of the concessions lately made to the Dissenters. 'For they are not half so angry as they pretend to be, in order by that bugbear to gain their point.' In short, any delay would not only be intolerable in its own right,

---

* It was suggested by Anglesey's biographer, his great-great grandson, that this letter-opening ought not to have surprised anyone conversant with the ways of the Irish post office at that date.

but worsen the situation; all agreed on the impossibility of 'burying this matter in oblivion', even for a short time.

Living as he did in a buzzing hive of political rumour, Viceroy Anglesey wanted to see Wellington's 'noble declaration', now being circulated among Curtis's friends of both religions, for himself. It was, after all, written by the British Prime Minister to an Irish Archbishop even if it was confidential. Curtis sent him the original. At this point Anglesey is supposed to have exclaimed that he hoped, he was inclined to think, that it looked good for the cause. This reaction was natural enough. His next step was more controversial. He decided to follow suit, as it were, and enable the publication of a letter of his own.[17] It could be argued that Wellington and Curtis between them had already forfeited the right to privacy, the one by writing and the other by circulating an extremely important statement without the knowledge of the King's Lord Lieutenant in Ireland.

Anglesey wrote back to the Archbishop on 23 December, saying that he had not previously known the Duke's precise sentiments on the Catholic Question. While he differed over the issue of 'oblivion' for a short while, he nevertheless urged that the Duke should be 'propitiated' in every way, all obstacles avoided, all personal and offensive insinuations suppressed, and ample allowance made for the difficulties of his situation. Let Parliament decide, and let the opposers of Emancipation be disarmed by 'the patient forbearance' as well as the 'unwearied perseverance' of its advocates.

Wellington's letter to Curtis of 11 December appeared slightly inaccurately in *The Times* – with a reference to 'the' settlement of the question, not 'a' settlement – on 26 December. Wellington noted curtly in a letter to the Archbishop on the same day: 'As Dr Curtis thought proper to publish this letter, though without the Duke's permission, he might as well have published an accurate copy of it.' The Archbishop responded with a long, hurt letter, denying that he had authorized publication, but admitting that he had permitted gentlemen to read it and even copy it with the express condition it would not be published. Their failure to observe this condition Curtis put down to the impossibility of keeping silent on such an issue: 'so great was the general wish to know your Grace's intentions'.

In contrast, Anglesey's subsequent letter of commentary, with its revelation about the Duke's new attitude to Emancipation, was printed in the *Dublin Evening Post* on 1 January 1829 by his own deliberate arrangement. He explained his reasons to his brother: 'It was to pacify the public mind that I consented to its being put forth.' He cited the meeting of the Catholic Association to be held the next day, when the most violent resolutions would have been adopted. 'The whole Country would have been in a blaze.'[18] On the other hand, '*I* could not address the public. *I* could not communicate with the Association.'

Horrified, the Home Secretary, Peel, ordered the Viceroy, already under notice, to quit his post immediately. Under the circumstances, it is certainly easy to understand the reaction of the sixty-five-year-old Earl Bathurst, long-time member of the government, an amiable but not brilliant Tory in the opinion of Greville. He was contacted in vain to fill the vacant position of Viceroy in Ireland: 'My dear Duke,' he replied. 'Nothing could induce me to go there as Lord-Lieutenant.'

The appointment went to the Duke of Northumberland, whose liberality as Ambassador Extraordinary to the Coronation of Charles X of France in 1825 had stunned the European nobility and boded well for Viceregal splendour. Mrs Arbuthnot was inclined to dismiss this Duke: she called him stupid and 'posing', although she had to admit he was rich as Croesus, with a wife covered in diamonds, and (no doubt for those reasons) very good-humoured and popular. Greville was even more dismissive: Northumberland was a very good sort of man, but with 'a narrow understanding, an eternal talker and a prodigious bore'. Greville believed, however, that the diamond-decked Duchess actually ruled her husband.[19]

Northumberland's stance on Catholic Emancipation was suitable enough for this particular tricky moment. He had voted against it, but in his letter of acceptance to the Duke confessed that 'I shall rejoice to see a settlement of this question originating with your Grace, as Prime Minister, in the House of Lords.' The

Duke of Wellington for his part begged the Duke of Northumberland to appoint the nephew by marriage of the King's beloved Lady Conyngham as an ADC. He added, with just a hint of a threat: he was anxious that Northumberland should not have the disadvantage of having declined the King's request, 'considering to what family belongs [he] for whom it is asked'.[20] The truth was that this was a trivial subject on which George IV could be easily pleased, compared to the far greater matters which lay ahead.

The departure of the Marquess of Anglesey on 19 January 1829 provided a dramatic illustration of the mindset of Irish society on what was, or was not, the eve of Emancipation. A witty Irishwoman spoke for many when, according to *The Times*, she exclaimed to the departing Viceroy: 'For God's sake don't make yourself so much beloved by us all: do something unpopular, that you may be left here a little longer.' That night Anglesey's wife Charlotte wrote of 'Such a mixture of wretchedness and *exultation* as I did not conceive possible.' [21]

At noon on a brilliantly sunny day, the Marquess left the Castle, wearing the Star of the Order of the Garter (granted by his sovereign). He passed between crowds of thousands on his way to that port which had been renamed Kingstown seven years earlier. Spectators wore black crêpe in their hats, and black crêpe hung from the windows. As Charlotte put it: 'To see you *torn* from a populace, from a Nation which perfectly adored you, and for no fault but that of having won their hearts!' The three Anglesey sons, William, Arthur and George Paget, were with their father. Charlotte's Irish maid, 'walking amongst the lower orders', reported that there was much sympathetic murmuring on this subject: 'There he goes with those dear Children who are as brave as himself – look at them riding in such a throng.'

On the one hand, Anglesey's ploy of publication had succeeded: the Catholic Association passed comparatively pacific resolutions the next day, and expressed themselves fortunate to have such an enlightened Lord Lieutenant. On the other hand, this Lord Lieutenant had been taken from them by the orders of the King – carried out by the government in London.

CHAPTER FIFTEEN

From RPeel to Repeal

'Oh! Member for Oxford, you shuffle and wheel
You have altered your name from RPeel to Repeal.'

Rhyme, February 1829

O<small>N</small> 12 JANUARY 1829, a week before Anglesey's tragic, tearful and triumphant departure from Ireland, the Home Secretary, Robert Peel, wrote a long letter to Wellington. He told him that if his resignation would be an 'insuperable obstacle' to Emancipation, he would stay.[1]

The body of the letter was reluctant if not outright mournful, and stressed Peel's personal desire to retire all over again – 'the single step which I can take that is at all satisfactory to my own feelings' – but the gist of it came at the end and was quite brief. As Prime Minister, 'you shall command every service that I can render in any capacity'. This reversal of his long-held determination has been described by Peel's biographer as 'one of the crucial decisions of his life'.[2] Peel attached a memo on the Catholic Question which could be laid before the King.

This came after the Archbishop of Canterbury and two of his fellow bishops had indicated to the Prime Minister that the attitude of the Church of England towards Catholic Emancipation,

symbolized by their persistently hostile voting in the House of
Lords, had not changed. The Archbishop of Canterbury, William
Howley, formerly Bishop of London, had succeeded Archbishop
Charles Manners-Sutton the previous July. The latter (father of
the Anti-Catholic Tory politician of the same name) had opposed
all concessions to the Roman Catholics, although he was more
liberal-minded towards Protestant Dissenters. Archbishop
Howley continued the tradition.

In late December 1828, Wellington complained to Mrs
Arbuthnot that he had been five hours 'with the Bishops' yesterday, and would be eight hours with them today on his excursion
to Windsor: 'really too much for any man'. Yet the gulf between
them had not been bridged: basically, the leaders of the Church
of England still believed that involving the Crown with the
administration of the Catholic Church (for example by paying
the clergy following Emancipation) 'would revive the old Cry of
Popery and Arbitrary Power'.[3] Wellington, however, considered
that was just where the danger lay: *from* Popery and Arbitrary
Power – a danger which Emancipation on certain conditions
would subvert.

With the King and the Church of England tacitly against him,
Wellington faced a couple of formidable foes. As Lord Holland
commented to Anglesey, the trouble was that the King was by
now far from cordial with his Prime Minister. Holland emphasized the royal feeling of rivalry which was no doubt rooted in
the original military triumphs of the Great Duke: the King disliked Wellington's power, 'and yet more his love of display of it'.
In practical terms, therefore – those terms which always mattered
so much to the Great Duke – Peel's support was what he most
needed at this moment, if any kind of peaceful settlement was
to be achieved. As Wellington told Peel in reply to his letter, 'I
tell you fairly that I do not see the smallest chance of getting the
better of those difficulties if you should not continue in office.'[4]
Above all it was essential that Peel should still be speaking for
the government in the House of Commons where the Duke, as a
peer, had no voice.

Wellington duly passed Peel's memo on to the King on 14

January, and the next day the King interviewed all those members of the Cabinet hitherto pledged against Emancipation. In the end King George, with reluctance, agreed to consider the whole question of Ireland. That of course meant the Abominable Catholic Question, in the disgusted phrase of the Anglican clergyman the previous year (with which the King would have undoubtedly agreed). But, ominously, the sovereign still reserved his right to reject the advice of his Cabinet – even if it was unanimous.

A fortnight later he was still asking Wellington questions which were a mixture of aggression and apparent bewilderment. On being told that Catholics were to be excluded from judicial offices connected with the Protestant Church, he was surprised that Catholics would be eligible for any judicial offices such as a Judge of the King's Bench. Then, on the question of limiting the number of Catholic MPs, he exclaimed: 'Damn it, do you really mean to let them into Parliament?', as though the reality of it had yet to strike him.[5]

Peel's record of opposing Emancipation was both long-held and publicly held. His own conservatism on the subject, coupled with an attachment to the Church of England, was a profound element in his character from early days. His voting record in the House of Commons conveyed a continued abhorrence of further Catholic Relief. Less than two years ago, he had been among the Cabinet ministers who resigned from the government when Canning took over from Liverpool: the issue was explicitly Emancipation. The previous August, Peel had first of all made it clear to Wellington that his own views on the subject were not 'materially changed', before admitting that some kind of settlement might be the lesser of two evils, given the 'most unsatisfactory' state of Ireland. But he had ended by stating his determination to resign from government in that case, at least while legislation went through; otherwise he would be seen to betray his own beliefs.

What had brought about the change? In one interview with Peel, the King had sulkily asked him why he, the King, was being asked to forgo his principles, while Peel was allowed to maintain his (by resigning so as not to be contaminated). It was not an unreasonable question; but in fact a sense of shame does not seem to have acted on Peel. Was it, then, the obvious political advantage of remaining with the Duke at this vital moment, when his support might well make the difference in bringing about Emancipation or not? If so, Peel would not be the first or last honourable politician to trim his sails to the prevailing wind – in order to stay with the fleet and possibly one day lead it.

Many years later, in his memoirs, published six years after his death, Peel rebutted the charge of political ambition. It was the welfare of the two nations which had concerned him and he swore, as he would swear in the presence of Almighty God, 'I was swayed by no fear except of public calamity.'[6] As for ambition, the immediate consequences to him were not exactly advantageous. It was notable, however, that this firm disavowal was followed by just a hint of something else: 'It may be that I was unconsciously influenced by motives less perfectly pure and disinterested – by the secret satisfaction of being

> ...when the waves went high,
> A daring pilot in extremity.'

Peel was quoting from Dryden's *Absalom and Achitophel*. Significantly, a British politician, making a study of Peel at the beginning of the twenty-first century, drew attention to the passage with the comment: 'The motives of politicians are neither more nor less straightforward than those of other human beings... mixed up in a genuine conversion was Peel's belief in Peel.'[7]

Certainly Peel's claim was justified that the immediate consequences to him were not advantageous: he would need all his self-belief in the next few months. That Ultra-Tory the Duke of Newcastle spoke for many when he recorded in his diary on 4 February: 'The whole affair seems to be of the blackest and most disgusting nature.' As for Peel personally, aristocratic disdain wrinkled its nose yet again: 'this cotton Spinner is a degraded wretch'.[8] Two notorious criminals, Burke and Hare, were tried for sixteen killings and Burke was executed at the end of January, their crime being to provide corpses for dissection by an Edinburgh doctor. The well-publicized trial and execution gave the caricaturists ample opportunity to make the comparison between the convicted murderers and Wellington and Peel, killers of the constitution.

The trouble for Peel began at once. It was the matter of his highly 'Anglican' constituency. Having begun his political career in 1809 with an Irish seat sponsored by Wellington (then Sir Arthur Wellesley), Peel had represented Oxford University in Parliament since 1817. His constituents were by definition Oxford graduates, many of whom were Anglican clergymen. Peel now wrote to the Dean of Christ Church (his old college) to tell him that he intended to bring in a bill in favour of Emancipation and offering his resignation if it was required. This would mean a by-election.

Peel duly resigned his seat on 20 February and, with some reluctance, did agree to be renominated for the same seat, instead of taking what would have been the easier if less courageous course: he could have simply shifted to a safe seat elsewhere. The campaign was bitter. This was, after all, a university where Convocation had just voted to stand against Emancipation.

A young undergraduate called William Ewart Gladstone was at Christ Church at the time, having arrived from Eton the year before. Still a Tory (he would strongly oppose Parliamentary Reform a few years later), he reported on Convocation to his brother and found the text of the regular Anti-Catholic Petition against further Relief for this year 'very gentle and moderate'.[9] Gladstone suggested that because the Petition was all in Latin, it might have saved the Roman Catholics many a hard word. *Peto! Peto!* [I demand! I demand!], cried great numbers of the Convocation. The Anti-Catholic Petition needed to be presented. Ironically enough, it was Peel himself, the new convert to the other side, who was actually asked to do so, since he was still the MP for the University.

Matters were not helped when, after a period of confusion during which Peel's intentions were not quite clear, Sir Robert Inglis stood against him: another Christ Church man but of a very different political conviction on this subject (not only was he an Ultra-Tory but he was also believed to have Evangelical tendencies).[10] The feelings of the Duke of Newcastle on the subject of Peel's treachery were expressed in Oxford more succinctly by a sign hammered out in iron nails on a prominent Christ Church door, by a group of offended Christ Church men: NO PEEL.*

The Earl of Ellenborough, on the other hand, a minister in the government, spoke for many of Peel's supporters when he exclaimed against the whole university world: 'God forgive me if I am wrong, but from what I saw of them at Cambridge, the persons I least respect are Fellows of Colleges, and I believe the Oxonians are even less liberal than the people of Cambridge.' At least Peel had shown himself '*a great man* by his equanimity in all that has taken place'.

In a sense Ellenborough was unfair to the university world: it was the clergymen who reacted angrily against Peel the traitor. Although many dons voted for him, the country clergymen who flocked in to register their indignation against him made sure that he was convincingly defeated: by 755 votes to 609. (The seventy-nine votes cast at Christ Church for Inglis could have won him the election.)

What happened next was that Sir Manasseh Lopes, a Sephardic Jew turned Christian, with a huge fortune based on Jamaican sugar, came to the rescue. Lopes, now in his seventies, had a back history of parliamentary involvement which included a spell in prison for electoral bribery. Despite this, he was currently both the Member for and patron of the Westbury pocket borough in Wiltshire, having bought it himself. Immediately he abandoned his seat. Peel was nominated hastily before another candidate could appear and the election took place. There were, however, defiant protests from the locals, which took the form of missiles, one of which hit Lopes himself, and broken windows in his own house. In the streets there were menacing demands, with threatening calls for silver coins in exchange for support.

Part of this honourable-dishonourable affair was the price

* Still to be seen opposite the Hall Staircase, off Tom Quad, in Christ Church: visible relic of a politician's change of mind.

to be paid for Lopes's compliance, which was a peerage: his price, that is. It was said he had already chosen the title of Lord Roborough, although the wits naturally pretended he would be Lord Rottenborough. The eventual payment was not a peerage for Lopes, but a consulate at Pernambuco for his nephew for which Peel paid, backing away – ungratefully, it can be argued – from the peerage that Lopes so much desired. (Peel certainly did not show gratitude when he reflected privately, 'what a torment this Jew is'.)

February in government was occupied by a process which a popular rhyme of the time, emphasizing Peel's change of heart, crudely designated:

> Oh! Member for Oxford, you shuffle and wheel
> You have altered your name from RPeel to Repeal.[11]

According to John Hobhouse in his diary, the Whig MPs had a subtler if more irritating way of commenting on the conversion: they could not help smiling openly at hearing from his mouth those arguments which he had so often opposed. But George 'Derry' Dawson, Peel's brother-in-law, whose Londonderry speech had aroused such a mixture of horror and anticipation in August, called it 'the happiest event that could be found recorded in the pages of Irish history for a long period' and prophesied the dawn of Irish prosperity after the long night of misery and wretchedness.[12]

The subject of the wheeling and shuffling was the detail of 'Repeal': the actual bill, and of course the vexed question of 'securities'. The measure had been officially announced in the House of Lords in the King's speech on 5 February. There was a reference to his Majesty's 'continued solicitude about the State of Ireland', before the request that the Houses of Parliament should review the laws which impose 'civil disabilities on his Majesty's Roman Catholic subjects'.[13]

Reaction was instantaneous. Many Tories, especially the grandees, expressed indignation at having been kept in ignorance: the Duke of Rutland announced his intention of retreating to Belvoir Castle and not voting; the Duke of Beaufort 'did not like what he heard', according to Greville. In the House of Commons,

Sir Robert Inglis – the Member for Ripon who would shortly displace Peel at Oxford – invoked 'the protestation of Protestantism' now at the feet of the Roman Catholics; he suggested offensively that his Majesty's ministers had yielded to the double intimidation of 'the Clare people', who were some of the lowest of the low in the south of Ireland, and the Dublin lawyers.

When Peel got to his feet on 10 February to justify his 'conversion', he talked on the contrary of Emancipation as being in the 'true interests of the British empire'. He was, he said, 'looking back to the past, and forward to the future'. He emphasized that his great object was to maintain the Protestant interest as inviolable. Peel had not abandoned his opinions but he had changed his cause; and he contended that he had a right to do so when he considered the critical state of the country.[14]

In an earlier period, it has been seen that the notion of 'securities' had troubled the English Catholic Church itself, leading to internal divisions. Exactly what control, if any, should the Crown be allowed over the Catholic Church in the United Kingdom in return for Emancipation? The old English Catholic aristocracy believed in some kind of compromise (of the sort that had long allowed them to lead their lives in peace while discreetly practising their religion), while many of the Catholic clergy, prominent among them Bishop John Milner, had explicitly denounced any kind of Veto on Catholic appointments. In consequence Milner had been thrown off the Catholic Board, to which he responded that if he was unfit for their company on earth, he hoped that God could make him fit for their company in Heaven.[15] But Milner was dead. There were of course many positions in between the two extremes, held by members of the Catholic community, rapidly increasing as it was with Irish immigration.

Quite early on in this new process, the Cabinet had abandoned the whole question of 'securities': this might be seen as a remarkable turnaround, given the long-drawn-out arguments on the subject, but it was in fact a testimony to the essentially pragmatic nature of the whole process. It was decided that the imposition of 'securities' would give the opposite message to the desired one of reconciliation. The same was felt about restricting by law the number of Catholic MPs. Catholics were explicitly barred from certain offices, that of the Lord Chancellor among them. The exclusion of Forty-shilling Freeholders from the Irish voting system, on the other hand, was a real concession to the indignant Irish landed gentry who were still attempting to cause trouble. The bar for voters was now lifted to ten pounds.

Would Daniel O'Connell be prepared to do the deal in return for Emancipation (which he of course saw as leading to the end of the hated Union)? It was ironic that at this point the more moderate people in Dublin were said to be furious with O'Connell for his publicly abusive language: 'violence, bad taste and scurrility' had made him lose the brilliance of his former promise. O'Connell might be lacking lustre these days by some fastidious standards, but Greville commented: 'There is no getting over the fact that it is he who has brought matters to this conclusion.' Part of this process was his canny ability to mix violent language – never violent conduct – with negotiation.[16]

On the same day, 10 February, in the House of Lords, the Earl of Longford, founder of the Irish Brunswick Club, specifically denounced Peel's biased view of Irish tranquillity, or rather the lack of it. Ireland was fine. Any trouble was entirely due to the Catholic Association, aided by 'deluded dupes and factious fools' (the final meeting was in fact two days later).[17] Brunswick Tom – referred to with dignity if not approval as 'my noble relative' by Wellington in his reply – grew increasingly heated. He admitted that he might have been betrayed into 'no ordinary warmth of expression', but there had been nothing equal to it since the Revocation of the Edict of Nantes. (In 1685 Louis XIV had removed that freedom granted to the Huguenots by Henry IV to practise their own religion; it led to persecution followed by widespread emigration.) It was an odd comparison since the Revocation removed a liberty and Catholic Emancipation granted it.*

---

* It is one of the pleasing ironies of history that a younger son of Brunswick Tom, Charles Reginald, became a (Catholic) Passionist priest known as Paul Mary Pakenham in 1851, after first serving in the army under his uncle the Duke of Wellington.

In fact, the Catholic Association dissolved itself on 12 February. Sheil, in moving the motion for dissolution which was carried, referred to it as 'prompt and voluntary'. The Association, to which so much was owed, did not allow itself to be extinguished by others. It was a brilliant move, suggested by the Whigs but part of the pragmatic attitude now being taken by O'Connell and the leading Irish Catholics. Maybe there had to be sacrifices to secure success. After all, things were undoubtedly going their way. Lady Morgan was at a party in Dublin three days later, composed of what she called the *débris* of the Ascendancy faction: 'the Orange ladies all looked *blue* and their husbands tried to look green'.[18]

This wheeling and shuffling was complicated by the need to consult the King, mainly at Windsor. That process again was bedevilled by the return of his brother the Duke of Cumberland on 14 February, to come to the aid of the 'Great Cause', as he had vowed to do in August. Wellington did his best to stop the Prince by appealing to his sense of duty: a royal duke should not be the leader of a violent party. The delicate question of the succession, which could never be totally absent from a hereditary system, featured once again. Wellington also hinted at what was certainly obvious to any student of the current Royal Family: two sixty-year-old men without legitimate children and a little girl were all that currently stood between Ernest and the throne; under certain tragic circumstances, if Providence so disposed, Cumberland might find himself in 'a most elevated situation' – in which case he would need to be 'the impartial arbiter of destinies' rather than allied to any particular party.

A letter to this effect was despatched via Sir William Knighton, travelling incognito. In a black comedy of errors, Ernest had already set out for England, sending his own letter to Knighton in London commanding '*good fires*' to be lit in his rooms. Ernest's letter also expressed anxiety about his brother's prodigious use of laudanum – something which, incidentally, was already causing serious concern to Knighton on the spot: this might lead to palsy and eventually death.[19] (And what use would a palsied King be in supporting the Great Cause?) The two men, Knighton and the

Duke of Cumberland, crossed in their journeys and Cumberland duly arrived unhindered. Once at the side of his royal brother at Windsor, he fulminated.

In vain, Wellington invited him to dine and put the points encased in the letter that had missed him. A few days later, Cumberland took his fulmination to the House of Lords.[20] The question he put to their lordships – and he emphasized that it was indeed the enormous question they now had to face – was whether 'this country was to be a Protestant country with a Protestant government, or a Roman Catholic country with a Roman Catholic government'. Compared to such blanket extremism from a royal prince, Lord Plunket's spirited suggestion from the other side seemed positively mild: he attempted to rechristen the Brunswick Clubs the 'Titus Oates Clubs' after the Anti-Popish villain, so that they should not be associated with the throne.

The next debate involving Cumberland followed in the House of Lords on 23 February and was subsequently known as 'The Night of the Three Princes';[21] it followed rather a different course. The Duke of Cumberland found himself opposed by his more liberal brothers, William Duke of Clarence and Augustus Duke of Sussex. It was Clarence who spoke the most telling words: 'He could not help suspecting that his illustrious relative had been so long abroad that he had almost forgotten what was due to the freedom of debate in this country.'

All the while Anti-Catholic Petitions came flooding into Parliament. There were lighter moments, seen from the perspective of history. Lord Eldon declared that he had a peculiar problem as he presented a Petition against any further concessions to the Catholics: it had been signed by a great many ladies. But let it be understood that there was no precedent for excluding ladies from their lordships' House. This led to some badinage with Lord King, who favoured Emancipation. Eldon suggested that many women had more knowledge of the constitution and more common sense than descendants of Chancellors (like Lord King). To this the latter replied with heavy-handed humour that he was sure the sentiments presented in the Petition were those of 'the old women of England'.[22]

The theme also emerged later in the Commons at the intervention of a London MP, Alderman Robert Waithman, a Welsh linen draper by origin, now in his sixties with a reputation for supporting Parliamentary Reform (he had also opposed the French wars and the horror of Peterloo). Despite these radical views, he complained that a new and extraordinary doctrine was being broached: an Hon. Member had suggested that even if a few children signed the Petition they had a right to do so, 'and women also'. Now Mr Waithman was as ready as any man to admit that women were very well in their proper place (Hansard recorded 'a laugh'), but he did not think they were in their proper place when they came forward to petition Parliament. If, however, they insisted, let them come forward in their proper 'profession'; he added meaningfully that these were 'ladies of a certain description', indicating what was sometimes known as the world's oldest profession.[23]

The true drama came at the end of February and it centred on the King, the King and his oath. On 25 February Wellington saw the King at Windsor and heard that he was not intending to agree to Emancipation after all. The Duke therefore arranged to return two days later, at which point he would announce in Parliament either that the King approved, or that his Majesty intended to dismiss his government. It was a brutal choice. On 27 February therefore Wellington had another long interview with the King, at which point he faced him with the alternatives again. It was incidentally the moment at which Peel was being defeated at Oxford. On Sunday, 1 March Lord Chancellor Lyndhurst was at Windsor. He went on from Windsor to the Duke's house at Stratfield Saye in Hampshire, where at 3 a.m. he had the Prime Minister woken to receive news of the continuing crisis.

On 4 March, on the eve of the presentation of the bill in the House of Commons, Wellington gave the King an ultimatum. Wildly, George IV talked of abdication with his Prime Minister, Peel and Lyndhurst in a session lasting nearly six hours. The King drank brandy and water throughout while he insisted that the Coronation Oath was sacred. The message was clear. He, the King, could not agree to this bill.

At which point all three ministers declared that they would resign. Peel (who had been returned as an MP on 3 March) would tell the House of Commons the next day that the King's servants were prevented from carrying out a measure which had already been announced in Parliament.

It was a hideously painful scene. Here was a manifestly ill man, talking wildly of abdication – but not necessarily meaning it or indeed meaning anything that he said. On the one hand he deserved sympathy in his obvious suffering. On the other, this sick man had the theoretical ability to dismiss his government; while his most intimate adviser, his brother Ernest, was urging him on in exactly the opposite direction of his government.

There was to be no beating about the bush by the ministers. The consequences of the King's decision were outlined to him. The King indicated that he understood. He said farewell, according to his usual custom, with a double kiss. George then assured his brother Ernest that he had not given way at any point.

What was to be done? The Duke of Wellington talked to the powerful Sir William Knighton, who murmured that the King was ill, and suggested tactfully that the Duke went to see Lady Conyngham. Fearing to find his Majesty already there, pouring out his troubles to his mistress, Wellington departed instead. By ten o'clock that night he was at a Cabinet dinner at the house of Lord Bathurst in London.

At Windsor, however, all was not lost. It was Knighton and both Conynghams who emerged as discreet heroes. They went to see the hysterical King, there was the added calming element of a good dinner, and finally they persuaded him that no other ministry was possible: the idea of summoning another government was a fantasy. Visibly distressed, the King wrote giving his agreement in a note to the Duke: 'My dear Friend. As I find the country would be left without an administration, I have decided to yield my opinion to *that* which is considered by the Cabinet to be the immediate interests of the country. Under the circumstances you have my consent to proceed as you propose with the measure.' The poignant phrase was in the last sentence: 'God knows what *pain* it costs me to write these words. G.R.'[24]

Wellington received the letter on his return from the Cabinet dinner and immediately sent it on to Peel at his house in Whitehall Gardens. Peel's reaction was wary. Let the King write *Approved* upon Wellington's letter of 2 March. So Wellington got to work again at midnight. The result was another letter to the King, who for once was woken early to receive it. Still in bed, the King wrote to assure Wellington that he had put the right construction on his own reply. He had indeed agreed to the Bill for Roman Catholic Relief.

It was now 5 March, the day on which the bill was to be presented in the Commons. Robert Peel, whose conversion had sparked off the last stage of the struggle, would be able to address the House of Commons once more as its Leader. The wearer of the crown had not in the end gone against the will of his government: Emancipation was proposed in the King's speech.

CHAPTER SIXTEEN

The Duel

*'Well, what do you think of a gentleman
who has been fighting a duel?'*

The Duke of Wellington to Mrs Arbuthnot,
March 1829

Robert Peel's speech to the House of Commons, in
which he intended to explain the absolute necessity of Catholic Emancipation, began at 7.30 in the evening on 5 March.[1]
It lasted for nearly five hours. Peel's opening sentence was as
dramatic as anything else, given what had been happening: 'I
rise as a Minister of the King and sustained by the just authority
which belongs to that character, to vindicate the advice given to
his Majesty by a united Cabinet.' Then he added: 'I yield to a
moral necessity I cannot control', before passing on to the crucial
statement: 'According to my heart and conscience, I believe that
the time is come when less danger is to be apprehended to the
general interests of the empire, and to the spiritual and temporal
welfare of the Protestant establishment in attempting to adjust
the Catholic Question, than in allowing it to remain any longer
in its present state.'

Like the King, Peel demanded sympathy for the pain he was

enduring. There was a quotation from Peel's favourite, Dryden, in *The Hind and the Panther*, which referred to the suffering involved in a change of mind:

> 'Tis said, with ease – but oh! how hardly tried
> By haughty souls to human honour tied –
> Oh! sharp convulsive pangs of agonising pride!

Peel then explained why there would be no Veto or 'securities': 'we willingly relinquish a "security" from which no real benefit will arise, but which might, after what has passed, detract from the grace and favour of the measure of relief'. Greville for one believed that these same pangs of agonizing pride led to the making of the best speech Peel ever delivered, and Mrs Arbuthnot recorded a generally similar view. On the other side it was probably a compliment that Sir Robert Inglis, now MP for Oxford University in Peel's place, thought it so bad that his previous constituents would be appalled. John Hobhouse wrote that 'it was difficult to believe our senses, and this was the Protestant champion'. As Lord Sefton commented to Hobhouse, 'My God! did you ever hear anything like that? There he goes, bowling them down, one after another.'[2]

Peel ended his bowling by quoting Livy in Latin to this effect: 'I would indeed like to please you but I much prefer to make you safe whatever your feelings towards me may be in the future.' Then he added: 'Sir, I will hope for the best. God grant that the moral storm may be appeased – that the turbid waters of strife may be settled and composed – and that, having found their just level, they may be mingled with equal flow in one clear and equal stream.'

The cheers in the House of Commons were heard as far as Westminster Hall. Greville reflected: if only the University of Oxford had been there! It was said that Peel's old father, Sir Robert Peel the first Baronet – who died the following year – had his speech read to him and declared: 'Robin's the lad after all.'[3] At last it seemed possible that the answer to that question the King had put to Wellington six weeks earlier – 'By God, do you mean to let them into Parliament?' – was 'Yes'. But of course, at the very end it would not be Wellington and his government who would let the Roman Catholics into Parliament: it was the monarch when he gave the Royal Assent. There had already been one short-lived hysterical scene over the inclusion of Emancipation in the King's speech; it might be a prelude to something more obdurate. In this context the continuing presence of the Duke of Cumberland made for danger.

The Catholic Relief Bill was given its first reading in the House of Commons on 10 March and the second reading was moved on 17 March. The date was of course St Patrick's Day, increasingly marked by celebration in England, as the Irish community swelled with immigration. Daniel O'Connell was in London but, as he told his wife Mary, he had not yet decided the timing of taking his seat in Parliament. He did, however, survive a challenge in the shape of a Petition to the House by four Co. Clare Freeholders, calling for his deselection; their argument was that there had been intimidation by the Catholic clergy. The Petition was dismissed and he was duly declared elected.

In spite of this, in spite of his earlier public victory in Co. Clare, there remained a huge question mark over O'Connell's actual admission to the House of Commons; it concerned the oath that he would take on entry. One of John Croker's correspondents in Dublin described him as being 'in a paroxysm of fear now that the hour approaches for performing the *Fee-faw-fum* of the Irish political giant at the bar of the House'. This derision did O'Connell less than justice, although Henry Hunt, the Radical MP, with less savagery, also believed he should try to take his seat. But the bill was not yet law, and any MP entering Parliament now was still faced with an effectively Anti-Catholic oath which O'Connell had always sworn he would never take, 'for [all] the wealth of the world'.[4] It was understandable that he wished to reserve himself for the symbolic moment of entry until the dreaded oath was amended.

On the eve of the introduction of the bill, Daniel O'Connell had written to Mary: 'tomorrow is the awful day, *big with the fate of Cato and Rome*', and, having quoted Joseph Addison's tragedy *Cato* (which American patriots such as George

Washington also loved), mocked himself: 'you see, my love, how poetic I am grown'.[5] Two days later he greeted the detailed Emancipation Bill as a 'great and glorious triumph' with no Veto and no ecclesiastical payments.

The additional bills to prevent the extension of the Jesuits and other monastic orders, and the 'bad, very bad' bill to raise the freehold qualifications, would hopefully be countered. In fact, the history of the Society of Jesus during this period was extremely complicated. In short, it had been suppressed by the Pope in 1773 in the brief *Dominus ac Redemptor*; nevertheless, there were Jesuits in England with their headquarters in Liège, where the Prince showed them an indulgent attitude. The Pope caused the restoration of the Society at the end of his captivity in 1814 at the hands of Napoleon; by 1829 there were reckoned to be over a hundred Jesuits in England, and, quite apart from Stonyhurst in Lancashire, even a small day school for boys in Norton Street (now Bolsover Street), near Regent's Park.

O'Connell was similarly optimistic to the Provincial of the Franciscan Fathers in Cork: the bill, on the subject of Catholic Orders, was 'insolent' and 'inexcusable' but unworkable in practice.[6] In short, he advised the Catholics to be quiet for the time being and remember there would soon be fellow Catholic MPs in Parliament, working on their behalf.

The Irishmen in London on St Patrick's Day made merry. In St Giles district (to the east of modern Oxford Street), long held to be the haunt of vagrants, O'Connell encountered hundreds of his elated compatriots with large shamrocks in their hats. 'God bless you, Counsellor!' they shouted, and a new cry was heard: 'Huzza for the Juke of Willington!'[7] This was at a moment when the Tory press were hissing with fury over the Duke's behaviour, coupled with that of Peel. In the genial spirit of the day, another Irishman had a helpful suggestion: 'By my soul, we are all terribly dry with shouting. I wish the Counsellor would open his heart and give us our Patrick's Pot.'* The Catholic grandees, however,

---

* In other words a drink, referring to a story told about St Patrick in a pub.

were less welcoming to their Irish co-religionist. On 6 March O'Connell complained to his wife that this time the Duke of Norfolk had not yet entertained him, and nor had any of the leading English Catholics: 'We have been invited only by the rich mercantile men' (which included 'rich Jews in the City').[8]

The debate on the second reading of the bill was marked by 'a rabid rant' from the Attorney-General. Sir Charles Wetherell accused Peel and Lyndhurst, the Lord Chancellor, in language that even Lord Lowther, who shared his views, thought too extreme to be effective. Many believed him to be drunk. Others commented on the vulgarity and coarse buffoonery of his speech. The frenzied gestures with which Wetherell accompanied his words were so great that his braces broke, and his breeches began to descend. This inspired a *bon mot* which Greville attributed to the Speaker: the only 'lucid interval' Wetherell had was that between his waistcoat and his breeches.[9]

Charles Wetherell was dismissed from the government on 22 March. So far the Duke of Wellington had pursued a conciliatory policy towards his colleagues, including Wetherell, who voted against the bill. He did not wish to be obliged to take in Whigs in favour of Emancipation to fill their places. Wetherell for his part had refused to resign his post, despite his strong feelings against Emancipation, in order, as he told his friends, to throw the onus of dismissing him on the government. Now Charles Wetherell's furious pomposity (including the entertainment provided by his breaking braces) was from any point of view hard to ignore. What this demonstrated, along with other similarly themed speeches from Ultra-Tories, was that while compromise was the new spirit of Wellington, the spirit of Anti-Popery remained deep, not only in the hearts of those designated the 'lowest orders', but in fact among those designated their governors.

Such tirades were not limited to the House of Commons. In the Lords, 'Roaring Hatton', in other words the Earl of Winchilsea, the hero of Penenden Heath to his followers, continued to harangue sympathetic fellow Brunswickers in his familiar style. The Anti-Catholic newspaper *John Bull* had printed one of his own rants in mid-February: 'Let the voice of Protestantism be heard from one end of the Empire to the other. Let the sound of it echo from hill to hill, and vale to vale. Let the tables of the Houses of Parliament groan under the weight of your Petitions; and let your Prayers reach the foot of the Throne.'[10] Part of his appeal, or otherwise, was of course the voice, that bellow which Mrs Arbuthnot declared she could hear right outside in the lobbies – less appropriate, as she pointed out, in the House of Lords than on Penenden Heath.

When Lord Winchilsea decided to make his views known in other ways, trouble, real trouble ensued. The story of Emancipation had begun with the bloodshed in the Gordon Riots. For a moment it looked as if the blood shed fifty-odd years later might be that of the Prime Minister. The duel which the Duke of Wellington was currently having with the forces of reaction – including the King – found a grim echo on 21 March. And the challenge to a duel actually came from the Duke of Wellington, not the Earl of Winchilsea.[11]

On 16 March a letter appeared in the *Standard* from Lord Winchilsea announcing that he was cancelling his subscription of £50 a year (nearly £4,000 today) to the newly founded King's College, London. This was because of the part that the Duke of Wellington had played in its foundation. It was the Duke who had been present at the opening meeting in June the previous year, flanked by archbishops and bishops, to reaffirm the place of religious teaching in education (unlike University College, then called London University, in 'Godless Gower St'). Winchilsea proceeded to accuse the Duke, in print, of an evil long-term plan to attack the constitution of 1688. He was using King's College as a stealthy way 'under the cloak of some outward zeal for the Protestant religion, [to] carry on his insidious designs, for the infringement of our liberties, and the introduction of Popery into every department of the State'.

Wellington twice demanded apologies for accusations which attributed shocking motives to him in promoting the inauguration of the College. Unabashed, Lord Winchilsea refused, unless the Duke made a public statement declaring that he had not been contemplating Catholic Emancipation in June 1828. This time it was Wellington who strongly and absolutely refused. He would not be called to account by Winchilsea. If it was a battlefield, the Iron Duke did not intend to be defeated on it.

Wellington's message, written at six-thirty in the evening, was unequivocal. It began: 'Since the insult, unprovoked on my part, and not denied by your Lordship, I have done everything in my power to induce your Lordship to make me reparation – but in vain ... Is a gentleman who happens to be the King's minister to submit to be insulted by any gentleman who thinks proper to attribute to him disgraceful or criminal motives for his conduct as an individual?' He went on: 'I cannot doubt of the decision which I ought to make on this question. Your Lordship is alone responsible for the consequences.' A formal challenge followed: 'I now call upon your Lordship to give me that satisfaction for your conduct which a gentleman has a right to require, and which a gentleman never refuses to give.'[12]

Sir Henry Hardinge, a Cabinet minister, was instructed as his second and Lord Falmouth, an Ultra-Tory colleague, would act for Winchilsea. The duel would take place very early the following morning, Saturday, 21 March. Battersea Fields was the site chosen. As it happens, much of the detail of this dramatic event is preserved in a report written that day by the doctor co-opted on behalf of the Duchess of Wellington. Dr John Hume bears witness to his complete astonishment when the 'persons of rank and consequence' he was summoned to attend turned out to be the Prime Minister and an opponent. Wellington said in 'a laughing manner, "Well, I dare say you little expected it was I who wanted you to be here."' Dr Hume could only agree. Wellington repeated the phrase of his challenge: he had no alternative. They then encountered Lords Winchilsea and Falmouth. Formal attempts were made by the anxious seconds to acquire suitable apologies which would have aborted the duel. It was too late.

Hardinge explained what was going to happen. Since he only had one hand – a war injury – Hume helped him to load Wellington's pistol. An instant's pause: then, according to custom, he spoke the words: 'Gentlemen, are you ready? *Fire!*'

In Dr Hume's version, Wellington 'presented '(raised) his pistol immediately, but seeing that Winchilsea did not do the same, hesitated for a moment 'and then fired without effect'. It emerged subsequently that he actually grazed his opponent's trouser leg with his shot. Winchilsea, according to Hume, did not present his pistol at all; but, once Wellington had fired, raised it and with deliberation 'holding his pistol perpendicularly over his head', fired into the air. It was over. Or so it seemed.

It turned out that Winchilsea had written a letter in advance which he handed to Lord Falmouth. He had also assured his second that he would not fire upon the Duke. Hardinge now demanded a total apology for the material Winchilsea had caused to be printed. Falmouth duly produced a letter of apology: it contained what Falmouth declared to be an admission that Winchilsea had been in the wrong. He had 'unadvisedly published an opinion' which had given offence to the Duke, and now offered to have this expression of 'regret' published in the *Standard*.

The crisis was not quite over. The Duke said in a low voice to Hardinge: 'This won't do; it is no apology.' It was true that the actual word 'apology' appeared nowhere, only regret being expressed. A brief nit-picking argument about actual wording now took place between the seconds, still at the scene of the duel; it was concluded only when Lord Falmouth took a pencil and inserted in the middle of Winchilsea's declaration for publication: '*(in apology) I regret...*'. Finally the Duke was able to depart, arriving to her complete astonishment at Mrs Arbuthnot's house while she was having breakfast. 'Well, what do you think of it, a gentleman who has been fighting a duel?' he said breezily on entry.

Dr Hume ended his detailed account of the affair with a positive paean of praise for the behaviour of Wellington: how the triumphant victor of Europe – 'fixing the boundaries of kingdoms and controlling by his single word the destinies of the world' – had shown himself 'calm, modest, unassuming, yet dignified, resolute and firm etc. etc.'. Hume even spared a word for Winchilsea, who had received the Duke's fire without betraying any emotion, but, as he raised his own pistol to fire into the air, seemed to have a faint smile, as if to say: 'Now, you see, I am not quite so bad as you thought me.'

The question remains: did the Great Duke really have no alternative but to fight a duel? He was nearly sixty (Winchilsea was still in his thirties). He was involved in negotiations for a crucial process in which his own participation was absolutely vital. Perhaps Dr Hume's lyrical praise of Wellington the victorious contained the key: Wellington had recently been obliged to curb all his aggressive instincts in the interests of compromise and welfare and had done so with admirable public equanimity. Now, for an instant, he let himself go.

It is interesting that Wellington did not gain the admiration of the world for his behaviour, personally courageous as it might be. Greville had the cynical reaction that the reprobate Winchilsea had made an ass of himself and positively wanted to be sent to the Tower. Mrs Arbuthnot loyally defended Wellington: if he had not fought, such insults would have been repeated all over again. But she admitted that it was the fashion to say that he should not have fought. He should have treated Lord Winchilsea with contempt, since the Duke's reputation for courage was 'too well-established to render such a measure necessary'.[13]

One person, however, who did tell the Duke that he was quite right to fight was the King. The Duke reported on his visit when he dined with the Arbuthnots on his return from Windsor. Harriet's account of the Duke's behaviour on that occasion does suggest rather touchingly a brief human moment in the life of the great military man (which might have turned to disaster but didn't, largely due to the behaviour of Winchilsea, who was a nightmare but a gentlemanly nightmare). The Duke was 'in high spirits and seemed rather pleased at having had a fight', noted Harriet.

In all other ways the King was very far from giving his approval to Wellington at this time. The crisis of his potential refusal had not gone away and would not go away until he had formally given the Royal Assent. The third reading of the Emancipation Bill took place in the House of Commons on 30 March. It was passed by a majority of 178. There were more Ultra speeches, but the bill was now on its way to the House of Lords. A majority there was theoretically more doubtful: the presence of Anglican bishops, who were against Emancipation, in the House signified danger. One of them, Charles Sumner of Winchester, did pledge support for Catholic Relief, but the Archbishop of Canterbury remained set against it.

Wellington moved the first reading on 31 March, and despite protests from the Ultras succeeded in establishing the second reading for 2 April. The debate lasted for three days, in the course of which Ultra speeches came from peers such as Lord Winchilsea's second, Lord Falmouth. On the other hand, there was a 'magnificent' speech in favour of Emancipation from the Whig Lord Grey and another from the Irish lawyer William Lord Plunket, recently ennobled and Chief Justice of the Common Pleas, previously that Whig MP who had spoken up for Irish interests after the death of Henry Grattan. It was notable that the steps of the throne were 'half covered with ladies', bearing witness to the continued passionate interest of 'the fair sex' in the political crisis.

John Cam Hobhouse for one was struck by Wellington's performance as a speaker – subject to much criticism in the past. The Duke spoke slowly but without hesitation and virtually without notes. 'The most striking part of his speech was when he alluded to his own experience of the horrors of civil war, and said he would willingly lay down his life to avoid one month of it.' The effect of this statement on his audience was visible: this was not so much the boasting of an orator but the sincere testimony of 'a great soldier'.[14]

Here Hobhouse had surely pointed to one of the strongest weapons in the duel for and against Emancipation: the reputation of the Iron Duke, who had within living memory controlled the destinies of the world, in his doctor's emotional description. The historian Macaulay, still in his twenties at the time (he was elected an MP the following year), was fond of repeating the story told to him by Lord Clarendon.[15] Asked on what terms the Iron Duke would recommend the Catholic Relief Bill to the peers, Lord Clarendon replied: 'Oh! it will be easy enough. He'll say: "My Lords! Attention! Right about face! March."' It was not quite like that; it was his reputation, not his martial manner, which secured him their agreement. But one symbolized the other.

The happy result was a majority for the government of 105. Part of this success was the defection of the bishops from the hostile side: ten of them voted for the bill. As the MP Charles Williams Wynn reflected on 7 April, 'at length we have a prospect of release from the Catholic Question'.[16]

The result at the end of the third reading on 10 April was roughly similar – and similarly joyous for the government. Daniel O'Connell wrote lyrically to Mary the next day: 'the ascendancy and superiority which neighbours had over you will be at an end the day you receive this letter'.[17] He had predicted to her a few days earlier that the bill would go through the following week and he would then arrange to take his seat; in short, Parliament would have to face what had changed. The Duke of Wellington came up to Lord Duncannon as the final vote was announced, and said cheerfully: 'Well, I said I would do it, and I have done it handsomely, have I not?' All that remained was to secure the Royal Assent.

But while the mood at Westminster was happily positive from the Catholic point of view, the atmosphere at Windsor was very different. As the Duke had told Mrs Arbuthnot's husband Charles in March, 'Nobody knows the difficulties I have in dealing with my Royal master, and nobody knows him as well as I do.' But he added firmly: 'I will succeed but I am as in a field of Battle, and I must fight it out my way.' When the results of the vote were known, the King exclaimed histrionically: 'Oh, the Duke of Wellington is King of England, O'Connell is King of Ireland, and I suppose I am only considered Dean of Windsor.' He also, even more histrionically, fancied himself as another persecuted (and subsequently executed) monarch, Louis XVI.[18]

The King's state of mind now becomes of vital importance: how much had it been affected either by the recent controversy over Emancipation or by the very different effect of his declining health – or a combination of the two? It was generally believed by those in the know that at this stage the King never heard or thought of Catholic Emancipation without being 'disturbed' by it.[19] It was as early as January, after all, that Lord Mount Charles, the son of Lady Conyngham, had told Greville that

he really thought that the King would go mad on the Catholic
Question. Mount Charles detected the influence of two men who
were dead, his father and his brother the Duke of York, and the
all-too-living Duke of Cumberland. On the subject of George III,
the present King was explicit if melodramatic: 'his Father would
have laid his head on the block rather than yield' to the demand
for Emancipation: 'he is equally ready to lay his there in the same
cause'.[20]

There is little doubt that George IV's growing obsession with
his father and the latter's fatal – in Catholic terms – rejection
of Emancipation at the time of the Union lay at the foundation
of his agitation. This was a very different mentality from that
of the young Prince who had favoured the Whigs, contracted a
marriage with a Catholic in the comely shape of Mrs Fitzherbert,
and welcomed Catholic refugees from the French Revolution.
But there were significant physical factors as well: Knighton's
concern over the royal use of laudanum, combined with a vast
intake of alcohol, was shared by many people. Not only did the
alcohol lead to extreme irritability, but occasionally there were
days of total stupor. In December the previous year Greville had
predicted the King would not last more than another two years.
It was a possibility that could never be overlooked.

In the meantime, Mrs Arbuthnot referred to the King's infant-
ile behaviour, the word 'child' constantly reoccurring. There were
his notorious fantasies, as when, incredibly, he lectured the Duke
of Wellington on his, the King's, own courage on the field of
Waterloo. (It was less than thirteen years ago; could George IV
seriously have imagined that he was present?) At the opening
of Parliament in 1824 the King had been described by Lord
Colchester as having the crown pressing heavily on his brow. The
point remained, five years later, that the crown was still pressing
on his brow and no other; the question of his right to refuse the
Royal Assent remained.

Of course, the very childishness and the fantasies made it
difficult to assess what action the King would actually take. He
had after all caved in quickly at the beginning of March when
Wellington and his government threatened resignation, together

with that sad note about the pain it caused him to do so. Now he had to decide – if decision was the right word. Any decision was a negative one in that he had to decide to refuse the Royal Assent to a measure passed in both Houses of Parliament and presented to him by his Prime Minister with full agreement of his Cabinet. Three days before the fatal moment, it transpired later, he told his surgeon that he was going to refuse.[21]

The oath sworn by George III in 1761, and repeated by his son in 1821, referred to 'the Protestant reformed religion established by law'; both Kings had promised to maintain and preserve inviolably 'the settlement of the united Church of England and Ireland' and 'the doctrine, worship, discipline and government thereof', as well as the rights and privileges of the bishops and clergy. But this bald statement of what was actually sworn ignores the indefinable but potent Anti-Papist tradition of history in which somehow the King's oath had got mixed up with the whole legality of the Hanoverian succession.

The mind of George IV, muddled by those two enemies of clear thinking, drugs and alcohol, with in this case the third destructive force of his increasing age, fixed on the oath as a sacred trust. His conscience forbade him to assent to the bill. At the same time Mrs Arbuthnot rudely commented about the King: 'everybody knows that he has no more conscience than the chair he sits on'.[22] But, like most scornful dismissals, this went too far. The King *did* have a conscience. Whatever the stories of his conduct, growing ever wilder – that he had personally ridden the winning horse at Goodwood, and won battles such as Salamanca as well as Waterloo itself – that did not exclude the possibility of genuine torments over a principle. He could still hear the voice of conscience in his ear, even if it was a wayward voice by any normal standard. The real question concerned his rights under the constitution to listen to it – and then insist that the awkward counsel of this delicate or zany royal conscience prevail, by blocking the bill.

Would the King then actually refuse to sign at the last moment, and if so what were the rights of the government in contrast? There have been constitutional critics of Wellington who have suggested that the inordinate attention he paid to the King's personal view was unnecessary at the time; that it was in some way old-fashioned. On one occasion, the military Duke was certainly sharp enough on the subject of the Duke of Cumberland, busy organizing Petitions and a march of 20,000 men on Windsor, to present them to their sovereign. Wellington exploded that if he did so, he would send the royal Duke to the Tower of London: 'One can never be safe with such an intriguing villain,' he commented.[23]

More sensibly, Wellington suggested to Cumberland that the best course would be to leave his proxy vote against the bill with the notoriously Anti-Catholic Earl of Eldon and go abroad. The implication was that he should spend more time with his family. Some of this campaign to get Cumberland to leave for the Continent – on the part of others, rather than Wellington – had the grimy tinge that press stories about royalty have had from time to time down the ages. There had always been those prurient rumours that Cumberland had fathered the illegitimate child of his sister Princess Sophia. Now the newspapers in favour of Emancipation such as *The Times* revelled in them.

Wellington's more dignified approach, suggesting a strategic retreat, laid itself open to a reproof from Cumberland, however: such a retreat would be 'unmanly and unworthy'. What would Wellington himself have said on the eve of the Battle of Waterloo if 'any General officer had come to your Grace and said: he had business which required him to go to his family?' Cumberland had his own histrionic moment when he declared: 'I would rather lay my head on the scaffold, feeling that I die in a good cause, than lead a life with shame and disgrace at the end of it.'[24] It must be remembered, in extenuation, that these references by the royal brothers to execution were made only thirty-odd years after the death of a monarch at the hands of his people; Louis XVI's fate was not remote history.

Once again, to be fair to the Duke of Cumberland, not only was his wife ill, but his beloved son was also very unwell. His letter implored the Duchess's understanding: 'Ach, God, how I wish I could [return]. I am, alas, the *only* one of the Royal Family except the King who is *Protestant*, faithful in this holy cause, if I quit all is finished... you know your Ernest, you know that he adores you, that he adores his child as no father could.' It was 'the feeling of *Duty*' which kept him from their side.[25] So the Duke remained. He presented over two hundred Petitions to the King in person and 150 to the House of Lords. His speeches emphasized that he opposed a breach in the constitution, not the Roman Catholics as such.

The Duke of Cumberland related in his memoirs how he had written a long letter to his brother begging him not to sanction the bill.[26] The King wept, but did not have the resolution to do that which in Cumberland's opinion would have taught Wellington that he would not submit to his 'overbearing and dictatorial manner'. It would also have immortalized him and secured the affection of his subjects. The eloquent letter was not enough.

Just as the short but extraordinary crisis of early March had been survived by the government, the King did actually give his assent on 13 April, for all his threats to the contrary. The Duke of Wellington prudently decided not to go down to Windsor personally to secure the royal signature lest his presence cause further upsets: 'that there should be no fresh discussion between them'. The sight of King Arthur might have incited King George to a further metaphorical duel.

Under the circumstances, then, George IV duly gave his assent. In doing so, he pointed out once again that he had 'never *before*' affixed his name 'with pain or regret' to any act of the legislature.[27] None of this altered the fact that the sovereign of the United Kingdom had assented to a bill to which he was thoroughly and openly opposed.

As a postscript, it was either delightful or depressing, according to the point of view of the observer, to find that King George IV soon took to calling the Act for Roman Catholic Relief 'his measure'. He was fond of saying that he always knew he should carry it at a canter; the Duke, however, was '*very nervous*!!'[28]

CHAPTER SEVENTEEN

Tale of Two MPs

*'Either to do me justice or to show themselves
the greatest rascals in existence'*

Daniel O'Connell, April 1829

'THE FIRST DAY OF FREEDOM!': this was how Daniel O'Connell headed one letter on 14 April 1829, the day after Catholic Emancipation became law in Britain and Ireland. Shortly before that, O'Connell had informed his wife that once the bill got the Royal Assent, he would proceed with what he called his experiment and arrange to take his seat. 'So as to compel *them* either to do me justice or to show themselves the greatest rascals in existence.'[1] As we have seen, O'Connell, an Irish Roman Catholic, had been duly elected for Co. Clare nine months earlier. The first Roman Catholic MP to be elected *after* the passage of the Act was, aptly enough, the English Earl of Surrey, son and heir of the 12th Duke of Norfolk. Their experiences were to be very different.

In the meantime, the reactions to the first day of freedom, and the giddy days which followed, were characteristically mixed, as reactions to Emancipation had always been. In the House of Lords it was no longer relevant that the Dukes of Cumberland

and Wellington demonstrably did not speak to each other: the royal Duke had lost out to King Arthur. At Windsor the situation was different. Lady Conyngham was frankly alarmed at the prospect of having the Duke of Cumberland there for so long. Even if the King's behaviour was in general rather more bearable since he had given the Royal Assent – Wellington, for example, found him not so much bad-tempered as cold – the Duke of Cumberland continued to make trouble. Sir William Knighton reported that the whole household was in awe of His Royal Highness. As for Lady Conyngham, the King was very much upset by the fact that she could not get on with Ernest, his favourite brother.

Duke Ernest did not in fact return to the Continent, but took up residence in his house in Kew. Rumours continued to swill round about his private life; there was the matter of a scandalous affair with Dolly Lyndhurst, the handsome if 'under-bred' wife of the Lord Chancellor, for example. His troublemaking did not cease. George IV himself was reported as saying: 'there never was a father well with his son, or husband with his wife, or lover with his mistress, or a friend with his friend, that he did not try to make mischief between them'.[2] So HRH the Duke of Cumberland continued to use his seat in the House of Lords in the future to denounce reforms with his usual vitriolic energy.

Elsewhere, congratulations were heaped upon the Prime Minister; only Lord Falmouth, recently Winchilsea's second in that potentially game-changing duel, stood by himself, 'sad and sombre'. For some it was difficult to take in. 'By God, it seems like a dream!', as his neighbour exclaimed to John Cam Hobhouse MP, as they sat as spectators in the Lords. From the opposite point of view, Brunswick Tom, Earl of Longford, wrote to his sister Bess: 'This morning the Popish bill passed by a very great majority.' He added that he would be truly happy to find he was mistaken in his views. He was not aware that Daniel O'Connell had told Mary on 11 April that the Ascendancy and superiority which her neighbours had over her would end the day she received his letter.[3]

Maria Edgeworth reflected that the Duke of Wellington must now be a happy man as well as a great one: he had after all prevented a civil war and saved both England and Ireland. As for Tom Moore, he came up with a characteristically original response: 'I started suddenly, after a few minutes reverie, from my chair and taking a stride across the room as if to make trial of a pair of emancipated legs, exclaimed: "Thank God! I may now, if I like turn Protestant!"'[4]

Not everyone rejoiced at the prospect of this freedom for themselves and others. The Duchess of Richmond had stuffed rats under a glass cover on her dinner table, pointedly awarded the names of Peel and Wellington. Lord Kenyon's maiden aunt thought the Duke of Wellington deserved hanging. The Duchess of Rutland was so horrified by it that she took to her bed, 'prostrate with alarm about Bloody Mary, Guy Faux and the Duke of Norfolk' in that order.[5]

The first instinct of Bernard, Duke of Norfolk, had in fact been the reverse of lethal: it was placatory, the historic attitude of the old English Catholics which had enabled them to survive. He left a note for the Duke of Wellington on 22 April, asking whether it would be right for the English Catholics to present an address to the King thanking him. Wellington's response was terse. They were trying to *efface* distinctions on the grounds of religion, not publicize them.[6] Imagine the opening: 'The Roman Catholics approach your Majesty for the last time as a body distinct from the rest of your subjects!' The answer was: 'No'.

So the Duke of Norfolk's actual lethal behaviour consisted of giving a banquet to celebrate. On 18 April, five days after the passing of the bill, he took his seat in the House of Lords, with Lord Dormer and Lord Clifford, the first Catholics to do so since the reign of Charles II. There were in fact only eight Catholic peers available – one duke, one earl and six barons – whereas 200 years earlier there had been at least twenty-two. The rest of the titles had one way or another slipped out of Catholic hands.

Lords Stafford, Stourton and Petre followed on 1 May, all bearing ancient Catholic names, part of a long recusant history; the ancestor of Lord Stafford had been executed in 1680 for his (fictitious) part in the so-called Popish Plot. William Stourton, who had escaped the threat of the French Revolution, had become the 18th Lord Stourton. He had then taken an interest in the poor of both countries, England and Ireland, publishing pamphlets on the subject. In particular he criticized the absenteeism of the Irish landlords; this led to a lack of public provision for the distressed, whose plight they were happily able to ignore from afar.

Now Stourton was able to take his seat in the united nation's Parliament, 'having, first, at the table, taken and subscribed the oath appointed to be taken by the Act of the present Session by Peers professing the Roman Catholic Religion'.[7] It so happened that Lord Clifford was extremely tall, as was another Catholic peer, Lord Arundell of Wardour, a kinsman of the Duke of Norfolk. 'What a pity we have so long excluded from our deliberations such a fine-looking set of men!' was the reaction of one lady spectator.

The personal background of Henry Howard, Earl of Surrey, the first English Catholic MP to be elected, was chequered, despite his high position in the peerage as direct heir to the premier Duke: his parents had divorced when he was four and he himself was married to an heiress whose powerful mother was suspected of bending him towards Protestantism. But Greville described him on his election to Brooks's Club as 'plain, unaffected, reasonable and good-natured', just what was needed now, under the circumstances which provided a combination of ancient privilege with a new opportunity.[8] He too was a handsome, upstanding man with many court connections, and would later hold distinguished offices in the Royal Household.

In the future, as Duke of Norfolk, he would acquire a satirical Marie Antoinette-and-the-cake reputation for advising the poor who could not afford bread to try curry instead (thus his nickname, Old Pepper and Potatoes).[9] He also became a nominal Protestant, although turning to the Catholic Church for the Last Sacraments at his death. For now he was returned for his father's borough of Horsham in Sussex, not far from Arundel Castle, on 4 May, the sitting Member retiring in his favour. His speech to his constituents was the very opposite of revolutionary. Surrey insisted that his patriotism was undiminished by his upbringing in 'a religion in some trifling respects different to you'. He hoped that both Catholics and Protestants would vie with each other 'in showing an attachment to the King and in maintaining the church as established by law'.

The Catholic *Orthodox Journal* dismissed the speech as 'cant'; it certainly displayed a diplomatic indifference to recent struggles. There was a public meeting at the London Tavern to congratulate him, and on 6 May he took the new oath which was the prelude to taking his seat; the hateful declarations against Transubstantiation, adoration of the Virgin Mary and the 'superstitious and idolatrous' Mass of the Church of Rome were no longer demanded. Six other Catholic MPs were elected for the House during this period. Like the peers, their names were resonant of Catholic history: Philip Henry Howard, Edward Petre, Henry Stafford Jerningham and Robert Throckmorton. Surrey, however, was the first person 'confessedly of his Communion' to do so since the Penal Laws. As Hansard commented, Lord Surrey MP was 'warmly greeted by many of his friends' in the House of Commons.[10]

In contrast to that was the chilly reaction to Daniel O'Connell given by the Cisalpine Club of the old English Catholics. A proposal to elect him was made by Charles Langdale, seconded by Thomas Stonor. O'Connell was blackballed. Although members resigned as a result, it was plain that even now Catholic Ireland was seen as a millstone round English necks; the phrase was that of Lord Petre in the previous century, a man who even then had been considered worthy to entertain George III magnificently at his house, Thorndon Hall. The Cisalpine Club was in fact soon changed into the Emancipation Club, and as such lasted fifteen years; worldly compromise to secure tolerance was no longer a necessary object of contemplation. The whole incident provoked a dry response from O'Connell. He described himself as having been '*black-beaned*', adding, 'but it was a strange thing of them to do; it was a comical "testimonial" of my services in emancipating them. It would be well, perhaps, if I could *unemancipate* some of them.'[11]

Daniel O'Connell made his long-awaited entry to the

Commons at the Bar of the packed House on 15 May.[12] The expectation of his appearance to take his seat under the provisions of the Roman Catholic Relief Bill 'occasioned a strong sensation'. The Gallery and the 'avenues' of the House were crowded, for there was a complication: a grotesque complication which did no credit to the government. Advantage was taken of the fact that O'Connell had technically been elected at a time when the old oath was valid, to demand that he took this previous oath instead of the new one (as sworn, for example, by Lord Surrey).

At five o'clock the Speaker of the House ritually asked if there were any new MPs. O'Connell rose from his seat under the Gallery and went to the table of the House, conducted according to custom by two sitting MPs, Lords Ebrington and Duncannon. *The Times* wrote afterwards of 'the silent, almost breathless attention with which he was received'. O'Connell already had his qualification papers and a certificate saying that he had taken the preliminary oaths. The Clerk of the House examined them and found them correct. At which point he produced a copy of the original oath,* as well as a copy of the New Testament. It was now that the Speaker formally told him of the situation concerning the oath he needed to swear. O'Connell bowed to the Speaker but showed no signs of moving.

For a few moments O'Connell said nothing but simply gazed back in silence. He then announced that as a Catholic he could not take this oath, although he would willingly take any new oath required. When this was formally reported to the Speaker, he ordered O'Connell to withdraw from the House.

Now Henry Brougham, Whig MP for Winchelsea, rose to speak in O'Connell's favour, only to be cut short by the Speaker with the barking words: 'Order! Order!' Once more O'Connell was ordered to withdraw. O'Connell bowed again and this time he withdrew. He still neither uttered nor attempted to utter a single word.

It was a masterstroke from the greatest orator of his age: what

---

* The oath in fact constituted several oaths together.

words could convey more than the unyielding, heroic silence of this man? The King of Ireland, as George IV had angrily termed him, had maintained all his royal dignity, compared to the petty vengeance of the English Establishment. As Creevey put it, 'one damned thing' had been allowed to taint the whole process of conciliation.[13]

O'Connell returned to his seat under the Gallery, while an angry debate ensued with many demanding that he should be heard, while Peel as Home Secretary maintained with energy that he had no right to speak.

On 18 May O'Connell reappeared. There was an interesting historic link for those who cared for such things: under the Gallery sat two French royals: the Duc d'Orléans (who would transform into King Louis-Philippe after the fall of the Bourbon dynasty a year later), and his son the Duc de Chartres. Together they observed one event in what was a revolutionary British situation.

O'Connell was called to address the House.[14] Although there were genteel English doubts about his flamboyant Irish style, his message was clear enough: it was the voice of his people that had sent him there. He made a long and detailed speech on the subject of the Commons which ended: 'My title to sit in it is clear and plain; and I contend that the Statute [of Emancipation] is all comprehensive in its intentions, in its recital, and in its enactments... But while I show my respect for the House, I stand here on my right, and claim the benefit of it.' In the words of Hansard, the honourable and learned gentleman – a reference to O'Connell's legal profession – bowed to the House and withdrew, amidst loud and general cheering. It so happened that one of the French royals had occupied his seat, and he therefore sat by the sergeant-at-arms.

Daniel O'Connell made a final appearance – for the time being – the next day. On 19 May he asked to see the oath in question, and was presented with it on large pasteboard cards. He proceeded to put on his spectacles. After studying it, he pointed to one assertion he knew to be false, and one he believed to be untrue. Then, in a voice of contempt, he declared: 'I therefore refuse to take this Oath' and dramatically flung his card away. He was then formally disqualified by the Speaker of the House of Commons on account of his refusal to take the oath – actually the previous oath in law. The seat for Co. Clare was declared vacant.

O'Connell fared no better with the real King of Ireland (and England). He duly presented himself at the royal *levée*. The last time he had set eyes on George IV was in 1821 when the King paid his famous visit to Ireland and promised to serve the country. At the newly named Kingstown he had presented George IV with a laurel wreath. Now O'Connell saw the King's lips move but could not hear what he said. O'Connell correctly kissed his hand and then passed on. Later it was reported in a Scottish newspaper that George IV had cursed 'an Irish subject'. O'Connell asked the Duke of Norfolk to explain to him what had actually happened. Norfolk did not beat about the bush. 'Yes. His Majesty said as you were approaching: "There is O'Connell! God damn the scoundrel." '15

Who was responsible for this vindictive decision, like so many acts of vengeance, self-defeating in its purpose? It was not after all likely to lead to warmer relations with O'Connell personally. It immediately secured still greater blasts of what would now be called the oxygen of publicity for the Irish leader – without keeping him out of the Commons for very long. Nobody could have supposed that the bold victor of Clare would be rejected in a new election, now that he could legally take his seat, in spite of the alterations to the franchise. O'Connell did explore a safe (but expensive) nominated seat, before going once again for Clare. Robert Peel, as Leader of the House of Commons, even though he supported O'Connell's appearance at the Bar, must take the responsibility. It was a short-sighted action, whereas Peel's conversion to Emancipation had been far-seeing.

Sure enough, in July Daniel O'Connell was once more elected unopposed. The Viceroy, the Duke of Northumberland, reported 'perfect tranquillity' where the electoral process was concerned. Yet Wellington still told Peel on 14 July that O'Connell's renewed election would be 'a great misfortune to the public interests . . .

I would do much to prevent it'. He hoped the county would not be terrified into voting for the Great Dan. It is only fair to say that O'Connell's opinion of the Great Duke in August was equally low: 'a narrow minded, single *idea'd* [sic] man, fit to be a great general with the aid of exceedingly brave troops but he is not a statesman nor a liberal nor an enlightened man'.[16] The truth was that both men had worked hard for what was in the short term the same objective: neither of them had turned into a saint – the sort of saint venerated at a shrine in their shared native Ireland.

Wellington's advice to Admiral Sir Thomas Pakenham, uncle of Brunswick Tom, on behalf of the Irish landed class, was more sensible.[17] The Brunswickers (including their shared connection, Tom Longford) were being very foolish. 'If men of property continued to quarrel about a religious question, which is decided, they must become victims of the more numerous class who have everything to gain and nothing to lose' from such a quarrel. Hang together and adhere to the government! That way the Brunswickers would be too strong and able to repel any injury which might be apprehended. In other words, keep calm and carry on.

So the celebrated green banners of the previous year might be faded and have to be bleached white. Green or white, the Clare by-election was another famous victory. It was left to bigots like the Duke of Buckingham to exclaim at the end of the year that the Catholics themselves were more and more disgusted with O'Connell: 'he should share the fate of an extinguished tallow candle, and die in his own stink'. But O'Connell's flame was not so easily extinguished. A friend jokingly slapped him on the back on the day that Emancipation was passed and quoted Shakespeare: 'Othello's occupation's gone.' O'Connell replied with a smile, referring to a possible future occupation: 'Isn't there a Repeal of the Union?'[18]

Daniel O'Connell had to wait until Parliament reassembled to commence his parliamentary career. He finally took his seat on 4 February 1830. He swore his oath on the left side of the table rather than the right, which took Members aback, but no official complaint was made. O'Connell then sat with a long-term ally, Sir Francis Burdett. One of the other five MPs who swore the oath at the same time, incidentally, was the twenty-one-year-old Marquess of Douro, heir to the Duke of Wellington, whose clear pathway into the House of Commons had been in marked contrast to O'Connell's own complicated route.[19]

When the Member for Co. Clare rose it was to comment on the King's speech, which had called for the relief of 'some' public distress.[20] O'Connell's beginning was plain enough (and might be echoed by many leaders down the ages): 'The people had sent him here to do their business.' In the discharge of that duty, he felt that he was authorized to express his humble opinion as to the state of the country. On the supposed partial nature of the public distress, O'Connell was quick to express astonishment at the Chancellor of the Exchequer for describing a certain 'oasis in the desert' – where there was no distress at all. 'Who would have thought it?' he asked with mock bewilderment: that was in Ireland! Under the circumstances it was surely the duty of the House to sit on, and on, 'from day to day', until it had finally managed to ascertain the causes of this surprising Irish public distress where it actually did occur. According to Hansard, this characteristic ironic flourish was greeted with cheers and laughter.

When the time came O'Connell voted with Sir Edward Knatchbull's amendment, which suggested distress should be described as 'general and extraordinary'. The amendment was defeated by fifty-three votes.

O'Connell had made his mark in the English Parliament as an elected Member, although the honour of being the first Roman Catholic MP had gone to the future Duke of Norfolk nine months earlier. Greville described O'Connell's debut as 'a successful one, heard with profound attention, his manner good and his arguments attended to and replied to'. Soon he was sufficiently versed in the way of the House to send urgently to Dublin for his court dress to be packed up and despatched by *the first* mail coach. He was to dine with the Speaker on Sunday and 'it seems one dines with him in Court Dress'.[21] This was the customary dinner given to the Opposition, and O'Connell was asked as a matter of course.

'I am fast learning the temper of the House,' reported O'Connell further, 'and in a week you will find me a constant speaker.' He added: 'There is more folly and nonsense *in* the House than anywhere out of it. There is a low and subservient line of thinking, there is a submission to authority which is to the last degree of debasing.' From the happy flow of denigration, one gets the impression that O'Connell was beginning to feel somewhat at ease.

Liberal issues in the modern sense soon occupied him. He spoke in favour of the Petition supporting Jewish Emancipation, just as he had earlier spoken out against slavery. Game laws and the monopoly of the East India Company engaged his attention, as did flogging in the army and blasphemy laws. Having begun by thanking the Jewish leader, Isaac Lyon Goldsmid, for his kindness to him in London, he went on to tell him that the Irish Christian community was the only one unsullied by acts of persecution of the Jews. It was 'an external and universal truth that we are responsible to God alone for a religious belief and that human laws are impious when they attempt the exercise of those acts'.[22] He was now able to pursue this counsel of perfection in the British House of Commons.

O'Connell arrived at a time when that deepening rift between Ultra-Tories and their more liberal colleagues over Emancipation and other matters was beginning to have a profound effect on the next vigorous public campaign: the Reform of Parliament itself. In February the Marquess of Blandford, heir to the Duke of Marlborough and Ultra-Tory MP, notoriously against Emancipation, actually joined an organization in favour of Reform. The new rules allowing Catholics into the House affronted him so deeply that he accused the government of giving in to 'Jesuits and Jacobins'. As a result, he thought that what the House actually needed was: Reform![23] Conversely, in the long battle for Reform ahead, the vote of the Irish MPs would play a significant part.

This was a period when George IV's health had passed from being a matter of anxious speculation to one of acute concern. In February, about the time of O'Connell's proper entry into the Commons, Sir William Knighton recorded in his diary: 'I conjecture that his heart is enlarged, much loaded with fat and that his Majesty's death will be sudden'. Bulletins began to be issued about his health at the end of April.[24] George IV died two months later, on 26 June 1830; a year and a quarter after his Royal Assent to Emancipation. That death would bring to an end a thirty-year period when the conscience of the King – two kings in succession – was one huge element in the great issue of the day, the Catholic Question.

CHAPTER EIGHTEEN

Bloodless Revolution

*'It is one of the greatest triumphs recorded
in history – a bloodless revolution'*

Daniel O'Connell, 14 April 1829

THE STORY OF CATHOLIC EMANCIPATION began with
blood: the Anti-Catholic Gordon Riots which followed a very
mild form of Catholic Relief in 1780. But it did not end like that.
Lord Byron had written that 'Who would be free, themselves
must strike the blow.' The remarkable thing about Catholic
Emancipation was how few blows as such were actually struck.
Fifty-odd years after the Gordon Riots, Daniel O'Connell hailed
the Emancipation Act as 'one of the greatest triumphs recorded
in history – a bloodless revolution more extensive in its operation
than any other political change that could take place.'[1]

What, then, was achieved in the glorious and bloodless
triumph? In the course of their long stand-off in March 1829,
the King had spent much time rambling on to the Prime Minister about his various detailed objections to the projected bill.
Wellington had to remind him that 'everything' was to be conceded to the Catholics; there would be infinite possibilities for
them in the future. And he repeated the words: 'Yes, everything.'

As Cardinal Wiseman would pronounce in 1863, 'The year 1829 was to us what the egress from the catacombs was to the Christians.'

Wellington's claim was not completely true, however. The elimination of the Irish Forty-shilling Freeholders from the electorate was one price O'Connell had to pay. As he had told his wife: 'That that [sic] is the only blot.'[2] The people who lost their vote were the kind of men who had brought him to power. 'An Act for the Relief of His Majesty's Roman Catholic Subjects (April 13 1829) 10. George IV. CAP. 7', as it was officially termed, undoubtedly had particular areas of discrimination. Certain roles and offices were still denied by law to Catholics even if they now had the right to vote.

Foremost among them was the role of the British monarch, and those within the line of the royal succession. The Act of Settlement of 1701 establishing a Protestant sovereign and heirs was not repealed. The text of the Emancipation Act was rigorous on the subject. It was true that Roman Catholics would no longer have to take the Oaths and Declarations against Transubstantiation, the Invocation of the Saints and the Sacrifice of the Mass, 'as practised in the Church of Rome', in order to qualify for sitting in Parliament, and for 'the Enjoyment of certain Offices, Franchises, and Civil Rights'. But the oath they would have to take instead promised to 'maintain, support and defend ... the Succession to the Crown ... limited to the Princess Sophia, Electress of Hanover and the Heirs of her Body being Protestants'.

In its language the new oath also recalled old sixteenth-century battles with the Pope and his foreign Church. There were to be no more sanctified assassinations by Catholics, in so far as such had ever existed: 'I do renounce, reject and abjure the Opinion, that Princes excommunicated or deprived by the Pope, or any other Authority of the See of Rome, may be deposed or murdered by their Subjects, or by any Person whatsoever.'

The Coronation Oath, in the form of the declaration in front of Parliament made by the sovereign, continued to cause dissension. William IV took the same effectively Anti-Catholic oath as his brother in 1831, and so did Queen Victoria. It was not until

Edward VII revolted that the oath was altered for his successor George V in 1910. King Edward objected to the wording of the declaration he was forced to read at the opening of his first Parliament, which repudiated Roman Catholicism in unequivocal terms.[3]

Before reading the speech from the throne, Edward VII was called by the Lord Chancellor, in accordance with the Bill of Rights of 1689, to repeat a declaration repudiating the doctrine of Transubstantiation and asserting that 'the invocation or adoration of the Virgin Mary or any other saint and the sacrifice of the Mass as they are now used in the Church of Rome are superstitious and idolatrous'. There was to be no evasion, equivocation or mental reservation whatever. King Edward saw it as a gratuitous insult to his Catholic friends, in which he resembled George III, with his Thomas Welds and Lord Petres. It was also, incidentally, the time of the Boer War in South Africa, in which Catholic soldiers were fighting on the British side. The Lovat Scouts, for example, recruited among Scottish Catholic Highlanders, was raised for service in the Second Boer War by the 14th Lord Lovat, descendant of Simon 11th Lord Lovat, executed for 'a deliberate and malignant purpose to ruin and subvert our present government' – in other words, for supporting the Stuart rebellion of 1745.[4]

King Edward compromised with a low voice which was scarcely audible, and then wrote to his Prime Minister, Lord Salisbury, asking for a change in the 'crude language' which was not in accordance with public policy at the present time. Salisbury agreed with him personally, but believed that there might be a Protestant backlash.

It was not until the reign of his son George V (who took the oath in its old form) that a bill was passed in both Houses which abolished the old declaration of 1689 and substituted the positive for the negative: a declaration 'that I am a faithful Protestant' who would maintain the enactments which secured the Protestant Succession to the throne as well as the throne itself. The Coronation Oath taken by Queen Elizabeth II on 2 June 1953 consisted of a similar positive statement. She would do her utmost to maintain in the United Kingdom the Protestant Reformed Religion which had been established by law. She also swore to maintain and preserve inviolably the settlement of the Church of England, as by law established in England; as well as preserve the rights and privileges by law of the (Protestant) bishops and clergy.*

Neither the Lord Chancellor specifically nor, by implication, the Prime Minister could be Roman Catholics. The latter would be precluded by the clause which forbade any Catholic to advise on ecclesiastical appointments, a duty which comes to the Prime Minister of a country in which there is an officially Established Church.† Other specific offices excluded were the Regent of the United Kingdom under whatever designation, Lord Lieutenant or Lord Deputy, that is the Chief Governor of Ireland, and His Majesty's High Commissioner to the General Assembly of the Church of Scotland.

There were minor clauses which in the event did not have a great deal of practical effect, such as restrictions on the general wearing of ecclesiastical habits in public. These were to be kept for private houses, and Catholic places of worship. The Jesuits and other monastic orders were to be subject to 'gradual Suppression and final Prohibition', which meant entry being forbidden to new recruits into the country and existing members registered. The territorial names of existing Protestant dioceses could not be used by 'any person'; that is to say, they could not be used for Catholic dioceses and there was a fine of £100 for anyone rash enough to persist in doing so. Catholic priests could not be Members of Parliament. At least the final clause showed a certain chivalry towards women: nothing here affected in any manner

---

* A 'Papist' had been forbidden to inherit the throne itself by the Act of Settlement, 170l, reiterated in the Acts of Union between Scotland, and later Ireland and England, of 1707 and 180l. The Royal Succession Act of 2013 did, however, remove the disqualification of a person who married a Roman Catholic from possible accession to the throne.

† In 2018 there has not yet been a Catholic Prime Minister in Great Britain: the Rt Hon. Tony Blair announced his conversion to the Catholic Church following his retirement as Prime Minister.

'any Religious Order, Community or Establishment consisting of Females bound by Religion or Monastic Vows'. Nuns evidently did not evoke the same primitive angry dread as monks.

When O'Connell hailed the glorious prospect of Emancipation, he added the caution that he was specifically referring to political rather than social change, which might break to pieces the framework of society. But his rejoicing in the lack of bloodshed was unrestrained. In an age which had seen the French Revolution and the Napoleonic Wars in Europe, rebellions in Ireland and wars in both North and South America, O'Connell's triumphant emphasis is easy to understand. And he was right, along with his colleagues in Ireland, to take the credit, given their constant emphasis on non-violence during their campaigns in a way that surprised contemporaries expecting something very different from the 'barbarian' Irish. The banning of all violence, including alcohol as conducive to it, during the Clare by-election symbolized a resolute new approach to demagoguery unfettered by customs of the past.

George IV had muttered under his breath about that 'blackguard O'Connell' the first time he saw the new MP at court after the Act was passed; but compared to 'blackguards' of the past such as Wolfe Tone and Robert Emmet, O'Connell's methods were very different. Banning of violence was negative, if crucial; in contrast the formation of the Catholic Association was strongly positive. Thomas Attwood, the English Radical, who would soon be plunged into the campaign for Parliamentary Reform, appreciated the point immediately: in May 1829 he hailed the Irish people who by 'union and organisation' in the Catholic Association (as opposed to violence by day and night) had lately obtained 'a glorious and bloodless victory'.[5] That too owed much to the inspiration of Daniel O'Connell.

The influence of particular individuals on the course of history remains and will always remain a subject of fascinating conjecture; hence the eternal spell of biography. It is, however, possible to say with certainty that O'Connell's charismatic character, his decisions, his gifts and the use he chose to make of them, his attitude to apparently insuperable obstacles, entitles him to emerge as one of the chief heroes of the fight for Emancipation. The ecstatic popular song which celebrated 'the Catholic Victory' is easy to understand:

The bondage of the Israelites our Saviour he did see,
He then commanded Moses for to go and set them free
And in the same we did remain suffering from our own
Till God he sent O'Connell, for to free the Church of Rome.[6]

What then of the obvious counterpart to O'Connell, on the side of the government? Greville commented at the time that the Duke of Wellington, being all-powerful, would receive all 'the honour of the day'; whereas success was really due to O'Connell and those who fought the battle on both sides of the water. It was not so simple. The contribution of the Great Duke should not be eliminated. Arthur Wellesley, Duke of Wellington, was also born in Ireland, like the Liberator, although a member of the Protestant Ascendancy. Nevertheless, his Irish background was one important element in his eventual realism on the subject of Emancipation. As Princess Lieven hissed at the Duke of Cumberland in a moment of aristocratic conservative revulsion, 'How mistaken we have been about Wellington, after all he is no more than an Irish adventurer.'[7] Since Ireland was all-important in the Catholic Question, it was certainly appropriate that at the end two Irishmen should face each other across the religious duelling ground with ritual pistols raised – which both finally decided not to use.

The pragmatic attitude of Wellington to politics would not always serve him (as his attitude to Parliamentary Reform, where he simply got it wrong, would shortly demonstrate). But it certainly served him on this occasion, and it served his country. Sir Francis Burdett, who supported Emancipation and would sit beside O'Connell at his first appearance in the Commons, was right to predict in May 1828 that if the bill passed, the Great Duke would add 'another wreath to the laurel of victory'.[8]

The Great Duke was able to employ his extraordinary authority, to project 'King Arthur' in the real King's bitter phrase, to bring about a change which a great many of his strongest supporters were loath to see. Just as Daniel O'Connell had his eye on the repeal of the Union as a consequence of Emancipation, the Duke of Wellington placed the peace and welfare of that actual United Kingdom above religious scruples and decided that Emancipation was necessary to secure it. The religious scruples included those of the sovereign, swept aside at the end in a masterly way that only Wellington could manage.

Sir Walter Scott, for example, had been a dedicated opponent of Relief for Catholics: Popery, he believed, was such a mean and depriving superstition. He would willingly have had 'the Old Lady of Babylon's mouth' stopped with a plaster.[9] Now he altered his mind in favour of Relief because his confidence was 'entirely in the Duke of Wellington'. Having done so, Scott signed a Petition in favour of the bill – no half-measures which 'do but linger out the feud' – and there were loud cheers in Parliament when his name was read out. Wellington must also be allowed his place as, in a very different sense from O'Connell, a hero of the struggle: neither the Duke nor the demagogue would necessarily have succeeded without the other.

On the personal level, the Ultra-Tory Protestants lacked a brilliant leader comparable to an O'Connell or a Wellington. This was a weakness for their cause. The rantings of Lord Winchilsea and his like were in a different class, although the emotion behind them was surely also genuine, the emotion of certain dedicated conservatives down the ages in a time of change. The conversion of the brilliant politician Peel from intellectual and emotional support for the Church of England to a position of compromise, from a sense of duty if not untinged with ambition, damaged him personally; at the same time it robbed the extreme Protestants of any really effective ally. What has been described by one biographer as 'a contemporary squib' announced a new Catholic feast day celebrating 'the Conversion of Saint Peel'.[10]

As for Peel himself, turncoats have never fared well at the hands of their former allies throughout history from Judas onwards. Peel was certainly no Judas: he was a man of honest conviction who had honestly changed his mind and had the courage to say so. Nevertheless, the slur would affect his standing in the Tory Party and the next great campaign for Reform.

There were other elements which contributed to the success of the struggle at that precise moment: the unlooked-for effect of the French Revolution in bringing Catholic refugees, including many in religious orders, to Britain was one. Papists were no longer necessarily the historic enemy, linked to that bogeyman the Pope. They were in fact fleeing England's Continental enemy, which was forbidding their religion. In offering practical compassion to Papists, the hosts conceived a new image of monks, nuns and other co-religionists. Meanwhile the Pope himself became a fugitive at the orders of that new notorious bogeyman, Napoleon, dispossessed from the historically threatening religious fortress of Rome.

From exactly the opposite point of view, the need for soldiers brought about by these wars placed a proper practical emphasis on the welfare of Irish and Scottish men who might be recruited and asked to fight for their country – the country which denied them the day-to-day practice of their religion. The military seniors were the first to appreciate the point. What harm did it do the men to have their Mass before going into battle? It certainly did not hinder recruitment. This was a practical consideration, nothing to do with the long tentacles of Rome. The fact that Catholic soldiers could die for a country which denied them the worship they wanted was constantly and rightly emphasized during the campaign for Emancipation.

The role played by the 'New World' of the Americas was also significant. References were frequently made during the long debates on the subject of Emancipation to the religious liberty which was part of the original constitution of the United States. It was praised, for example, by Daniel O'Connell; a natural reference given the level of Irish emigration across the Atlantic at that period. These emigrants themselves in many cases remained supportive by word – and money and even the threat of armed intervention – of their fellow Catholics still in their native land. Similarly, the success of Simón Bolívar provided a living example that freedom was there for those who fought for it, and showed themselves to be heroes in the process.

The influence of a certain kind of cry for liberty, voiced by many poets of the time, was more complicated, however. Here the mythical machinations of the Popish Church could still be seen in medieval terms; cartoon monks could still be envisaged as up to no good at all, certainly not encouraging the spread of freedom. In the same way, the Whigs, roughly speaking, always stood in favour of Emancipation, as being a liberal attitude which chimed with their innate predisposition towards reform. But it should be remembered that Lord Holland, admirable, tolerant Whig grandee as he might be, was capable of outbursts in private against the Pope.

The lesson of history on the subject of prejudice is a painful one: so long as it lingers, the trickle of malice can always turn unexpectedly into a spring torrent. Anti-Catholicism in England was certainly not eliminated in 1829, just as permanent peace was certainly not achieved in Ireland. It was in 1829 that Thomas Wyse wrote in his *Historical Sketch of the Late Catholic Association* that the single word Emancipation 'contained within itself the panacea for all the sufferings of Ireland' – with hindsight, a touchingly optimistic view.[11] It is for this reason that the discreet, enduring, long-term influence of the old Catholic families should not be overlooked. They might be insufficiently ardent in Sheil's dismissive phrase, but in the words of Abbé Sieyès, asked how he fared in the Revolution: they survived. They had endured through hard times.

Once the complication of the Stuart challenge to the throne, military and otherwise, was over, their very endurance proved a factor in counterbalancing the image of Catholics as foreigners. They might be educated abroad, through no fault of their own, but foreigners they clearly were not: these were friends of the King at the highest part of established society, with their large country estates and discreet rooms or mausoleums or other dwellings which might just be Catholic chapels. It would also be wrong in this context to ignore the contribution of the people, nameless, who served them down the ages, nameless but faithful

to their masters and the Catholic Faith. There were weavers and
labourers such the Wilcocks, Baldwins and Charnlys of Walton-
le-Dale in Lancashire, as well as the Norfolks, Welds and Petres.

The influence of diplomat-clerics should not be forgotten. Cardinal Consalvi died five years before Emancipation was granted,
but had played an important part both during his visit to London
and generally in Rome at a very tricky time for the Papacy,
including his handling of the estate of the last Stuart, Cardinal
Henry of York. In his sophisticated way, he would surely have
enjoyed the scene in Rome after Nicholas Wiseman, the new
Rector, decorated the façade of the English College with lanterns
spelling *Emanzipazione Cattolica*. Some Italian passers-by, believing that a new saint had been canonized, struck their breasts
with the invocation *Santa Emancipatione, ora pro nobis.*[12] Then
there were the Protestant champions in Parliament at roughly
the same period, such as Henry Grattan, whose oratory deserves
acknowledgement in the achievement of legislation.

The attitudes of the earlier Catholic English clerics such as
Bishop Milner in refusing to bow to suggestions of compromise
like the Veto, although seemingly a dangerous game at the time,
and one which delayed perhaps some form of Emancipation,
resulted in the final Act being free of 'securities', which was
generally regarded by Catholics as a triumph.

Lastly, returning to the biographical theme, the passions and
prejudices of the two kings involved were obviously of crucial
importance. Contrasted as they were in character, they united in
the end in standing for what they perceived to be the immutable
values of the Hanoverian Protestant dynasty. The whole story
would have been very different if George III had not protested
against the Emancipation which was half promised at the time of
the Union of Britain and Ireland in 1801.

After that, the fact has to be faced that George IV remained
unwilling to give his Royal Assent to the bill until the very end.
He did so finally, 'with pain and regret', in what was a notable
surrender by the Crown to the will of the government. Most of
the population of the British mainland – although pollsters did
not as yet exist to confirm it – probably agreed in their hearts

with their monarch, not their Parliament. A caricature of April 1829 by the satirist William Heath gives that lurking national reluctance pungent expression. A huge, terrified John Bull – the patriotic symbol – lies helpless, held down by Robert Peel, while a demonic Wellington, as Dr Arthur, forcibly administers medicine down his throat with the words: 'Hold him fast, Bob – I'll soon make him swallow it – there it goes Johnny, you will be quite a different man after this.' John Bull, in short, was on the side of the King, not the Catholics.

Let Sydney Smith, staunch Protestant friend of liberty, have the last word.[13] When Emancipation became law, he wrote to a Catholic friend: 'I rejoice in the temple which has been reared to Toleration and I am proud that I worked as a bricklayer's labourer at it – without pay, and with the enmity and abuse of those who were unfavourable to its construction.' There were many discreet labourers, as well as the political bricklayers themselves, who had the right to feel proud of the progress made in 1829. And there would be many toilers in the future on the ever-fragile structure of that temple to Toleration. In the meantime all honour is due to those who, with a variety of motives and in many different ways, laid the bricks for Catholic Emancipation.

REFERENCES

PROLOGUE

1. Colley, p. 332; Bence-Jones, p. 23; Gwynn, p. 36
2. de Castro, p. 107 *et seq.*
3. Kelly, *Susanna*, p. 82 *et seq.*
4. George, p. 109
5. Edgeworth, *Harrington*, p. 383 *et seq.*; Haywood and Seed, p. 5
6. Haydon, p. 173
7. Leys, *Catholics*, p. 130
8. *Walpole*, p. 457; Gilmour, p. 346 *et seq.*
9. Hibbert, *King Mob*, p. 12 *et seq.*
10. Ibid., p. 30
11. Haydon, p. 209
12. Mathews, pp. 226–41; Knights, p. 52
13. *Henry IV Part 2*: Prologue, Scene 1; Haydon, p. 250; Hibbert, *King Mob*, p. 28
14. Stourton, 'Lord Petre', p. 117; Martin, p. 45
15. Sheils, pp. 113–14
16. de Castro, p. 194
17. Brooke, p. 218
18. de Castro, p. 108
19. Aitken, pp. 205–6
20. Kynaston, p. 61; Martin, p. 47
21. Hibbert, *King Mob*, p. 161
22. *Lord George Gordon's Narrative*, BL Add. Mss. 42,129
23. Gilmour, p. 3

CHAPTER ONE:
That Fallen Worship

1. de Lisle and Stanford, p. 33; Haydon, p. 185
2. Butler, *Historical Memoirs*, vol. II, p. 199
3. Stourton, 'Lord Petre', p. 115 *et seq.*
4. *Letters and Notices*, vol. XLV
5. Evans, p. 456
6. Hattersley, p. 213
7. Museum of London Catalogue, *Great Fire Exhibition*
8. de Lisle and Stanford, p. xv
9. Ibid., p. 15
10. Hattersley, pp. 150–51
11. Haydon, p. 254; *Eighteenth-Century British Erotica II*, vol. I, *passim*
12. Choudhury, p. 33 *et seq.*
13. Fothergill, p. 103
14. Ibid., p. 136
15. Brooke, p. 366
16. Mathew, p. 168
17. Bence-Jones, p. 49
18. Walton-le-Dale registers,

passim; *The Tablet*, 23 May 2015
19. James, p. 14 *et seq.*
20. Petre, p. 40 *et seq*; Bence-Jones, p. 120 *et seq.*
21. Petre, p. 44
22. Hibbert, *George* III, p. 165
23. Ibid., p. 225; Robinson, *Dukes*, p. 154
24. *Walpole*, p. 73
25. Petre, p. 48
26. Scott, p. 26
27. Snape, p. 12 *et seq.*
28. Ibid., p. 31

CHAPTER TWO:
Nothing to Fear in England

1. Robinson, *Dukes*, p. 171 *et seq.*
2. Gwynn, p. 160; Ellis, p. 123; Bossy, p. 341
3. Amherst, vol. II, p. 38; p. 86, n. 1
4. Leys, 'The Rights of Women', pp. 83–8
5. Amherst, vol. II, p. 59 *et seq.*
6. Colley, p. 5
7. Bence-Jones, pp. 82–3
8. Amherst, vol. II, p. 1
9. Berkeley, p. 183 *et seq.*
10. *Stourton*, vol. II, pp. 371–2
11. Aveling, p. 341
12. Amherst, vol. II, p. 232 *et seq.*
13. Jerningham, vol. I, pp. 33–4
14. Taylor, p. 123; Jerningham, vol. I, p. 34
15. Fraser, *Unruly Queen*, pp. 33–5
16. Bence-Jones, p. 106
17. Mathew, p. 161 *et seq.*; Berkeley, p. 176 *et seq.*; Bence-Jones, p. 47 *et seq.*
18. Leys, *Catholics*, p. 212, n. 2; Berkeley, p. 194 *et seq.*
19. Leys, *Catholics*, p. 212

20. Pakenham, *Year of Liberty*, p. 25 *et seq.*; Tomko, p. 24

CHAPTER THREE:
The Royal Conscience

1. Gwynn, p. xviii; Gash, *Peel*, p. 147
2. Gash, *Peel*, p. 174; Edgeworth MSS, 28 May 1828
3. Sadleir, p. 150
4. de Tocqueville, p. 118 *et seq.*
5. *Lady Morgan's Memoirs*, vol. II, p. 260; Southey, vol. VI, p. 35
6. Brady, p. 284
7. Pückler-Muskau, p. 221
8. Pearson, p. 129
9. Mullett, pp. 195–6; Norman, *Anti-Catholicism*, p. 27
10. Butler, *Eldest Brother*, p. 260
11. Ehrman, p. 499 *et seq.*
12. *Faithful Account*, pp. 52–3
13. Bew, *Castlereagh*, p. 59
14. Arbuthnot, vol. I, p. 181; Bew, *Castlereagh*, p. 173 *et seq.*
15. Bew, *Castlereagh*, p. 527
16. Hibbert, *George III*, p. 313
17. Ehrman, p. 495 *et seq.*
18. Ehrman, p. 510
19. Pares, p. 137
20. Brooke, p. 367
21. Hibbert, *George III*, p. 316
22. Hansard, 25 April 1825
23. Butler, *Eldest Brother*, p. 263

CHAPTER FOUR:
Green Shores of Liberty

1. O'Brien, p. 75 *et seq.*
2. Hibbert, *George IV* (1972), p. 227
3. *Works ... Smith*, p. 307
4. Throckmorton, p. 147; p. 92
5. Hinde, *Canning*, p. 11 *et seq.*
6. Ibid., p. 100

7. Geoghegan, *King Dan*, p. 13 *et seq.*
8. MacDonagh, p. 46
9. Wyse, vol. II, p. lxxiii
10. Ibid., p. lxxii
11. Creevey, vol. II, p. 183
12. *Lady Morgan's Memoirs*, vol. II, p. 225
13. O'Brien, p. 91 *et seq.*
14. Hurd, p. 22
15. Magee, p. v *et seq.*
16. Ibid., p. 75 *et seq.*
17. Ramsay, p. 46
18. Gash, *Peel*, p. 155
19. Peel, *Sketch of the Life*, p. 105
20. Magee, p. 151 *et seq.*
21. Ibid., pp. 163–4

CHAPTER FIVE:
Cardinal Tempter

1. Butler, *Historical Memoirs*, vol. II, App. Note, p. 467
2. Amherst, vol. II, p. 141 *et seq.*
3. Ibid.
4. Robinson, *Consalvi*, pp. 106–7; Consalvi, *Mémoires*, p. xxvi; Ward, *Eve*, vol. II, p. 91 *et seq.*
5. Ellis, p. 120
6. Ward, *Eve*, vol. II, p. 94
7. Robinson, *Consalvi*, p. 143; Ellis, p. 171, n. 2 ; Stuart, p. 213
8. Robinson, *Consalvi*, p. 91
9. Wiseman, p. 66
10. Stuart, p. 216 *et seq.*
11. Royal Archives [RA] GEO / ADD / 4 / 35 n.d. [1811?]
12. Hardman, p. 89
13. Ward, *Eve*, vol. II, p. 93
14. RA GEO / ADD / 4 / 35 n.d. [1811?]
15. Ellis, p. 145
16. Robinson, *Consalvi*, p. 108
17. Hibbert, *George IV* (2007), pp. 396–7

18. Leslie, p. 143
19. Irvine, p. 204
20. G.E.C., vol. VI, p. 512, note a
21. Robinson, *Dukes*, p. 171 *et seq.*; Robinson, 'Arundel's Bibliophile Dukes', pp. 20–23
22. Robinson, *Dukes,* p. 149
23. Ibid., p. 191 *et seq.*
24. Ward, *Eve*, vol. II, p. 132
25. Ibid., p. 173 *et seq.*; Tomko, p. 40 *et seq.*
26. Amherst, vol. II, pp. 114–19
27. Ibid., vol. II, p. 14
28. Hansard, 25 February 1813
29. Hansard, 30 May 1815
30. Bourne, *Palmerston*, p. 230
31. Geoghegan, *King Dan*, p. 147 *et seq.*
32. O'Connell, *Life and Speeches*, vol. II, p. 209

CHAPTER SIX:
Grattan the Great

1. Geoghegan, *King Dan*, p. 162
2. MacDonagh, p. 137; Edgeworth, *Harrington*, vol. I, p. 307; Hibbert, *George III*, p. 135
3. Geoghegan, *King Dan*, p. 159 *et seq.*
4. Hansard, 9 May 1817
5. Ibid.
6. Gash, *Peel*, p. 209
7. Gaunt, p. 8; Hansard, 3 May 1819
8. Hansard, 3 May 1819
9. Geoghegan, *King Dan*, p. 175
10. Sheil, vol. II, p. 164; *History of Parliament*, Plunket; Colley, p. 327
11. Hansard, 28 February 1821
12. O'Connell, *Life and Speeches*, vol. II, p. 242
13. Arbuthnot, vol. I, p. 8

14. Ibid., vol. I, p. 81
15. Strong, p. 374 *et seq.*
16. Ibid., p. 409
17. Hibbert, *George III*, p. 316

CHAPTER SEVEN:
Serving Ireland Royally

1. MacDonagh, p. 175; Fagan, vol. I, p. 262
2. Arbuthnot, vol. I, p. 120; Cloncurry, p. 235
3. MacDonagh, p. 177
4. Sheil, vol. I, p. 18
5. Hibbert, *George IV* (2007), p. 621 *et seq.*
6. Smith, *George IV*, p. 194
7. Campbell, p. 187
8. Bew, 'Ireland under the Union', p. 87
9. Hibbert, *George IV* (2007), p. 623
10. Smith, *George IV*, p. 195
11. Ibid., p. 196 *et seq.*
12. Hibbert, *George IV* (2007), p. 629
13. Campbell, p. xi
14. Hibbert, *George IV* (2007), p. 759
15. Bostrom, p. 169 *et seq.*
16. Owenson, p. 21 *et seq.*
17. Campbell, p. 176; Hibbert, *George IV* (2007), p. 759
18. Kelly, *Ireland's Minstrel*, p. 39
19. Ibid., p. 219
20. Hibbert, *George IV* (2007), p. 636
21. Hilton, p. 288 and n. 335
22. Colchester, vol. III, p. 231
23. Butler, *Eldest Brother*, pp. 530–31
24. Longford, p. 57
25. Cloncurry, p. 237; Longford, p. 121
26. G.E.C., vol. IV, p. 238; Longford, p. 162
27. Hibbert, *George IV* (2007), p. 388
28. Colchester, vol. III, p. 241
29. Ibid., p. 257
30. Hansard, 30 April 1822

CHAPTER EIGHT:
Millstone

1. Ellis, p. 31
2. Tomko, p. 36; p. 89
3. Hansard, 21 April 1812
4. Tomko, p. 47 *et seq.*
5. Southey, vol. III, p. 339
6. Ibid., vol. II, p. 320
7. Phillips, pp. 125–36
8. Lingard, p. 15
9. Cattermole, p. 173
10. Colchester, vol. III, p. 268
11. Ibid., vol. III, p. 300
12. Holland House Papers, BL Add. Ms. 52175 fol. 117
13. Gwynn, p. 218 *et seq.*
14. Geoghegan, *King Dan*, p. 196 *et seq.*
15. Ibid., p. 202 *et seq.*
16. O'Ferrall, *Catholic Emancipation*, p. 74
17. Kelly, *Bard of Erin*, p. 391
18. Moore, *Captain Rock*, p. 221
19. Robinson, *Dukes*, p. 191; Hansard, 18 June 1824
20. Robinson, *Dukes*, p. 191; Colchester, vol. III, p. 336
21. O'Ferrall, *Catholic Emancipation*, p. 83

CHAPTER NINE:
A Protestant King

1. Geoghegan, *King Dan*, p. 206 *et seq.*
2. Gash, *Peel*, p. 369 *et seq.*

3. W.D.C.M., vol. IV, pp. 254–5
4. Sheil, vol. II, p. 194 *et seq.*
5. Campbell, p. 83
6. Navickas, p. 115; Mathew, p. 184
7. Muir, *Stonyhurst*, p. 69 *et seq.*; p. 123
8. *O'Connell Correspondence*, vol. III, p. 132
9. Ibid., vol. III, pp. 130–31
10. Sheil, vol. II, p. 220 *et seq.*
11. *The Times*, 18 May 1825
12. *History of Parliament*, Sir Francis Burdett
13. Sheil, vol. II, p. 204
14. Moore, *Memoirs*, vol. II, p. 158
15. Hansard, 1–23 March 1825
16. Geoghegan, *King Dan*, p. 219
17. Hansard, 18 April 1825
18. Fraser, *Princesses*, p. 5; Amherst, vol. I, p. 229
19. Arbuthnot, vol. I, p. 71; Hansard, 25 April 1825
20. Geoghegan, *King Dan*, pp. 219–20
21. Machin, p. 59; Hood, p. 253
22. Gwynn, p. 229
23. *Lady Morgan's Memoirs*, vol. II, p. 225
24. Aspinall, *Letters*, vol. III, p. 126, n. 1; Butler, *Eldest Brother*, p. 513
25. Sheil, vol. I, p. 332; Butler, *Eldest Brother*, p. 511 *et seq.*
26. Arbuthnot, vol. I, p. 243; p. 243, n. 2
27. Aspinall, *Letters*, vol. III, p. 126, n. 1
28. Hobsbawm, p. 138
29. Moriarty, p. 356
30. Ibid., pp. 357–63

CHAPTER TEN:
Noise of No Popery

1. Machin, p. 68
2. Brown, p. 113; Machin, p. 71
3. Aspinall, *Letters*, vol. III, pp. 126–7
4. *Works ... Smith*, p. 556; pp. 487–534
5. Pearson, pp. 134–5
6. Tomko, p. 113
7. Machin, p. 71
8. Kelly, *Ireland's Minstrel*, p. 198
9. *History of Parliament*, vol. I, pp. 221–7
10. O'Ferrall, *Catholic Emancipation*, p. 122; Geoghegan, *King Dan*, p. 231
11. Wyse, vol. II, p. 71
12. Gwynn, p. 235
13. *History of Parliament*, Leslie Foster
14. Pakenham, *Soldier Sailor*, p. 185; *History of Parliament*, vol. VI, p. 619
15. *History of Parliament*, vol. I, p. 226
16. Brown, p. 116
17. Aspinall, *Letters*, vol. III, p. 184
18. Jerningham, vol. II, p. 187
19. Aspinall, *Letters*, vol. III, pp. 152–3
20. Ibid., vol. III, pp. 176–7; p. 174
21. O'Ferrall, *Catholic Emancipation*, p. 149
22. Pückler-Muskau, p. 83
23. Aspinall, *Letters*, vol. III, p. 181
24. Greville, *Diaries*, p. 19
25. Arbuthnot, vol. I, p. 71; p. 403
26. Machin, p. 88; Geoghegan, *King Dan*, p. 239

CHAPTER ELEVEN:
Mr Canning

1. Greville, *Diaries*, p. 19; Hinde, *Canning*, pp. 433–4
2. Hinde, *Canning*, pp. 433–4
3. Peel Papers, BL PP Add. Mss. 40343 + 63
4. Hansard, 5 March 1827
5. Machin, p. 91
6. Kelly, *Bard of Erin*, p. 433
7. Colchester, vol. III, pp. 472–3
8. Hansard, 2 May 1827
9. Hansard, 1 May 1827
10. Byron, 'The Age of Bronze' (1823); O'Ferrall, *Catholic Emancipation*, p. 154
11. Longford, p. 139; Hansard, 2 May 1827
12. Longford, p. 115
13. Aspinall, *Letters*, vol. III, p. 228
14. Willis, *Ernest Augustus*, p. 173; Mitchell, *Holland House*, p. 116; Holland House Papers, BL Add. Mss. 51318–52254
15. Machin, p. 100; Aspinall, *Letters*, vol. III, p. 222
16. Le Marchant, p. 351
17. Hinde, *Canning*, p. 448
18. Longford, p. 143
19. Ibid., p. 144 *et seq.*
20. MacDonagh, p. 232 *et seq.*
21. *O'Connell Correspondence*, vol. III, p. 340
22. Ibid., vol. III, pp. 344–5
23. Bartlett, p. 328; O'Connell, *Life and Speeches*, vol. II, pp. 449–50; *O'Connell Correspondence*, vol. III, pp. 348–9
24. Greville, *Diaries*, p. 21
25. Aspinall, *Letters*, vol. III, p. 358; Holland House Papers, BL Add. Mss. 51318–52254
26. Smith, *Grey*, p. 248

27. *O'Connell Correspondence*, vol. III, p. 374

CHAPTER TWELVE:
O'Connell's Boldest Step

1. Ellenborough, vol. I, p. 3; Pakenham, *Soldier Sailor*, p. 187
2. Geoghegan, *King Dan*, p. 257
3. *History of Parliament*, Charles Wetherell
4. W.D.C.M., vol. IV, p. 194
5. Butler, *Eldest Brother*, p. 527
6. Anglesey, *One-Leg*, p. 184
7. Hansard, 26 February 1828
8. Hansard, 18 March 1828
9. Anglesey Papers, D 619/27/A, 10 April 1828; 13 May 1828
10. Hansard, 8 May 1828
11. Anglesey Papers, D 619/27/A, 13 June 1828
12. Hibbert, *George III*, p. 365
13. Willis, *Ernest Augustus*, p. 170; Aspinall, *Letters*, vol. III, pp. 197–8
14. Fraser, *Princesses*, pp. 190–91
15. Ellenborough, vol. I, p. 143
16. *History of Parliament*, Vesey Fitzgerald
17. Hurd, p. 119
18. Geoghegan, *King Dan*, p. 250 *et seq.*
19. O'Ferrall, *O'Connell*, p. 62
20. Sheil, vol. I, p. 97
21. Gwynn, pp. 244–5
22. Hilton, p. 387; W.D.C.M., vol. IV, p. 565; Geoghegan, *King Dan*, p. 255 *et seq.*
23. W.D.C.M., vol. IV, pp. 565–6
24. Geoghegan, *King Dan*, p. 255
25. Sheil, vol. II, p. 293 *et seq.*; Anglesey Papers, D 6171/27/A, 13 June 1828; O'Ferrall, *O'Connell*, p. 63; Anglesey,

One-Leg, p. 199; Bartlett, p. 342

26. Geoghegan, *King Dan*, p. 257
27. Boyce, p. 57; O'Ferrall, *Catholic Emancipation*, pp. 197–8
28. Banim, vol. II, p. 6; Gwynn, p. 246
29. Bourne, *Palmerston*, p. 293
30. Sheil, vol. II, p. 308 *et seq.*
31. Pückler-Muskau, p. 211 *et seq.*

CHAPTER THIRTEEN:
Brunswickers

1. *History of Parliament*, Vesey Fitzgerald
2. Pückler-Muskau, p. 211 *et seq.*
3. MacDonagh, p. 255
4. Geoghegan, *King Dan*, p. 262 *et seq.*
5. Peel, *Memoirs*, pp. 181–2
6. Greville, *Memoirs*, vol. I, p. 217
7. *History of Parliament*, George Dawson
8. *O'Connell Correspondence*, vol. II, p. 409
9. W.D.C.M., vol. V, p. 298
10. Aspinall, *Letters*, vol. III, p. 438
11. Machin, p. 132
12. *O'Connell Correspondence*, vol. III, p. 403; Pakenham MSS, W.A. Williamson, 28 October 1828
13. *Westmeath Journal*, Pakenham MSS
14. W.D.C.M., vol. IV, p. 229; p. 154
15. *O'Connell Correspondence*, vol. III, p. 403
16. Arbuthnot, vol. II, pp. 196–8
17. W.D.C.M., vol. IV, pp. 565–70

18. Arbuthnot, vol. II, p. 198 *et seq.*
19. W.D.C.M., vol. V, pp. 133–6
20. Gwynn, p. 261
21. W.D.C.M., vol. V, p. 588; Moriarty, pp. 362–70
22. Gash, *Peel*, p. 537
23. Southey, vol. V, pp. 196–7; Pearson, p. 130; Hansard, 2 May 1827
24. *O'Connell Correspondence*, vol. III, p. 380

CHAPTER FOURTEEN:
Boot-and-Spur Work

1. Sheil, vol. II, p. 315 *et seq.*
2. Machin, pp. 140–42
3. Arbuthnot, vol. I, p. 218
4. Hempton, pp. 136–8
5. Hylson-Smith, p. 264
6. Machin, p. 120, n. 2
7. O'Ferrall, *Catholic Emancipation*, p. 214
8. Howell-Thomas, p. 130; W.D.C.M., vol. V, p. 314; pp. 324–5
9. Anglesey, *One-Leg*, pp. 205–6
10. Ibid., p. 211; W.D.C.M., vol. V, p. 280
11. W.D.C.M., vol. V, p. 275
12. Ellis, p. 128
13. W.D.C.M., vol. V, pp. 308–9
14. Ibid., vol. V, p. 326
15. Anglesey, *One-Leg*, p. 213
16. W.D.C.M., vol. V, pp. 352–3
17. Anglesey, *One-Leg*, p. 215
18. Ibid., p. 216
19. Greville, *Memoirs*, vol. I, p. 242; Arbuthnot, vol. II, p. 232
20. W.D.C.M., vol. V, p. 453
21. Anglesey, *One-Leg*, p. 217

CHAPTER FIFTEEN:
From Peel to Repeal

1. W.D.C.M., vol. V, p. 436
2. Gash, *Peel*, p. 546
3. Machin, p. 159; Muir, *Wellington*, p. 331
4. Anglesey Papers, D619/27/A, 12 January 1829; W.D.C.M., vol. V, p. 452
5. Ellenborough, vol. I, p. 325 *et seq.*
6. Peel, *Memoirs*, p. 188
7. Hurd, p. 117
8. Muir, *Wellington*, p. 335
9. Morley, vol. I, p. 52 *et seq.*
10. Nockles, p. 350, n. 79
11. Briggs, p. 232
12. O'Ferrall, *Catholic Emancipation*, p. 240 *et seq.*
13. Hansard, 5 February 1829
14. Hansard, 10 February 1829
15. Amherst, vol. II, p. 114
16. Greville, *Diaries*, p. 25
17. Hansard, 10 February 1829
18. MacDonagh, p. 265 *et seq.*; *Lady Morgan's Memoirs*, vol. II, p. 271
19. Willis, *Ernest Augustus*, pp. 175–6; Aspinall, *Letters*, vol. III, p. 458
20. Hansard, 19 February 1829
21. Hansard, 23 February 1829
22. Colley, p. 279
23. Hansard, 19 March 1829
24. Hibbert, *George IV* (2007), p. 743 *et seq.*

CHAPTER SIXTEEN:
The Duel

1. Hansard, 5 March 1829
2. Gash, *Peel*, pp. 470–76; Greville, *Diaries*, p. 26; Machin, p. 173; Gwynn,

p. 267; Hobhouse, vol. IV, pp. 308–9
3. Hurd, p. 119
4. *O'Connell Correspondence*, vol. IV, p. 31; p. 30
5. Ibid., vol. IV, p. 18
6. Turnham, p. 32; *Farm Street*, p. 11; *O'Connell Correspondence*, vol. IV, pp. 32–3
7. Wardroper, p. 144
8. *O'Connell Correspondence*, vol. IV, p. 21
9. Machin, p. 174; Hobhouse, vol. III, p. 311; Greville, *Diaries*, p. 27
10. Hansard, 11 March 1829; Machin, p. 154
11. W.D.C.M., vol. V, pp. 526–7; Longford, pp. 186–90
12. W.D.C.M., vol. V, pp. 537–8
13. Greville, *Memoirs*, vol. I, p. 276; Arbuthnot, vol. II, pp. 257–8
14. Hobhouse, vol. III, p. 316
15. Trevelyan, vol. I, p. 147, n. 1
16. Machin, p. 179
17. *O'Connell Correspondence*, vol. II, p. 43
18. Greville, *Memoirs*, vol. I, p. 269; Ellenborough, vol. II, p. 7; Colchester, vol. III, p. 612
19. Anglesey Papers, D 619/27/A, 25 January 1829
20. Greville, *Memoirs*, vol. I, p. 235; Hibbert, *George IV* (2007), p. 743
21. Hobhouse, vol. IV, p. 323
22. Wardroper, p. 133
23. Arbuthnot, vol. II, p. 254
24. Willis, *Ernest Augustus*, p. 185
25. Ibid., p. 188
26. Ibid., p. 193 *et seq.*
27. W.D.C.M., vol. V, p. 580
28. Hobhouse, vol. III, p. 320

CHAPTER SEVENTEEN:
Tale of Two MPs

1. *O'Connell Correspondence*, vol. IV, p. 45; p. 41
2. Greville, *Memoirs*, vol. I, p. 218
3. Hobhouse, vol. III, p. 319; Pakenham, *Soldier Sailor*, p. 192; *O'Connell Correspondence*, vol. IV, p. 43
4. Pakenham, *Soldier Sailor*, p. 193; Kelly, *Ireland's Minstrel*, p. 217
5. Mitchell, *Whig World*, p. 130
6. Ellenborough, vol. II, p. 22
7. *Stourton*, vol. II, p. 677
8. *History of Parliament*, Surrey
9. Robinson, *Dukes*, pp. 195–7
10. Geoghegan, *Liberator*, p. 1; Hansard, 6 May 1829
11. *O'Connell Correspondence*, vol. IV, pp. 59– 60 and n. 4
12. Hansard, 15 May 1829; Geoghegan, *Liberator*, pp. 1–2; Gwynn, pp. 279–80
13. Longford, p. 197
14. Hansard, 18 May 1829; Geoghegan, *Liberator*, p. 4
15. Gwynn, p. 281
16. W.D.C.M., vol. VI, p. 68; p. 60; *O'Connell Correspondence*, vol. IV, p. 124
17. Pakenham, *Soldier Sailor*, p. 195
18. W.D.C.M., vol. VI, p. 346
19. Geoghegan, *King Dan*, p. 270
20. Hansard, 4 February 1830
21. Greville, *Diaries*, p. 32; *O'Connell Correspondence*, vol. IV, p. 124
22. Geoghegan, *Liberator*, p. 18; *O'Connell Correspondence*, vol. IV, pp. 95–6
23. Fraser, *Perilous Question*, p. 30
24. Smith, *George IV*, p. 269

CHAPTER EIGHTEEN:
Bloodless Revolution

1. *O'Connell Correspondence*, vol. IV, p. 45
2. O'Ferrall, *Catholic Emancipation*, p. 251
3. Ridley, p. 371 *et seq.*; Roberts, p. 798; Lee, *Edward VII*, pp. 22–5
4. Riding, p. 496
5. Cannon, p. 192
6. O'Ferrall, *Catholic Emancipation*, p. 263
7. Charmley, p. 173
8. Hansard, 8 May 1828
9. Johnson, vol. II, pp. 1101–2
10. Gaunt, p. 30
11. Wyse, vol. II, p. lv
12. Skinner, p. 201
13. Pearson, p. 217

SOURCES

This list gives bibliographical details of books and articles cited in the References. Place of publication is London, and edition is hardback unless otherwise stated. The proceedings of the Houses of Parliament in Hansard are given by date of entry, which applies equally to hardback and online publication.

Aitken, Jonathan, *John Newton*, pbk, 2007

Amherst, W.J., *The History of Catholic Emancipation and the Progress of the Catholic Church in the British Isles (chiefly in England) from 1771 to 1820*, 2 vols, 1886

Anglesey, Marquess of, *One-Leg. The Life and Letters of Henry William Paget, First Marquess of Anglesey, K.G.*, 1963

Anglesey Papers, Public Record Office, Belfast, Northern Ireland

[Arbuthnot] *The Journal of Mrs Arbuthnot*, ed. Francis Bamford and the Duke of Wellington, 2 vols, 1950

Aspinall, A. (ed.), *Letters of George IV, 1812–1830*, 3 vols, 1938

Aspinall, A., *Politics and the Press 1780–1850*, 1949

Aveling, J.C.H., *The Handle and the Axe. The Catholic Recusants in England from Reformation to Emancipation*, 1976

Banim, John, *The Anglo-Irish of The Nineteenth Century. A Novel.*, 3 vols, 1828

Bartlett, Thomas, *The Fall and Rise of the Irish Nation. The Catholic Question 1690–1830*, Dublin, 1992

Beckett, J.V., *The Aristocracy in England 1660–1914*, Oxford, 1986

Bence-Jones, Mark, *The Catholic Families*, 1992

Berkeley, Joan, *Lulworth and the Welds*, Gillingham, Dorset, 1971

Bew, John, 'Ireland under the Union 1801–1922', see Bourke and McBride

Bew, John, *Castlereagh. Enlightenment, War and Tyranny*, 2011

[BL] British Library, London

Bodleian Library, Oxford

Bossy, John, *The English Catholic Community 1570–1850*, pbk, 1979

Bostrom, Irene, 'The Novel and Catholic Emancipation', *Studies in Romanticism*, vol. 2, no. 3, 1963

Bourke, Richard and McBride, Ian (eds), *The Princeton History of Modern Ireland*, Princeton, NJ, 2016

Bourne, Cardinal (Introduction), *Catholic Emancipation. 1829 to 1928. Essays by Various Writers*, 1929

Bourne, Kenneth, *Palmerston. The Early Years 1784–1841*, 1982

Boyce, D. George, *Nineteenth Century Ireland*, rev. edn, 2005

Brady, C., *J.A. Froude*, 2013

Briggs, Asa, *The Making of Modern England 1784–1867*, New York, 1959

Brooke, John, *George III*, 1972

Brown, David, *Palmerston*, New Haven and London, 2010

Butler, Charles, *The Book of the Roman-Catholic Church. In a series of letters addressed to Robert Southey, Esq., LLD on his 'Book of the Church'*, 2nd edn, 1825

Butler, Charles, *Historical Memoirs respecting the English, Irish, and Scottish CATHOLICS from the Reformation to the present time*, 4 vols, 1819

Butler, Iris, *The Eldest Brother. The Marquess Wellesley 1760–1842*, 1973

Campbell, Mary, *Lady Morgan. The Life and Times of Sydney Owenson*, pbk, 1998

Canning Papers, British Library

Cannon, John, *Parliamentary Reform 1640–1832*, reprint, Aldershot, 1994

de Castro, J. Paul, *The Gordon Riots*, Oxford, 1926

Cattermole, P.J., 'John Lingard. The historian as apologist.' Thesis, University of Kent, 1984

Challoner and His Church. A Catholic Bishop in Georgian England, ed. Eamon Duffy, Foreword by Cardinal Hume, 1981

Charmley, John, *The Princess and the Politicians*, 2005

Chedzoy, Alan, *Seaside Sovereign*, Wimborne, Dorset, 2003

Choudhury, Mita, *The Wanton Jesuit and the Wayward Saint. A Tale of Sex, Religion, and Politics in Eighteenth-Century France*, University Park, PA, 2015

The Church of England c.1689–c.1833. From Toleration to Tractarianism, ed. John Walsh, Colin Haydon and Stephen Taylor, Cambridge, 1995

Cloncurry, Valentine Lord, *Personal Recollections of the Life and Times*, 2nd edn, 1850

Cobbett, William, *Rural Rides*, ed. Ian Dyck, pbk, 2001

Colchester, Charles Lord (ed.), *Diary and Correspondence of Charles Abbot, Lord Colchester*, 3 vols, 1861

Colley, Linda, *Britons. Forging the Nation 1707–1837*, 1992

[Consalvi] *Mémoires du Cardinal Consalvi*, ed. J. Crétinau-Joly, 1895

[Creevey] *The Creevey Papers*, ed. Sir Herbert Maxwell, 2 vols, 2nd edn, 1904

Davis, R.W., 'The Tories, the Whigs and Catholic Emancipation, 1827–1829', *English Historical Review*, vol. 97, January 1982

Davis, R.W., 'Wellington and the "Open Question": The Issue of Catholic Emancipation, 1821–1829', *Albion: a Quarterly Journal concerned with British Studies*, vol. 29, 1997

Dickens, Charles, *Barnaby Rudge*, ed. Clive Hurst, Introduction and Notes by Iain McCalman and Jon Mee, pbk, Oxford, 2008

Edgeworth, Maria, *Harrington, A Tale*; and *Ormond, A Tale*, 3 vols, 1817

Maria Edgeworth's Letters from Ireland, ed. Valerie Pakenham, Dublin, 2018

Edgeworth MSS, Special Collections, Weston Library, New Bodleian Library, Oxford, *English Historical Review*

Ehrman, John, *Pitt. The Consuming Struggle*, pbk, 1996

Eighteenth-Century British Erotica II, vol. I, ed. Janine Barchas, General Introduction by Alexander Pettit, 2004

Ellenborough, Edward Law, Lord, *A Political Diary 1828–1830*, ed. Lord Colchester, 2 vols, 1881

Ellis, John Tracy, *Cardinal Consalvi and Anglo-Papal Relations 1814–1824*, Washington DC, 1942

Essex Recusant, vol. 6, no. 1, April 1964, Brentwood, Essex

Evans, Richard J., *The Pursuit of Power: Europe 1815–1914*, 2016

Fagan, William, Esq., MP, *The Life and Times of Daniel O'Connell*, 2 vols, Cork, 1847

A Faithful Account of the Processions and Ceremonies observed in the Coronation of Kings and Queens of England, exemplified in that of their Late Most Sacred Majesties King George III and Queen Charlotte, 1820

Farm Street Archives, 114 Mount Street, London W1

Farm Street. The Story of the Jesuits' Church in London, Michael Hall, Sheridan Gilley and Maria Perry, 2016

Fothergill, *The Cardinal King*, 1958

Fraser, Antonia, *Perilous Question. The Drama of the Great Reform Bill 1832*, pbk, 2014

Fraser, Flora, *Princesses. The Six Daughters of George III*, 2004

Fraser, Flora, *Unruly Queen. The Life of Queen Caroline*, 1996

Gash, Norman, *Lord Liverpool. The Life and Political Career of Robert Banks Jenkinson, 2nd Earl of Liverpool, 1770–1828*, 1984

Gash, Norman, *Aristocracy and People. Britain 1815–1865*, pbk, 1994

Gash, Norman, *Mr. Secretary Peel. The Life of Sir Robert Peel to 1830*, pbk, 2011

Gaunt, Robert A., *Sir Robert Peel. The Life and Legacy*, 2010

[G.E.C.] G.E. Cokayne, *The Complete Peerage of England, Scotland, Ireland, Great Britain, and the United Kingdom*, 13 vols, reprint 1982

Geoghegan, Patrick M., *Robert Emmet*, pbk, 2nd edn, Dublin 2004

Geoghegan, Patrick M., *King Dan. The Rise of Daniel O'Connell 1775–1829*, pbk, Dublin, 2010

Geoghegan, Patrick M., *Liberator. The Life and Death of Daniel O'Connell 1830–1847*, pbk, Dublin, 2012

George, M. Dorothy, *London Life in the Eighteenth Century*, 1925

Gibson, William, *The Church of England, 1688–1832. Unity and Accord*, Abingdon, Oxfordshire, 2001

Gilmour, Ian, *Riots, Risings and Revolution*, pbk, 1993

Gooch, G.P., *History and Historians in the Nineteenth Century*, 1913

Grell, O.P., Israel, J.I. and Tyacke, N. (eds), *From Persecution to Toleration. The Glorious Revolution and Religion in England*, Oxford, 1991

[Greville] *The Diaries of Charles Greville*, ed. Edward Pearce with Deanna Pearce, 2006

[Greville] *The Greville Memoirs, 1814–1860*, ed. Lytton Strachey and Roger Fulford, vol. I, 1938

Gwynn, Denis, *The Struggle for Catholic Emancipation. 1750 to 1829*, 1928

Hague, William, *William Wilberforce*, pbk, 2008

Hardman, John, *Louis XVI*, 2016

Hattersley, Roy, *The Catholics. The Church and its people in Britain and Ireland, from the Reformation to the present day*, 2017

Haydon, Colin, *Anti-Catholicism in Eighteenth Century England c.1714–80. A Political and Social Study*, Manchester, 1993

Haywood, Ian and Seed, John (eds), *The Gordon Riots. Politics, Culture and Insurrection in Late Eighteenth-Century Britain*, Cambridge, 2014

Hempton, David, *Methodism and Politics in British Society 1750–1850*, 1984

Henriques, Ursula, *Religious Toleration in England 1787–1833*, 1961

Hibbert, Christopher, *King Mob. The Story of Lord George Gordon and the Riots of 1780*, 1959

Hibbert, Christopher, *George IV. Prince of Wales, 1762–1811*, 1972

Hibbert, Christopher, *George III. A Personal History*, 1998

Hibbert, Christopher, *George IV. The Rebel Who Would be King*, Foreword by Amanda Foreman, pbk, 2007

Hill, Jacqueline R., 'National Festivals, the State and "Protestant Ascendancy" in Ireland 1790–1829', *Irish Historical Studies*, vol. 93, 1984

Hilton, Boyd, *A Mad, Bad, and Dangerous People? England 1783–1846*, pbk, 2008

Hinde, Wendy, *Catholic Emancipation. A Shake to Men's Minds*, Oxford, 1992

Hinde, Wendy, *George Canning*, 1973

History of Parliament, D.R. Fisher, 7 vols, Cambridge, 2009

[Hobhouse] Broughton, Lord (John Cam Hobhouse), *Recollections of a Long Life*, ed. Lady Dorchester, vols III and IV, 1910

Hobsbawm, Eric, *The Age of Revolution: Europe 1789–1848*, 1962

Holland House Papers, British Library Add. Mss. 51318–52254

Hood, Alban, 'The Throckmortons Come of Age: Political and Social Alignments, 1826–1862', see Marshall and Scott

Howell-Thomas, Dorothy, *Duncannon. Reformer & Reconciler 1781–1847*, Norwich, 1992

Hunt, Tristram, *Building Jerusalem*, pbk, 2005

Hurd, Douglas, *Robert Peel. A Biography*, pbk, 2008

Husenbirth, F.C., *Life of John Milner*, Dublin, 1862

Hylson-Smith, Kenneth, *The Churches in England from Elizabeth I to Elizabeth II*, vol. II, *1689–1833*, 1997

Inchbald, Elizabeth, *A Simple Story*, ed. and notes by J.M.S. Tompkins, Introduction by Jane Spencer, Oxford pbk, 2009
Irvine, Valerie, *The King's Wife. George IV and Mrs Fitzherbert*, London, 2004

James, Serenhedd, *George Errington and English Catholic Identity in Nineteenth-Century England*, Oxford, 2016
[Jerningham] *The Jerningham Letters. Excerpts from the Correspondence and Diaries of the Hon. Lady Jerningham and her daughter Lady Bedingfield*, ed. Egerton Castle, 2 vols, 1896
Johnson, Edgar, *Sir Walter Scott*, vol. II, 1970
Jolliffe, John, ed., *English Catholic Heroes*, Leominster, 2008
Jones, Edwin, *John Lingard and the Pursuit of Historical Truth*, Foreword by Norman Davies, Brighton, 2004

Kelly, Linda, *Susanna, the Captain and the Castrato. Scenes from the Burney Salon*, 2004
Kelly, Linda, *Ireland's Minstrel. A Life of Tom Moore: Poet, Patriot and Byron's Friend*, 2006
Kelly, Ronan, *The Bard of Erin. A Life of Thomas Moore*, Dublin 2008
Knights, Mark, 'The 1780 Protestant petitions and the culture of petitioning', see Haywood and Seed
Kynaston, David, *Till Time's Last Sand. A History of the Bank of England 1694–2013*, 2017

Le Marchant, Sir Denis Bt, *Memoir of John Charles, Viscount Althorp, 3rd Earl Spencer*, 1876
Lee, Sir Sidney, *King Edward VII. A Biography. The Reign 1901 to 1910*, 1925
Lee, Stephen M., *George Canning and Liberal Toryism 1801–1827*, Royal Historical Society, Suffolk, 2008
Leslie, Anita, *Mrs Fitzherbert. A Biography*, New York, 1960

Letters and Notices. Emancipation Centenary Events, vol. XLV, Roehampton,1930

Lewis, Clyde T., 'The Disintegration of the Tory-Anglican Alliance in the Struggle for Catholic Emancipation', *Church History*, vol. 29, no. 1, March 1960

Leys, M.D.R., 'The Rights of Women. An Eighteenth-Century Catholic "Petition"', *The Month*, February 1960

Leys, M.D.R., *Catholics in England 1559–1829. A Social History*, 1961

Lingard, Rev. J., *Observations on the Laws and Ordinances which exist in Foreign States relative to the Religious Concerns of their Roman Catholic Subjects*, 1817

de Lisle, Leanda and Stanford, Peter, *The Catholics and their Houses*, 1995

Longford, Elizabeth, *Wellington. Pillar of State*, 1972

MacDonagh, Oliver, *The Hereditary Bondsman. Daniel O'Connell, 1775–1829*, 1988

Machin, G.I.T., *The Catholic Question in English Politics, 1820 to 1830*, Oxford, 1964

Magee, John, *The Trial of John Magee Proprietor of the Dublin Evening Post*, reprint, New Delhi, 2013

Marshall, Peter and Scott, Geoffrey (eds), *Catholic Gentry in English Society. The Throckmortons of Coughton from Reformation to Emancipation*, Farnham, 2009

Martin, Christopher, *A Glimpse of Heaven. Catholic Churches in England and Wales*, 2007

Mathew, David, *Catholicism in England. The Portrait of a Minority: its Culture and Tradition*, 3rd edn, 1955

Mathews, Susan, '"Mad misrule": the Gordon Riots and conservative memory', see Haywood and Seed

McDowell, R.B., *Public Opinion and Government Policy in Ireland 1801–1846*, 1962

McDowell, R.B., *Ireland in the Age of Imperialism and Revolution 1760–1801*, Oxford, 1979

Mitchell, Leslie, *Holland House*, 1980

Mitchell, Leslie, *The Whig World*, pbk, 2007

Moore, Thomas, *Memoirs, Journal and Correspondence*, ed.
Lord John Russell, 8 vols, 1856

[Thomas Moore] *Memoirs of Captain Rock, the Celebrated
Irish Chieftain, with some account of his Ancestors, written
by Himself*, 5th edn, 1824

*Lady Morgan's Memoirs. Autobiography, Diaries and
Correspondence*, 2 vols, 1862

Moriarty, Thomas F., 'The Irish-American Response to Catholic
Emancipation', *The Catholic Historical Review*, vol. LXVI,
July 1980

Morley, John, *The Life of William Ewart Gladstone*, vol. I, 1903

Mount, Ferdinand, *English Voices. Lives, Landscapes, Laments,
1985–2015*, 2016

Muir, Rory, *Wellington. Waterloo and the Fortunes of Peace,
1814–1852*, 2006

Muir, T.E., *Stonyhurst*, rev. edn, Cirencester, 2006

Mullett, Michael A., *Catholics in Britain and Ireland,
1558–1829*, 1998

Museum of London Catalogue, *Great Fire Exhibition*, 2016

Navickas, Katrina, *Loyalism and Radicalism in Lancashire,
1789–1815*, Oxford, 2009

Nockles, Peter, 'Church Parties in the pre-Tractarian Church
of England 1750–1833: the "Orthodox" – some problems
of definition and identity', see *The Church of England
c.1689–c.1833*.

Norman, Edward, *The English Catholic Church in the
Nineteenth Century*, Oxford, 1984

Norman, E.R., *Anti-Catholicism in Victorian England*, 1968

O'Brien, Paul, *Shelley and Revolutionary Ireland*, 2002

O'Connell, Daniel, *The Life and Speeches*, ed. his son John
O'Connell MP, 2 vols, 1846

The Correspondence of Daniel O'Connell, ed. Maurice R.
O'Connell, vols III–IV, 1974–77

O'Ferrall, Fergus, *Catholic Emancipation. Daniel O'Connell
and the Birth of Irish Democracy 1820–30*, Dublin, 1985

O'Ferrall, Fergus, *Daniel O'Connell*, Dublin, 1997

O'Gorman, Frank, *Voters, Patrons and Parties*, Oxford, 1989

O'Gorman, Frank, *The Long Eighteenth Century*, 1997

Owenson, Sydney, *The Wild Irish Girl*, ed. Lady Morgan, 1846

Pakenham, Eliza, *Soldier Sailor. An Intimate Portrait of an Irish Family*, 2007

Pakenham MSS, Pakenham Archives, Tullynally Castle, Co. Westmeath, Ireland

Pakenham, Thomas, *The Year of Liberty. The Great Irish Rebellion of 1798*, 1969

Pares, Richard, *King George III and the Politicians*, pbk, 1973

Pearson, Hesketh, *The Smith of Smiths. Being the Life, Wit and Humour of Sydney Smith*, pbk, 2009

Peel Papers, British Library

Peel, Sir Laurence, *A Sketch of the Life and Character of Sir Robert Peel*, 1860

[Peel] *Memoirs of the Rt Hon. Sir Robert Peel. Part One, The Roman Catholic Question 1828–9*, ed. Lord Mahon and the Rt Hon. Edward Cardwell MP, 1856

Petre, M.D., *The Ninth Lord Petre*, 1928

Phillips, Peter, 'John Lingard', see Jolliffe

Pollen, Rev. J.H., SJ, 'The Eve of Catholic Emancipation', *The Month*, April 1913

[Pückler-Muskau] *Puckler's Progress. The Adventures of Prince Pückler-Muskau in England, Wales and Ireland, as told in letters to his former wife, 1826–1829*, trans. Flora Brennan, 1987

[RA] Royal Archives, Windsor Castle, Berks

Ramsay, A.A.W., *Sir Robert Peel*, 1928

Riding, Jacqueline, *Jacobites. A New History of the '45 Rebellion*, 2016

Ridley, Jane, *Bertie. A Life of Edward VII*, 2012

Roberts, Andrew, *Salisbury. Victorian Titan*, 1999

Robinson, John Martin, *Cardinal Consalvi 1757–1824*, 1987

Robinson, John Martin, *The Dukes of Norfolk,* rev. edn, pbk, Chichester, 1995

Robinson, John Martin, 'Arundel's Bibliophile Dukes', *The London Library Magazine*, 2017

Sadleir, Michael, *Bulwer: A Panorama. Edward and Rosina 1803–1836,* 1931

Schofield, Nicholas and Skinner, Gerald, *The English Vicars Apostolic 1688–1850*, 2009

Scott, Geoffrey, 'The Throckmortons at Home and Abroad 1680–1800', see Marshall and Scott

Sheil, Rt Hon. Richard Lalor, MP, *Sketches of the Irish Bar.* Memoir and notes by R. Shelton Mackenzie, 2 vols, New York, 1854

Sheils, William, 'Richard Challoner', see Jolliffe

Skinner, Fr. Gerard, *The Life of Fr. Ignatius Spencer: The English Noble and the Christian Saint*, Leominster, 2018

Smith, E.A, *Lord Grey 1764–1845*, Oxford, 1990

Smith, E.A., *George IV*, 1999

[Smith] *The Works of The Rev. Sydney Smith*, new edn, 1850

Snape, Michael, *The Redcoat and Religion. The Forgotten History of the British Soldier from the Age of Marlborough to the Eve of the First World War*, New York, 2005

Southey, Rev. Charles Cuthbert (ed.), *The Life and Correspondence of the late Robert Southey*, 6 vols, 1849–50

Stourton, James, 'Robert 9th Lord Petre', see Jolliffe

[Stourton] *The History of the Noble House of Stourton, of Stourton in the County of Wilts*, compiled under the supervision of Charles Botolph Joseph, Lord Mowbray, Segrave and Stourton, 2 vols, privately printed, 1899

Strong, Roy, *Coronation. A History of Kingship and the British Monarchy*, 2005

Stuart, Dorothy Margaret, *Dearest Bess. The Life and Times of Lady Elizabeth Foster afterwards Duchess of Devonshire from her Unpublished Journals and Correspondence*, 1955

Taylor, Stephen, *Defiance. The Life and Choices of Lady Anne Barnard*, 2016

Throckmorton, Sir John Bt, *Considerations Arising from the Debates in Parliament on the Petition of the Irish Catholics*, 1806

Thurston, Rev. Herbert, SJ, *The Darkness Before the Dawn (1700–1791)*, Catholic Truth Society, 1929

de Tocqueville, Alexis, *Journeys to England and Ireland*, ed. J.P. Mayer, 1958

Tomko, Michael, *British Romanticism and the Catholic Question. Religion, History and National Identity 1778–1829*, 2011

Trevelyan, Sir G.O., Bt, *The Life and Letters of Lord Macaulay*, Preface by G.M. Trevelyan, 2 vols, Oxford, reissued 1978

Turnham, Margaret H., *Catholic Faith and Practice in England 1779–1992. The Role of Revivalism and Renewal*, Woodbridge, 2015

Wall, Maureen, 'The Rise of a Catholic Middle Class in Eighteenth Century Ireland', *Irish Historical Studies*, vol. II, 1958

[Walpole] *The Letters of Horace Walpole, Earl of Orford*, ed. Peter Cunningham, 9 vols, 1861–6

Ward, Bernard, *The Dawn of the Catholic Revival in England 1781–1803*, 2 vols, 1909

Ward, Bernard, *The Eve of Catholic Emancipation*, 3 vols, 1803–1829, reprint 1970

Wardroper, John, *Wicked Ernest. The truth about the man who was almost Britain's king. An extraordinary royal life revealed*, 2002

[W.D.C.M] *Despatches, Correspondence, and Memoranda of Field Marshal Arthur Duke of Wellington, K.G.*, ed. his son the Duke of Wellington, K.G., vols III–VI, 1870–1877

[Wesley] *The Journal of the Rev. John Wesley, A.M.*, ed. Nathaniel Curnock, vol. VI, 1915

Wheeler, Michael, *The Old Enemies. Catholic and Protestant in Nineteenth-Century English Culture*, Cambridge, 2006

White, Terence de Vere, *Tom Moore. The Irish Poet*, 1977

Willis, G.M., *Ernest Augustus Duke of Cumberland and King of Hanover*, 1954

Willis, Richard, 'William Pitt's Resignation in 1801: Re-examination and Document', *Bulletin of the Institute of Historical Research*, vol. XLIV, 1971

Wiseman, Nicholas, Cardinal, *Recollections of Four Popes and of Rome in their Times*, n.d.

Wyse, Thomas, *Historical Sketch of the late Catholic Association of Ireland*, 2 vols, 1829

Zamoyski, Adam, *Phantom Terror. The Threat of Revolution and the Repression of Liberty, 1789–1848*, 2014

Ziegler, Philip, *Addington. A Life of Henry Addington, First Viscount Sidmouth*, 1965

Ziegler, Philip, *William IV*, pbk, 1971

INDEX